OPER... MILITARY RESOURCES

A Book Full of Resources for All Branches of Military and Their Families

KIMBERLY SUCHEK

Operation: Military Resources
A Book Full of Resources for All Branches of Military and Their Families

©2011 by Kimberly Suchek
Published in 2011 by Creative Freedom, LLC

ISBN: 978-0-9847284-0-4

Contact the publisher at: kim@MilitaryResourceBooks.com

Editing, layout, cover design, publishing consulting and author coaching provided by Alane Pearce, Author Coach at Alane Pearce Professional Writing Services LLC http://AlanePearce.com. Turning writers into published and promoted authors.

Contact Alane at alane@AlanePearce.com.

Cover photograph of girl and flag used by written permission of the photographer Andrew Jenkins, Owner-Canfield Jenkins House of Photography. Contact them at 989-227-8441 to schedule your deployment family photos.

Other photography royalty free stock photos from http://dreamstime.com.

ENDORSEMENTS

What others are saying about
OPERATION: Military Resources

"This book is phenomenal. While I'm quite familiar with most of the programs published in this book, the programs I did not know about was an eye opener, which I plan to take advantage of. I'm very appreciative that Kim has a love for the military family; you can tell that she loves this family from her efforts in this book. Great Job Kim!"

Lieutenant Colonel Leonard D. Rusher
1-182 Field Artillery Battalion Commander Michigan Army National Guard

"This book really is a great resource for military families!"

Senator Rick Jones
24th District, Michigan State Senate

"Finally! Someone has put all the websites and what they are about in one place so our veterans and their spouses/families don't have to go to several different areas to find a resource! I highly endorse this book to all our veterans and families. Great job Kim!"

Raymond Ladd
Transitional Assistant Advisor for ANG, State of Michigan
Master Sergeant, US Army (RET)

"Very useful book! This book is full of need to know resources and contacts that will help military personnel and their families. It will benefit anyone connected in any way with military service; whether it be through relatives, friends, or employment."

Miner W. Roth CSM Ret.
(Past Michigan State Command Sergeant Major/Senior Enlisted Adviser 1999-2005)
(Currently Yellow Ribbon Support Specialist, Michigan)

ABOUT THIS BOOK

I have written this book to offer support to service members and their families and to help them easily access information and resources that are available. During my positions at Joint Force Headquarters and Operation Homefront assisting military families and in speaking with friends who are military, I was surprised by the lack of knowledge about these resources among service members and senior leadership–even those who had been in the military for many years and deployed numerous times. I was also sick and tired of hearing, "You must have a couple paychecks in the bank for an emergency situation!" as their only and best piece of advice. (In this economy…RIGHT!!)

I could not understand how military families did not know what was available for them, and I was surprised at the lack of attention senior leadership gave to this. How could service members not understand their G.I. Bill or spouse scholarships, or not know about grants to assist when something breaks or to help their children with tutoring and education?

I am hoping this book can be a better resource to military families than the advice to "have some money in savings." (Which is good advice, also!) There are so many organizations in our communities who offer help and assistance to the military; I thought it would be helpful to list them all in an easy-to-use resource book.

I am sure in the creation of this book I have forgotten a resource or failed to list a full description or condition regarding one. This would be my mistake and I apologize in advance for any inconvenience this may cause. I did try to list everything pertinent and I have personally verified each of the resources listed in this book. At the time of writing this book these resources were being offered, but we all know things can change. I'm sorry if you find any of these resources out of business. Feel free to contact me if you have a resource for military families that I can include in my referrals and in future editions of this book.

If you see the symbol "*" beside an organization's name, it indicates that I have both used the organization myself and can professionally recommend them, or I know someone who used them. Usually I will make a comment about a group or resource I have used.

Best wishes to all and thank you to all these organizations and volunteers who take time away from their own families to help make the lives of military families better.

ABOUT THE AUTHOR

Kimberly Suchek is passionate about quality of life issues for military families. She has been married to an Army National Guard soldier for 13 years and lives and understands the many challenges the military lifestyle presents before, during and after deployments; she is concerned that military families do not know about all the programs and organizations there are to help during the different transitions of military life. "There is never any reason a military spouse should feel alone," says Kimberly.

Kimberly is past president of Operation Homefront of Michigan, Family Assistant Coordinator for The Army National Guard out of Joint Force HQ and Grand Ledge Armory and a DEERS Operator. She was also a patrol officer for six years. Although she holds an Associate's Degree in Criminal Justice, she is currently working on a teaching certificate along with a degree in creative writing. She loves being outdoors gardening, enjoys traveling to new places and spending time with her husband, daughter, family and friends.

ACKNOWLEDGMENTS

With any awesome creation it takes a team to get it done and done correctly. I would like to thank my editor, Alane Pearce, for her guidance in teaching me the business and not only for her hard work but also for understanding my vision and helping to guide it onto paper. It takes a visionary to be able to understand someone's vision and not be in the same room as they are. You are that and more.

I want to thank Ray Ladd for his assistance with the health insurance chapter and 1LT Steven Haggarty for his assistance with the education chapter. Your help and insight are greatly appreciated.

I would like to thank my family and friends for your patience and understanding of missed days together and no phone calls.

To my husband, Steve, and daughter, Cheyenne, thank you for your support and understanding when I missed events, didn't cook and when I'd lock myself in my office for days at a time. I love you and appreciate your love and support.

And thank you Cheyenne for allowing me to put your beautiful picture on the front of this book. You get more beautiful every day!!

DISCLAIMER

Some of the information contained in this book has come directly from the organization's brochure or website; I did this so I didn't misrepresent an organization by inferring or interpreting their organization's mission.

No endorsements by The Department of Defense or the US Armed Forces are implied to Kimberly Suchek, this book nor the organizations listen herein.

At the publication of this book in December of 2011, the websites and organizations listed in this book were operational. The author of this book, and anyone associated with the publication of this book, is not responsible for a link that doesn't work, an organization that no longer exists, or any other issues associated with the reader's experience with an organization listed here.

This book is meant to be a source of help for military families, but not a definitive list nor an official endorsement of any para-military organization listed herein. We did our best to make sure all the links in this document work; if a link doesn't work, we are sorry. With almost 300 pages of them, we were bound to miss a few! Just let us know and we'll fix it in the next book.

If you know of a resource not listed in this book, please contact the author at http://militaryresourcebooks.com and suggest it for future editions of this book.

Watch for state editions of this book coming soon!

Find out more at http://militaryresourcebooks.com.

DEDICATION

During the writing of this book, I could not help but think of my Grandmother Nettie. She had been encouraging me for a couple of years to write this book, telling me how one was never written and how I wanted to create it because fate was waiting for me. I don't know if that was true, but it was a wonderful thought. Well Grandma (Joe Joe), this book is dedicated to you. I thank you for always being there for me through all the years. I know some were quite rough with me, but the memories you have given my daughter and me are priceless. I miss you and I love you! I wish you were here; you deserved to be a part of this creation.

I GOT YOUR BACK

by Autumn Parker

I am a small and precious child, my dad's been sent to fight...
The only place I'll see his face, is in my dreams at night.
He will be gone too many days for my young mind to keep track.
I may be sad, but I am proud.
My daddy's got your back.

I am a caring mother; my son has gone to war...
My mind is filled with worries that I have never known before.
Everyday I try to keep my thoughts from turning black.
I may be scared, but I am proud.
My son has got your back.

I am a strong and loving wife, with a husband soon to go.
There are times I'm terrified, in a way most never know.
I bite my lip, and force a smile, as I watch my husband pack...
My heart may break, but I am proud.
My husband's got your back...

I am a soldier...
Serving proudly, standing tall.
I fight for freedom, yours and mine, by answering this call.
I do my job while knowing, the thanks it sometimes lacks.
Say a prayer that I'll come home.
It's me who's got your back.

This poem is used by written permission from the author, Autumn Parker

TABLE OF CONTENTS

BASIC INFORMATION YOU SHOULD KNOW

You may have heard about the police department and firefighters having their own tight group of friends and their tendency to run with their own. In the same way, the military has its own culture and community and the typical white house with the picket fence with a mom and dad home every night with the kids is NOT the norm! Instead, the military life "normal" is one parent gone most of the year on a deployment or in training. The norm is one parent home, holding down the fort and making sure everything is done all while trying to regularly update the missing spouse to promote a feeling of inclusion for the military member. These updates are usually accomplished by Skype, email, phone calls, letters or other creative means of communication. Each spouse in a military marriage deals with issues that the average married couple would never encounter, never find important and in some cases would never understand. It takes a unique person to be able to live the military life and be successful at it. I hope this book can assist you in your journey.

There are a few basic tools military families should have in place, or at least have a basic understanding about. So I want to outline them briefly here.

Defense Enrollment Eligibility Reporting System (DEERS): DEERS is simply a database of those who are eligible for TRICARE and other military benefits. In the military, unless you and your family are registered in DEERS you do not exist. Service members get automatically enrolled when they enter the military, but even their status and rank/status changes need to be updated. After you are registered in DEERS, you can take advantage of the same benefits your service member enjoys, such as a military ID card which allows you on bases, TRICARE health care, shopping at the Base Exchange and Commissary, discounts at stores and flights on space A travel (discussed later).

To enroll, go with your service member to a DEERS site on base and your service member will fill out a DD Form 1172 (an application for Department of Defense Common Access Card and DEERS Enrollment) for each eligible family member and be prepared to provide identification, which needs to include one picture ID (driver license, passport, state id card) and supporting documentation such as a marriage and birth certificates and Social Security Cards.

Don't forget to update DEERS as needed. For example, you'll need to notify DEERS for death certificates, newborns, service member's retirement information, etc. The service member must be with you when you enroll in DEERS and get your ID card unless he is deployed under Title 10 Orders. If this is the case, bring a copy of your spouse's orders, power of attorney paperwork (some sites want to see this documentation) along with other supporting documentation. If you are not available to be at a DEERS site with your service member when he is updating, he/she may print out an extra copy of the 1172 Form and bring it to you to go an obtain your military ID card (and dependents) without your sponsor present. This form will allow you 30 days from time it was printed.

Any time you or your service member experience a significant life event, update DEERS within 30 days. If you don't, you may experience a break in your benefits.

If you need assistance locating an ID office, visit the Rapids Site Locator at http://www.dmdc.osd.mil/rsl/appj/site?execution=e1s1. You can search for the nearest office by Zip code, city or state. After you have that information, make sure you call the office to verify its location and business hours first. Most sites only issue ID cards certain days of the week and/or at certain times of the day.

If you are the spouse of a service member, dependent child over the age of 10 or the child from divorced or single parents, no matter the age, you need to get an ID card. Remember, military ID cards have to be renewed every four years or when a service member has a change of status from non-active duty to active duty. Military ID cards are also your health insurance cards www. dmdc.osd.mil.

HEALTH CARE (TRICARE)

One of the most significant financial benefits service members and their families receive from the military is free health care when they are on Title 32 and 10 orders and discount health care cost when they are state employees (technicians) for the military working in the armories. The last time I checked, less than 50% of the civilian workforce has medical insurance and far fewer have dental, vision or prescription drug coverage. Most civilian retirees do not have employer-provided health care and if they do the costs, such as premiums and copays, randomly go up or items drop off the covered list. Sometimes coverage is not even guaranteed to last through their retirement. And they almost never have vision or dental coverage. However, those employed in, or retired from, the armed forces—and their families—have access to very affordable, quality health care and insurance guaranteed for life by the U.S. government.

Here is a brief rundown of health care plan choices. This includes, spouse, widow/widower (if not remarried), unmarried children under age 26 and dependent parents and in-laws. Also, former spouses qualify if they are not remarried and they are not eligible for private medical insurance. I will not go into major detail about the different options but this is something you will need to review in more detail; please review the TRICARE website for specifics http://www.tricare.mil/.

- **TRICARE "Standard"** provides you with the greatest flexibility to choose health care providers, without a referral or pre-authorization, but it also costs the most. It is available worldwide

- **TRICARE "Extra"** is more restrictive and less expensive. You pay the same annual deductible as those with Standard; however your share of medical costs is 5% less. This plan is only available in the continental United States (CONUS).

- **TRICARE "Prime"** is like an HMO and is geared toward preventive care. It is the least expensive option, but your choice of health care providers is limited. You pay very little and in some cases, nothing at all.

All active-duty service members and activated Guard and Reserve are **required** to enroll themselves and their family into TRICARE Prime or one of the TRICARE options, depending on where they live and work. All other eligible beneficiaries **may** choose to enroll in TRICARE Prime. If eligible beneficiaries don't enroll in TRICARE Prime, they are automatically covered by TRICARE Standard and Extra.

A few things you need to keep in mind when using TRICARE: There is a difference between "authorized" health care providers that are part of a network and "authorized" providers that are non-network providers, and also between participating providers and non-participating providers.

The difference (besides lots of money) is...

- **Authorized** health care providers may be part of a **network** of contracted providers who accept TRICARE negotiated payments and file claims for you.

- **Other Authorized** health care providers are **non-network** providers, they have no contract with TRICARE and they limit their services to a case-by-case-basis. You may or may not be able to access TRICARE paid services from authorized non-network providers. You will want to ask if they are familiar with TRICARE before you use their services if they are new to you.

- **Participating** providers accept TRICARE benefits as payment in full, file claims for you and won't bill you for additional costs for their services.

- **Non-Participating** providers may charge you up to 15% more than the TRICARE allowable charge. You may be responsible for paying for treatment at the time of service and filing your own claims with TRICARE for reimbursement.

TRICARE will only pay for care provided by **authorized** providers. Medicare certified hospitals must participate in TRICARE for inpatient care. However, for outpatient care, providers have the choice whether or not to become authorized providers.

Just ask your doctors before you use their services. If they are not authorized, explain that you do not wish to go to another doctor. Most do not want to lose business and it is easy enough for them to call TRICARE and fill out a form to keep your business. To find out if your provider is TRICARE authorized, check with your regional TRICARE service center at http://tricare.mil/contactus.

Also, if you are a state military worker and you have health insurance that you pay for, while you are on active duty orders, your premium is paid for by the federal government. This is very helpful if you have dependents. While you are deployed they use whatever health care you had as primary and then use TRICARE as secondary insurance. This will take care of most health care bills and prescription costs while deployed. Check with your local HMO office for more details.

The Catastrophic Cap for active duty and National Guard is $1,000. Retirees, family members of retirees, survivors, or former spouse is $3,000 per fiscal year.

ADDITIONAL TRICARE SERVICES

TRICARE Prime Remote: If you live more than 50 miles away from a military treatment facility your family can still participate in a program very similar to TRICARE Prime—it's called TRICARE Prime Remote. Instead of obtaining treatment at your local military treatment facility, you see a local civilian health care provider who is part of the TRICARE authorized network. Activated Guard and Reserve members and their families are eligible also. For more information about TRICARE prime remote visit http://mybenefit/home/ overview/plans/primeremote.

If using TRICARE Prime Remote and having requested medical assistance, go to www.mytricare.com and you can verify if your bill has been approved through your TRICARE program. If you go to the doctor before it is approved, you can pay for it and get reimbursed at a later date.

Please Note: There is a difference between TRICARE Prime and TRICARE Prime Remote. When a Guard or Reserve member gets activated, they have a choice; TRICARE Standard or TRICARE Prime Remote (NOT Prime). After deployment military families fall into TAMP, which will be Standard TRICARE. If they wish to have TRICARE Prime or TRICARE Prime Remote they will need to re-enroll.

TRICARE Prime Overseas: This works the same as TRICARE Prime in areas where there are military facilities and a network of civilian providers. The difference is if a provider is not available in your location, you may have your share of point-of-service costs waived by getting your primary care manager to refer you to a regional medical service center, which is a TRICARE authorized health care provider. But the point of service option is NOT available to active-duty military or activated Guard or Reserve members. For assistance with TRICARE Prime Overseas, call 888-777-8343 or visit http://mybenefit/home/ overview/plans/primeoverseas.

TRICARE Reserve Select: Available worldwide to most selected Reserve members and their families while not on active duty. You have the freedom to manage your own health care and utilize any TRICARE authorized provider. You may also access care at a military treatment facility. With TRICARE Reserve Select you get health care coverage for service members and dependents for $253 per month with an annual deductible of $50 or $150 per individual and $100 or $300 for the family each fiscal year, except when you receive treatment at a military treatment facility, then no deductible applies.

Cost range is dependent on rank. Your share of most medical services, device and supplies costs including outpatient, clinical preventive, laboratory and X-ray, maternity, ambulance and emergency services are 15% of allowable charges if approved and provided by a network provider. If services are rendered by a non-network provider, your share of allowable charges is 20%. Your cost for hospitalization, newborn care or inpatient skilled nursing treatment is over $15 per day, subject to a $25 minimum. In most cases there is minimal or no cost to access to treatment at a military treatment facility. Generally you have to pay for services when they are rendered and seek reimbursement by submitting a claim form to TRICARE Reserve Select.

TRICARE Reserve Select is an excellent option if you and your family are eligible. This program provides comprehensive health care at a reasonable cost and includes the TRICARE prescription drug coverage.

Updates to the TRICARE program that started in 2011 are as follows:

TRICARE Young Adult (**TYA**): A new premium-based health care plan for adult dependent children up to age 26. It can be purchased after eligibility coverage ends at age 21, or 23 if enrolled in a full course of study at an approved institution of higher learning. TYA provides access to medical and pharmacy benefits, but does not include dental.

TYA-TRICARE Standard is available worldwide, but TRICARE Prime will not be available until a later date. TYA participants may visit any TRICARE authorized provider, network or non-network provider but care at a military treatment facility is on a case by case basis only. TYA does not need a referral for any type of care but some services may require prior authorization. The type of provider determines how much the out-of-pocket expenses will cost. Just remember visiting a network provider will result in less out of pocket, in addition to the convenience of having the network provider file the claims directly.

Requirements to remember:

- TYA must be a dependent of an eligible uniformed service sponsor. If the sponsor is a non-activated member of the Selected Reserve of the Ready Reserve or of the Retired Reserve, the sponsor must be enrolled in the TRICARE Reserve Select or TRICARE Retired Reserve for the dependent to be eligible to purchase TRICARE Young Adult coverage.

- TYA must be unmarried, at least 21 but not yet 26 years old (NOTE: those enrolled in a full course of study at an approved institution of higher learning and their sponsor provided 50% of their financial support, their eligibility may not begin until age 23).

- Dependent is not eligible to enroll in an employer-sponsored health plan based on his or her own employment and not otherwise eligible for other TRICARE coverage.

- TYA is *pay-to-play* program requiring eligible dependents to apply a monthly premium. TYA premium rates are established annually on a calendar year bases. The 2011 monthly premium is $180 per month.

VISION BENEFITS

TRICARE Prime participants must be age three (3) and older–(there are special rules for newborns and infants or if you or a family member has diabetes) and are entitled to vision benefits, including comprehensive eye exams once every two (2) years. You don't even have to work through your primary care manager for a referral or authorization unless you can't or don't want to see a network provider. TRICARE covers some surgeries and treatments for diseases and conditions of the eyes. You can even get free eyeglasses from your local military treatment facility.

Vision exams are only provided to military members and families who have TRICARE Prime coverage. Those families covered by TRICARE Standard or Extra are not eligible unless the exam is necessary due to a covered medical condition. For additional information about all military health programs, visit the TRICARE website at http://www.tricare.osd.mil.

DENTAL BENEFITS

The TRICARE Dental Plan (TDP) is available to the military families of active duty or activated Guard or Reserve. Active duty and activated Guard and Reserve receive free dental care from the military dental treatment facilities. If a facility is not close to you then you can have your treatment approved by TRICARE prior to treatment from your dental office.

Dental Insurance is a premium-base insurance; TRICARE monitors it, but it is contracted through United Concordia Companies, Inc. The TRICARE Dental Program (TDP) is portable and is covered worldwide, so when your sponsor changes duty stations, you don't have to change dental plans. Coverage and costs on TDP changes for National Guard and Reserve members and their families as the sponsor's status changes from inactive to active duty. Your cost will be less, so remember to keep your DEERS information up-to-date. You are eligible for TDP if you are family members of active duty uniformed service personnel, family members of the National Guard and Reserve Service Member who are active duty and not active. Family members include spouses, unmarried children (including step-children, adopted children and court-appointed wards) under 21. Unmarried children are eligible up to the end of the month in which they turn 21 and may be eligible up to age 23 in certain circumstances. Sponsor must have 12 months remaining on obligation of the military (this is waived if deployed or being deployed).

Those not eligible for Dental Insurance are: Active duty service members including National Guard and Reserve members called or ordered to active duty for more than 30 days; retired service members and their families; former spouses, parents and parents in law, disabled veterans, and foreign military personnel.

I will not go into all costs and amounts related to TDP, please review the details online at www.tricaredentalprogram.com or call 800-866-8499 if you are in United States and 888-418-0466 OCONUS.

There are a few things I would like you to keep in mind when you are deciding on dental coverage:

- For eligible family members the monthly premiums for TDP are $11.58 for one person and $28.95 for two or more. First monthly premium is due upon enrollment, if your spouse is on active duty you can have premium deducted from his/her paycheck. If spouse is not activated, service members' premium will be taken from paycheck and families will be billed separately. Keep in mind premiums are cheaper when service member is activated, so make sure you update when necessary.

- The maximum annual benefit any one beneficiary can receive is $1,200 and lifetime maximum orthodontic benefit is $1,500 per beneficiary.

- Once enrolled in TDP, you must continue the coverage and pay premiums for at least 12 months. After the first 12 months your enrollment commitment is only month-to-month. Also, if you enroll after 21st of the month, coverage does not start until the beginning of the following two months. For example, if you enroll June 14, coverage starts July 1st. If you don't enroll until June 21, coverage will not start until Aug. 1st.

- The TRICARE dental plan covers all the costs for diagnostic, emergency and preventive services. This is all based on your service member's status and rank. If you need assistance enrolling in the TRICARE Dental Plan, contact United Concordia at 888-622-2256 or www.ucci.com.

PRESCRIPTION DRUG COVERAGE

If you are using TRICARE health care benefits, you are eligible for the TRICARE Prescription Drug Plan. The coverage is the same for all military health care plans and is available worldwide. There are four (4) different ways to have your prescriptions filled:

- **Military Pharmacy:** The military treatment facility pharmacy is your best option if your prescription is available there. You can get a 90-day supply at no cost. It's a good idea to call ahead to verify that your prescription is available.

- **Mail Order Pharmacies:** This is a great alternative if your prescription drug isn't available through the MTF. You can save money, but you must plan in advance. Depending on the pharmacy, the mail service and your location, it could take several days to receive your prescription. For more information visit the TRICARE mail order pharmacy program online at http://www.express-scripts.com/tricare.

- **Network Pharmacies:** If your prescription needs to be filled **immediately** and it is not carried by your local MTF, you will need to obtain it through a network pharmacy. To find a network pharmacies go to http://member. express-scripts.com/web/pharmacylocator/openpharmacylocator. do?portal=dodcustom&net=1991.

- **Non-Network Pharmacies:** The more expensive option is non-network pharmacies. These pharmacies do not partner with TRICARE and you will have to pay full price for your prescriptions.

If you have access to the Internet, the easiest way to enroll in any TRICARE program is online at http://www.tricare.mil/mybenefit/home/medical. You will need certain information to complete your enrollment application whether you are enrolling online, mailing your application or faxing it. Go to the website and follow steps to set up your profile. Once your application has been processed you will receive a package by mail, including a welcome letter identifying your primary care manager, if one has been assigned to you, and enrollment card for each family member who is enrolled, and a copy of the TRICARE Handbook.

**As of the printing of this book, there are a few things you need to be aware of regarding TRICARE. They will soon be changing their pharmacy copayments to encourage pharmacy home delivery. As of October 1, 2011, there are no copayments for generic prescription medications for 90- day supplies through TRICARE Home Delivery while the copayments for the same medication will increase from $3 to $5 at retail pharmacies.

The following are changes to the TRICARE pharmacy copayments effective October 1, 2011:

- Generic formulary drugs purchased at retail pharmacies will go from $3 to $5.
- Generic formulary drugs purchased through the Home Delivery option will go from $3 to $5 for a 90-day supply.
- Brand name formulary drugs from retail pharmacies will go from $9 to $12.
- Non-formulary medications will go from $22 to $25 in both retail and Home Delivery.
- Brand name formulary drugs purchased through Home Delivery will have the same $9 copayment.

**As of the printing of this book Express Scripts (company that manages TRICARE prescription-drug benefits) and Walgreens will no longer be doing business together beginning January 1, 2012. Walgreens has publicly announced it will stop participating as a provider in the Express Scripts pharmacy network. You can go to www.Express-Scripts.com/TRICARE/ pharmacy for a complete list of local participating network pharmacies if you have not received a letter from Express Scripts with a list of the closest 3 pharmacies to your residential area.

**As of the printing of this book the Department of Defense announced that military retirees enrolling in TRICARE Prime after October 1, 2011 will pay an additional $2.50 per month for individual members and $5 per month for members and family. The increase takes the annual premium rate from $230 (individual) and $460 (family) to $260 and $520 respectively. This

increase only affects those who enroll after October 1, 2011. It will not affect currently enrolled retirees until October 1, 2012. For more information, go to http://militaryadvantage.military.com/2011/09/tricare-fees-go-up-this-week/#ixzz1ZjINkZtN.

OTHER SUPPORT WITHIN THE MILITARY

There are times when you feel like you need more support than you are getting and you can't go to the unit or you don't wish to burden family or friends. There are other resources for you, and you don't have to live near an installation to use them.

- **Chapel:** Some bases offer services and ceremonies at the chapel on base. Even bases that do not have a chaplain offer support to service members and families before, during and after deployments. Remember, most chaplains have deployed and faced the same issues that you and your family are going through. Chaplains have many resources and are confidential.

- **Family Support Centers:** Family Support Centers hold a wealth of resources and provide loads of information about military life including deployments, before and after, financial management, job search, moves, volunteer opportunities, marital, family and individual (confidential) counseling, and more.

- **Clubs and Groups:** There are various clubs and groups within a base and off base in which you can participate. These can consist of Family Readiness Groups, church groups and spouse clubs. There are also organizations such as the Veterans of Foreign Wars (VFW), American Legion and Operation Homefront, just to name a few. These are terrific resources that can help you feel a great sense of belonging while befriending and communicating with people who understand what you are going through.

- **Family Advocacy Programs (FAP):** Sometimes in our lives, things happen that are out of our control. If that happens, or if you or anyone you know is a victim of abuse or even just major stress, the counselors and experts at Family Advocacy can help. FAP is your resource for child and spouse abuse prevention as well as preventive education classes, such as crisis management, parenting and anger management. They even have support groups for new parents and parents of deployed single soldiers.

- **Military Acronyms:** Helpful site for you to learn the abbreviations and acronyms that are widely used in the military world. http://www.dtic.mil/doctrine/dod_dictionary/index.html

- **Glossary Information:** This site features a glossary of terms relating to military quality of life programs as well as other links to additional glossaries that you may find helpful. http://glossarist.com/glossaries/government-politics-military/military/default.asp

MILITARY PAY

I was so surprised when I would help the spouse of a service member with financial issues and find they had **NO CLUE** as to how much their service member earned. Sometimes they would come to me with no knowledge of how to read an LES (Leave and Earnings Statement), or with incorrect or no financial information from the service member. And sometimes they were deliberately miss-informed. They were clueless about such concepts as special pay, allowances, raises, flight pay etc. I know I will probably have many service members upset with me for letting the "cat out of the bag" so to speak, but don't military families go through enough? Why should a spouse have to sacrifice more than they already do, or scramble to find money to fix something when the service member has the money and the spouse does not know?

So hold your hats spouses, it's going to be a bumpy ride! Basic pay, allowances and special pay are affected by your service member's military occupation, pay grade, where they are stationed and deployment status. I will attempt to give you just a brief description of these so that you can see what may apply to your family and goals.

Basic Pay: This is your service member's base paycheck and they are the same across all branches of the service. The only differences in basic pay are pay grade and, to a small degree, the number of years your service member has been in the service.

Additional Pay: Your service member may qualify for additional pay because of any unique training or specialty, where his/her duty station is located and whether they are in a combat zone. Your family may also receive allowances for food, clothing and shelter.

The following is a list of specialty pay and bonuses:

- **Hazardous Duty Pay:** While your service member is deployed overseas on Title 10 Orders, he/she is usually getting paid more money. The activities and situations they are exposed to dictate the compensation.
  - $225 per month for Hostile Fire and Imminent Danger Pay: Additional pay for those occasions when your service member is subject to hostile fire or explosion.
  - $50 to $150 per month for Hardship Duty Pay: For service member living and working in extremely difficult living conditions or enduring excessive physical hardship.

- $150 per month for Hazardous Duty Incentive Pay: In addition to living and working in a danger zone, under extremely difficult living conditions, your service member may also perform particularly hazardous duties such as jumping out of airplanes or handling explosives.

- $150 to $350 per month for Hazardous Duty Incentive Pay for Flying: Service member or aircrews (except pilots) receive this additional pay. Pilots are paid additionally for their job specialty but it is in a different category.

  Your service member is only entitled to any two of these hazardous duty pays that apply at any one time.

- **Unique Training or Specialty Pay:** Each branch of the armed services pays extra if the service member acquires the unique skills or specialized training for certain military occupations; he/she may also be eligible for certain bonuses. For example, aviation officers earn an extra $125 to $840 per month. Sea duty brings $50-$730 a month, and diving duty up to $340 per month. Proficiency in a foreign language that has been deemed critical can earn up to $1000 per month in extra income.

- **Special Bonuses:** The military offers certain bonus to help encourage service members to continue longer retention of its service members. This can be important for not only specialty fields but also for the extra cost it would be to retrain service members.

- **Re-enlistment:** Bonuses vary depending on training, specialty, willingness to accept undesirable assignments and length of service. It is sad to think after so many years they no longer get bonuses to re-enlist but that is the way the government works.

- **Pilot:** Up to $25,000 per year for aviators remaining on active duty after the end of their initial enlistment.

- **Nuclear:** Up to $20,000 one-time bonus is available to naval officers upon their selection for nuclear power training duty. An additional annual pay of up to $22,000 is provided for their technical qualifications for duty in nuclear propulsion plants. And if they sign a long-term contract, they may be entitled to an additional $25,000 bonus each year.

- **JAG:** Up to $60,000 is available to officers who complete ten years of service as a judge advocate.

- **Medical:** Special pay is awarded to medical officers if they agree to remain on active duty for at least one year after their service obligation. Remaining on active duty after their initial service obligation period provides up to $14,000 per year of additional pay.

- **Dental:** Up to $30,000 is available to officers who contract to serve on active duty for over four years. An additional $7,000 to $27,000 per year is paid for their unique skills, and even more if they are board certified.

- **Veterinary:** Veterinary officers are eligible to receive awards of $2,000 to $5,000 per year depending on their years of service. In addition they receive an extra $100 per month in special pay.

- **Special Warfare:** Officers who remain on active duty in special warfare service for at least one year may be entitled to receive a continuation bonus of up to $15,000 per year for each year they serve on special warfare duty.

ALLOWANCES

In addition to their basic paycheck with any additional special pay they may earn, your military member receives a family allowance if he is married or has other dependents. These allowances are to help cover increases in the cost of living, as well as additional expenses related to food, clothing and shelter if they live off base.

- **Cost of Living Allowance (COLA):** The cost of living varies from city to city. Since basic pay is the same no matter where you live, the military will provide a monthly cost of living allowance (COLA) to help make up this imbalance in compensation. COLA depends on the assigned duty station, pay grade, length of time in the service and whether there are dependents. If you live in a location that the military regards as a high cost area, you will receive a COLA increase whether you live on base or off. Visit www.military.com/cola to calculate the current COLA adjustment for various locations and your personal situation.

- **Basic Allowance for Subsistence:** This shows as BAS on your pay stub and is intended to offset the cost of food for the military member NOT THE FAMILY. The amount is adjusted annually. The monthly BAS paid to an officer is about $200 and the amount provided to enlisted is almost $300. This allowance is paid to all military members whether they dine in the mess hall or off base. Be careful with this though, as government-provided meals are only partially subsidized.

- **Clothing Allowances:** Service members receive a one-time payment clothing allowance after commissioning to buy clothing. Enlisted receive uniforms and an annual clothing maintenance allowance. If your service member is required to wear civilian duds as part of his duty assignment, the service will provide an allowance for this additional expense.

- **Per Diem:** While traveling on official military business, the military member is entitled to a daily allotment to reimburse them for the cost of food and lodging so the military member does not have to use money out of their pockets to pay for the business trip. To check the per diem rate for your state, go to http://perdiem.hqda.pentagon.mil/perdiem.

- **Housing Allowances:** Basic Allowance for Housing (also known as BAH) is provided to service members to adjust for the additional costs of living off base. The actual amount of BAH is based on the local rental housing market, pay grade and number of dependents. Keep a couple of things in mind when you are adding up the housing allowance; first, BAH is a set amount and your actual housing expense can be higher than your BAH. You can review this at http://www.military.com/benefits/military-pay/basic-allowance-for-housing-rates. Second, BAH is paid out automatically when you apply for off base housing and if you and your spouse are both employed by the military, each of you is entitled to the BAH. If you live together, one of you can claim BAH with dependents and the other must register at the single rate. You should have the service member with the highest pay grade claim dependents so you receive the highest BAH.

- **Overseas Housing Allowance:** If a service member is stationed overseas and lives off base, they don't receive BAH. Instead they receive Special Overseas Housing Allowance, or OHA. This allowance is intended to offset the actual coast of rent, utilities and recurring maintenance expenses. Unlike BAH, OHA is NOT a set monthly amount. While you are eligible for OHA, you also qualify for a move-in housing allowance to cover the purchase of necessities; one-time fees, such as real estate agent fees or lease taxes; and reimbursements for required security expenses. If you are unable to stay in government housing when you first report to a permanent duty station outside of the USA (OCONUS) for some other reason beyond your control, you may be eligible for an overseas temporary lodging allowance; generally up to 60 days.

- **Dislocation Allowance:** A military member or family must periodically relocate due to a change in duty stations or as required by the government. A dislocation allowance or DLA ranging from about $1,800 to nearly $4,000 is granted to help offset your relocation expenses. The DLA rate is dependent on pay grade. This allowance does not apply toward the costs your family incurs locating to the first duty station after initial training.

- **Family Separation Allowance (FSA):** When your service member is away for more than 30 days, you are entitled to the Family Separation Allowance of $250 per month. If your service member is assigned to a permanent duty station where dependents are not allowed or if your spouse is on duty on board a ship at sea for more than 30 days, you will be entitled to the FSA.

TIME OFF AND LEAVE

Military members earn two and a half (2 ½) days leave per month, or 30 days each year. Service members leave can accumulate for up to 75 days-over two full years and if they don't use it they will lose it.

Active duty unable to take leave because of operational duties may carry forward as many as 120 days leave for up to three to four years depending on circumstances. This carryover happens automatically. If the active duty member retires or transitions out of the armed forces with unused leave, they may receive a cash buyout of their unused leave. Enlisted service members may now sell back up to 30 days of special accrued leave earned in a combat zone or designated contingency operation. This is an especially valuable benefit because payment for leave earned under these circumstances is not taxed, however you can't cash out more than sixty (60) days' worth of leave.

MILITARY PROVIDED LIFE INSURANCE

I was surprised at how many spouses and young newly-enrolled service members did not know about this benefit, and I was also surprised at how many service members do not keep this up-to-date when they got married or divorced. This is something that needs to be taken seriously. If you get married and you still have your parents on the policy as the beneficiary (and your parents hate your spouse) your parents (or whomever is listed) will get the money. NOT your spouse! This is a situation I have come across time and time again. And in several of these situations the parents (or whoever was listed as beneficiary) did not give any assistance to the spouse. This needs to be taken seriously: **MAKE SURE LIFE INSURANCE POLICIES ARE UPDATED!!**

The military provides service members and family members with access to high-quality, affordable group life insurance. Again, I will briefly touch on the subject. Contact your local unit or Family Assistance Center for more information.

Service Members Group Life Insurance (SGLI) is available to all active duty and members of the National Guard and Reserves. Active duty personnel are automatically covered for $400,000 of death benefits, and policy payments are allotted out of the paychecks at $29 a month. The premium cost to insure your Reservist who is not on active duty is $25 per year for $250,000 of insurance. If a service member wishes to reduce, change or cancel coverage they need to fill out the SGLI Election and Certificate Form 3286 and turn in to their HMO office.

This coverage stays in effect for the duration of the military career and converts into Veterans Group Life Insurance (VGLI) with no medical underwriting upon transitioning from the military. Just remember conversion from SGLI to VGLI **MUST** take place within 120 days of retirement to avoid medical underwriting.

If you wish to have more life insurance coverage, here is a list of companies that are military friendly (basically because they don't have a war clause).

Check out the following web sites for additional information.

- www.usaa.com (my favorite)
- www.usba.com

- www.moaa.org (officers)
- www.navymutual.org (Navy and Marines)
- www.aafmaa.com (Army and Air Force)
- www.afba.com

Along with the $29 monthly payment for SGLI at $400,000, a $1 per month premium is automatically included for Traumatic Injury Protection coverage (TIPC). This is a mandatory coverage and provides benefit between $25,000 and $100,000 if your soldier sustains one of the following **Traumatic Injuries:**

- Loss of sight, speech or hearing
- Loss of one hand or foot, or a major injury to the hand
- Severe paralysis, burns or brain injury

The military also provides a **Families Service Member Group Life Insurance Policy (FSGLI).** This policy covers $200,000 for your spouse and $10,000 for each of your dependent children. The cost for your spouse under 35 is $5.50 a month (deducted from your paycheck) and no cost coverage for dependent children. This premium increases at a very affordable amount every five years. For more information on FSGLI visit www.insurance.va.gov/sglisite/fsgli/sglifam.htm.

LEGAL RIGHTS/LEGAL ISSUES

As a military family you have many legal rights and protections. Laws have been passed to secure these rights; unfortunately some people will try to abuse military families. Make sure you are aware of your rights and do not be afraid to use them. One of the biggest rights you have is called **"The Service Members Civil Relief Act" (SCRA) also known as Soldiers & Sailors Relief Act.** This law helps insure your family's legal rights. The law covers all active duty service members, activated Guard and Reserve, and their dependent family members. These laws were put in place to allow your service member to focus on the job and minimize undue financial hardship on the military family. To further minimize hardship on your family, the Armed Services provide legal assistance to all active-duty, Guard and Reserve members, and their dependent family members. I will list some of the highlights of the SCRA that you should familiarize yourself with:

- **Limit on Interest Rates:** Interest rates that the service member must pay on any loan or debt that they had **prior** to active duty are limited to no more than 6% a year. **However,** this cap on your interest rates is **NOT** automatic. You must contact your lender in writing and request this benefit change. They will require a copy of your service member's orders and sometimes a copy of the Power of Attorney. Remember these are debts that include both spouses names and/or military member's name alone but **NOT** debts that list only spouse name. Some companies, like SEARS and

Military Star card, will even go farther and put your account on a deployment hold. This means you are NOT required to make payments on the account while your military member is deployed. This will not affect your credit rating negatively. *These companies deserve praise for making this extra gesture. For some families this really helps!!* Speak to your creditors and you will be surprised at how many will go the extra mile.

- **Stay of Proceedings:** If you are involved in a lawsuit you can request a delay, if the delay is necessary due to your service member's service. For example, if the service member cannot show up for court. This **DOES** include child support cases and custody cases.

- **Statute of Limitations:** Your active-duty service member's service to our country will not be taken into account when determining the statute of limitations on legal proceedings brought by or against you.

- **Health Insurance Reinstatement:** If the service member has health insurance prior to reporting to active duty, SCRA requires your civilian health insurance company to reinstate coverage when the service member completes their service.

- **Home Foreclosure Protection:** Your mortgage company can't foreclose on you if you have a mortgage prior to active duty and you can prove that military service is the reason you can't afford to make your mortgage payment. **Remember, mortgages also fall under the 6% cap.**

- **Eviction Protection:** Your landlord also has to be more flexible if you are renting your home and can't keep up with your rent payments because of your service member's duty. They are also required by law to let you out of any contract if you get activated or PCS'd (moved) without any backlash of court or marks to your credit report.

- **Business Lease Termination:** Your service member can terminate a business lease (even one that has both your names on it) contract that you or your spouse had prior to active duty if reporting to duty would make continuing that lease unreasonable. That does not include walking away from back payments or abandoning the building the minute orders are issued. You will be responsible for all past payments through (most cases) the end of the next month. You must give the lease holder/landlord written notice along with a copy of your orders and in some cases power of attorney paperwork if the spouse is cancelling on behalf of the service member. Remember this includes leasing cars and in some cases recently purchased cars.

- **Eliminates Double Taxation:** If you or your service member work in one state, but your legal residence is in a different state, SCRA prevents the state in which you're employed from taxing your income. Only your state of residence may tax your income. (Hopefully your legal residence is one of the few states without state income tax).

Remember the new ruling is that spouses no longer have to change residency every time they move. Make sure your tax accountant is aware of this when you are doing your taxes.

In addition to the protections provided by **SCRA,** Guard and Reserve families and service members receive additional protections under the **Uniformed Services Employment and Reemployment Rights Act (USERRA).** The biggest provision under **USERRA** is the law that requires employers to re-employ Guard and Reserve members when they return from deployment. The exception would be if the company went out of business. Not only is the employer required to re-employ service members returning to the civilian work force, but employers must also re-employ the reservist in a position comparable to the one they had prior to going on active duty along with full seniority, pay and any further benefits they had.

Most states have a **Legal Assistance Centers** (JAG) for military families that assist if you are having trouble with any legal issues or any of your rights under the laws. In addition to answering questions about your legal rights and protections, your legal assistance center can assist you by drafting a will and creating health care directives and powers of attorney. Legal assistance attorneys can also answer questions and give advice about your income taxes or any other personal legal issues. Remember this is at **NO COST** to you.

To find a legal assistance center near you visit http://legalassistance.law.af.mil/content/locator.php. Also your JAG office can assist with some legal issues and may have this contact information at hand.

Don't forget your **Family Support Center!** They are loaded with resources and contact information about benefits for military families. Most centers are staffed with people who've been through transitions, deployments and reunions. They have spouses in the service and kids in the local schools. The staff can help you locate discount day care (**NACCRA**) and get you information about programs for the kids and summer camps. They will also have information about grants and scholarships.

POWER OF ATTORNEY

I have spoken of this document briefly above so I want to state again how important it is to have one in place, not only during deployments but also in day-to-day life. This document enables you to appoint someone to make financial decisions and manage your financial affairs in the event that you can't do this for yourself. Most couples appoint each other as their financial power of attorney. But, you should also select a successor, so that in the event your spouse is unable or unavailable to perform these services, you've got a backup. Your **military legal assistance office** can also assist you in obtaining these documents.

You should also consider a Living Trust and/or Living Will and a Durable Power of Attorney for health care. I should also mention **"Accounting for ownership and beneficiary designation"** which means all assets that transfer by title or beneficiary designation upon death avoid probate. You can reduce probate expenses and hassles by maximizing your use of appropriate ownership classifications. There are many specifics regarding this so I advise counsel with your legal advisor.

MILITARY SERVICE MEMBER

In this section I will be listing some services that are for service members before, during and after deployment. Subjects will range from counseling, jobs, health, records and more. Please remember this includes female service members too.

CAREER/TRANSITIONS

Army Career and Alumni Program: The Army Career and Alumni Program (ACAP), provides soldiers and eligible family member's transition and job assistance services at most Army installations. ACAP services include pre-separation counseling and employment assistance. For more information go to: http://myarmybenefits.us.army.mil/Home/Benefit_Library/Federal_Benefits_Page/Army_Career_and_Alumni_Program_(ACAP).html

Army National Guard Apprenticeship Program Initiative (GAPI): A partnership of the Department of Labor (DOL) and the Veterans Administration (VA) that is designed to help soldiers improve their job skills and establish a lifetime career. This program is an "earn while you learn" experience whereby soldiers learn new concepts and skills and obtain national certification in one of over 100 trades while earning a wage. These trades are mapped to over 200 military occupational specialties (MOSs) and eligible soldiers receive VA educational benefits while they pursue an apprenticeship program. The apprenticeship combines an educational curriculum with on the job training supervised by a trade professional or supervisor. Apprenticeship training takes one to five years to complete or 2,000 documented work hours to become fully qualified in an occupation or trade. For more information regarding this program, go to http://www.army.mil/standto/archive/2010/07/14/.

Bureau of Apprenticeship and Training (BAT): The website lists apprenticeship program sponsors recognized and registered by the BAT. Apprenticeship programs are sponsored and operated on a voluntary basis by individual employers, employer associations, or partnerships between employers and labor unions. The data is updated on a monthly basis. It is presented by state and by county; occupations are in alphabetical order, followed by the employers who have a registered program for that occupation. To view apprenticeship programs offered by different states, go to http://www. aboutmasci.org.

Business Assistance For Veteran Business-Owners: There are many basic assistance needs that you can get for free. For example, business startup, business plan writing, basic contracting, marketing, networking, business development, growth, and similar types of help can all be found at no cost. Veteran programs continue to multiply, and a few free and low cost programs include:

- Veterans Business Outreach Centers www.usa.gov/vetcenter
- SBA Office of Veterans Business Development www.sba.gov/vets
- Entrepreneurship Bootcamp for Veterans with Disabilities www.whitman.syr.edu/ebv
- Women Veterans Igniting the Spirit of Entrepreneurship www.whitman.syr.edu/vwise
- National Center for the Veteran Institute for Procurement www.nationalvip.org
- Center for Veterans Enterprise www.vetbiz.gov
- Southwest Veterans' Business Resource Center www.wherecommunitiesserveveterans.org
- Inc./Joining Forces Military Entrepreneurs www.inc.com/militaryentrepreneurs
- National Veteran-Owned Business Association www.navoba.com
- Veteran and Military Business Owners Association www.vamboa.org
- Veterans Business Network www.veteransbusinessnetwork.com
- Veteran Franchises www.veteranfranchises.com
- Military.com www.military.com/benefits/veteran-benefits/veterans-in-business

Also, every government agency has an office specifically established to help small businesses get work with their agency. These are usually called the Office of Small and Disadvantaged Business Utilization www.osdbu.gov/members.html or simply the Office of Small Business Programs. All have veteran business programs; some have more in-depth programs than others but they all offer valuable information and host free or inexpensive veterans outreach events.

Career Assistance Program Loan: If you are an active duty Army or Air Force member in grades from E-6 through E-9, W01, CW2, or O-1 through 0-3 and can use a little financial assistance, you may be interested in the Career Assistance Program. This program offers a one-time only $5,000 loan at 1.5% annual percentage rate with a 48-month repayment schedule through the military allotment system. There is no penalty for early repayment. To qualify, you must be an AAFMAA member with $250,000 of term or $50,000 of Value-Added Whole life Insurance, on active duty and be able to initiate a government allotment. Loan proceeds provided through a free checking account at Armed Forces Bank. To request an application for the Career Assistance Program, contact a Membership Coordinator at 877-398-2263 or email at: membership@aafmaa.com.

CareerOneStop: Site offers career resources and workforce information to job seekers, students, businesses, and workforce professionals to foster talent development in a global economy. http://careeronestop.org

Center for Veteran Enterprise (Veteran Business Opportunities): Vetbiz. gov is a Veteran resource information web site designed to assist veteran entrepreneurs who want to start and expand their businesses in the federal and private marketplace. This site provides up to the minute information from the federal government as it pertains to service disabled and veteran owned small businesses. http://www.vetbiz.gov/

Center for Workforce Development: Troops to Energy Jobs Program. www.cewd.org.

Civilian Employees: Civilian federal employees who are members of the uniformed services and who are called to active duty (or volunteer for active duty or full-time National Guard duty) are entitled to the following rights and benefits. Please go to this site and review. http://www.opm.gov/oca/compmemo/2001/2001-09A.asp

Coast Guard Academy Alumni Association: Offers various resources and information. Check out their Career Center at http://www.cgaalumni.org/s/1043/start.aspx

Department of Veteran Affairs: Resource for providing jobs to veterans who are looking for VA opportunities. These job postings are ONLY open to veterans and related job status. http://www.va.gov/vecs

Employer Partnership of the Armed Forces: Connects qualified reservists and veterans with civilian employers to achieve a mutually beneficial relationship. Reservists and National Guard members can take advantage of the programs online portal. Employer Partnership offers career support to soldiers, dependents, and retirees along with resume tips and career development advice. There are over twenty program support managers located throughout the nation to assist service members with job placement and in some cases working one-on-one. For more information, visit the website at www.employerpartnership.org.

*Employer Support for the Guard and Reserve (ESGR): Employer Support for the Guard and Reserve (ESGR) is a Department of Defense Organization that operates as a staff group within the Office of the Assistant Secretary of Defense for Reserve Affairs (OASD/RA), which is in itself a part of the Office of the Secretary of Defense. In this environment, civilian employers play a critical role in the defense of the nation by complying with existing employment laws protecting the rights of workers who serve in the Reserve component. *This is a great organization and I have worked with them in the past. They are very quick to defend a soldier's job, make sure you check out the site to see all the laws that employers have to abide by.* http://www.esgr.org/site. For the state of Michigan your contact is Mr. Gary Aden at 517-481-7909.

E-VETS: Assists veterans preparing to enter the job market. It includes information on a broad range of topics, such as job search tools and tips, employment openings, career assessment, education and training, and benefits and special services available to veterans. The e-Vets resource advisor will provide a list of web links most relevant to your specific needs and interests. http://www.dol.gov/elaws/evets.htm

Goodwill Industries International: They have resources to help military members and military spouses write resumes and find jobs. www.goodwill.org

Helmets to Hardhats: This site provides assistance to military service members, Reservists and Guardsmen to transition from active duty to a career in the construction industry. Helmets to Hardhats connects veterans into promising careers in construction by assisting with building your profile, assist with searching and applying for careers, connect you with other veterans and their staff of construction industry and military professionals. For more information go to http://www.helmettohardhats.org/.

Hiring our Heroes: The U.S. Chamber of Commerce along with the U.S. Department of Labor Veterans' Employment and Training Service (DOL VETS) launched this nationwide effort in March of 2011 to bring job fairs to cities across the nation. The fairs are designed to help veterans and military spouses find meaningful employment, and to motivate companies to actively recruit veterans and military spouses. Hiring our Heroes includes 100 job fairs where employers and potential job candidates can meet. In addition to connecting job-hunting military spouses with employment today, the goal is to raise solid awareness among civilian companies about military spouses and all they have to offer as employees. For more information about this program and to see if they are coming to your state or one close to you, you can go to http://www. uschamber.com/veterans/events.

Hire A Hero: An online job board and community of choice for those who have served our country. Hire a Hero has helped thousands of veterans and their spouses connect to employers who value their service, work ethic and loyalty to our country. To learn more about Hire a Hero or other programs, you can email info@hireahero.org or go to the website at http://www.hireahero.org/.

Hire Vets First: Is a comprehensive career website for hiring veterans. No matter your occupation, you will find the resources you need for matching employment opportunities with veterans. http://hirevetsfirst.do/gov

Income Verification and Means Testing: 800-929-8387

Job Connection Education Program (JCEP): Provides assistance to Guard and Reserve service members and their spouses who are unemployed and/or under-employed to help find careers. Offered by the Army National Guard, dedicated training and development specialists and a skilled business advisor will assist participants in making their job connections. Texas was chosen as the first site for the Job Connection Education Program with officers in the Fort Worth Sandage Armory and the Houston Westheimer Armory. JCEP is now in Iowa assisting service members and their families, hopefully this is a program that will expand to other states soon. For more information go to http://www. jcep.info/.

Job Corps – Pilot Program: This program is open for young veterans aged 20-24 years old. It provides free housing and offers training in more than 100 career fields, such as construction, automotive repair, information technology and advanced manufacturing. Labor's Veterans Employment and Training Service in partnership with the Job Corps will enroll veterans and place you at either Atterbury Job Corps Center in Edinburgh, Indiana, Earle C. Clements Job Corps Center in Morganfield, Kentucky or Excelsior Springs Job Corps Center in Excelsior Springs, Montana. Depending on the career choice, veterans will train from eight months to two years and receive a basic living allowance. Upon successfully completing the program you will receive a credential or certificate qualifying you in your specific trade. Upon graduation, vets also can obtain help with job placement; resume drafting and job-interviewing skills. For more information, including how to enroll, call 1-800-733-5627 or access www. recruiting.jobcorps.gov.

Military Franchising (JOBS): If you are looking to earn extra income on the side and operate a business out of your home, a home-based franchise may interest you. This website is a list of home-based franchise opportunities for military spouses and veterans. Click here to find "military-spouse/veteran friendly" home-based franchise opportunities. http://www.militaryfranchising. com/spouse/default.aspx

Military to Medicine: A partnership of Inova Health System. If you have healthcare experience, they can put you to work through their National Healthcare Career Network of hiring employers. If you need to acquire civilian healthcare credentials, and/or if healthcare is a new career, then Inova will provide online training leading to in-demand, entry-level healthcare jobs. Military to Medicine serves transitioning service members, National Guard, Reserve, veterans, wounded warriors and their caregivers, and military spouses. Learn more at www.militarytomedicine.org.

Military and Veteran Associations: Members of the military community have the opportunity to join or otherwise benefit from several types of associations and organizations. Ranging from fraternal to charity, the military-specific organizations can provide advocacy, help you network to access job opportunities, tap into benefits, lobby congress or find support. Click on the link at this site to navigate; it is far too long to put in this book. http://www.military.com/military-report/military-and-veteran-associations-012411?ESRC=miltrep.nl

National Association for Uniformed Services: Offers a variety of assistance from scholarships, resources, vacation discounts and news. Visit http://www.naus.org/ for updated information.

NEXSTEP: A Department of Labor funded program designed to provide eligible military spouses, DoD civilian employees and activated National Guard and Reservist with training so they can successfully enter, or re-enter the workforce. Visit http://www.military.com/spouse/cf/0,,cf_nexstep_091905,00.html for further information regarding this program.

Office of Personnel Management (OPM) – Federal Jobs for Veterans: Certain veterans, principally those who are disabled or who served on active duty during specified times, are entitled to preference for federal civil service jobs filled by open, competitive exams. Preference is also provided for widows/widowers not remarried, mothers of personnel who died in service, and spouses of service-connected disabled. This preference includes five or ten points added to passing scores on examinations. Individuals interested in federal information should contact the personnel officers of the federal agencies in which they wish to be employed. Or, contact any Office of Personnel Management (OPM) Service Center. The centers are listed in telephone books under U.S. Government, or you can visit the web site at http://www.opm.gov. Federal job opportunities can be found at http://www.usa.jobs.opm.gov. Also check out http://www.fedshirevets.gov.

Transition Assistance Advisors (National Guard and Veterans Affairs): The National Guard has placed a Transition Assistance Advisor at each of the State Joint Forces Headquarters to serve as the statewide point of contact and coordinator for easy access to Department of Veterans Affairs benefits and to provide assistance in access to entitlements through the Military Health System (TRICARE). Transition Assistance Advisors (formerly State Benefits Advisors) assist National Guard members with access to care and enrollment at VA healthcare facilities near their home of record. They also assist National Guard members and their families in applying for other VA entitlements and benefits such as compensation and pension for disabilities, insurance, loan guarantee, vocational rehabilitation/employment (VRE) and educational benefits. Additionally, they work with other Joint Forces Headquarters staff members and Directors of State Family Programs to build a state coalition of support with VA and community organizations for Guard members and their families to access in their community.

While the program was set up to primarily take care of Guard members and their families, Transition Assistance Advisors provide critical support and facilitate the integration for the delivery of VA and community services to all members of the active and reserve components.The state coalition is a model that ties together the resources of the Department of Defense, Department of Veterans Affairs, National Guard, and state and local community resources in an effort to ensure Guard members and their families receive the benefits and support to which they are entitled. Unlike active component members who return to a specific military base with onsite support and services for the service member and family, reserve component members return to their communities and civilian employment. The state coalition provides a community based network of support of VA, state and community resources to assist Guard and Reserve members at the local level. Transitional Assistance Advisors can be reached through the National Guard Family Program website at: http://www.jointservicessupport.org/ResourceFinderSearchFilter.aspx.

For more information about Transition Advisors you may also go to-http://turbotap.org/portal/transition/lifestyles/Introduction/National_Guard_Transition_Assistance_Advisor

Mr. Ray Ladd, POC for Michigan ANG, 517-990-1111 email at raymond.ladd@us.army.mil.

Transition Assistance Program (TAP): A site designed specifically to assist service members leaving active duty. This site will provide assistance with resume writing, financial planning, interviewing and job fairs for service members and other services. Retirees can start the process two years before leaving the military. For active duty, the law requires the military to offer TAP services–such as employment workshops or other seminars, often run by Department of Labor employees—at least 90 days before discharge. While the DoD Transportal site contains valuable information and resources, you should use this site as part of a comprehensive program of transition and employment assistance. http://www.turbotap.org and TAP–transitions assistance guide for demobilizing members of the guard and reserves: http://www.transitionassistanceprogram.com/portal/transition/resources/.

Troops 2 Roughnecks: Trains vets for jobs on oil and gas rigs. www.troops2roughnecks.com

Troops to Teachers: A program that helps veterans in efforts to become certified teachers under state law, and then provides placement assistance to appropriate schools. The program does not alter or circumvent existing teacher certification requirements. Troops to Teachers is funded by the U.S. Department of Education and managed by the U.S. Department of Defense. For more information about this great program go to http://www.proudtoserveagain.com/.

USAJOBS: The sole site where DoD job openings are listed. Features include USA Jobs, online resumes, a personal career management home, an option to make resumes searchable by agency recruiters, and an option to create and store letters. For current federal employees, the site provides information about career and job opportunities, leadership, insurance, pay and leave, benefits, work life, retirement and other topics of interest. http://www.usajobs.opm.gov/

U.S. Chamber of Commerce Hiring our Heroes Program: You can visit www.uschamber.com/veterans and www.facebook.com/hiringourheroes.

Veteran Employment Center - Veteran Job Site. http://www.military.com/veteran-job?ESRC=army.nl

Veterans Employment and Training Service (VETS): VETS assists veterans and service members with resources and expertise to assist and prepare them to obtain meaningful careers, maximize their employment opportunities, and protect their employment rights. For more information, go to http://www.dol.gov/vets/.

VMET: The Verification of Military Experience and Training (VMET) Document, DD Form 2586, helps service members verify previous experience and training to potential employers. VMET documents are available only through Army, Navy, Air Force, and Marine Corps Transition Support officers and are intended for separating or retiring service members who have at least six months of active duty service. Service members should obtain VMET documents from their Transition Support office within 12 months of separation or 24 months of retirement. Call the Veterans Question Hotline at 1-800-455-5228.

VetJobs: This website assists veterans, spouses and family members find quality jobs with employers worldwide. Vetjobs is partially owned by VFW and has been endorsed by various other veterans' service organizations. Vetjobs employment assistance section has all the tools and guidance needed to find jobs. It will start out with a career assessment, assistance on interviewing, writing resumes and other services. It also lists all legitimate job boards by occupation and location in the U.S. For employers, VetJobs is a flat-fee site that has the largest reach possible into the veteran job-candidate market. Additionally, VetJobs has been effective for those employers who need candidates with security clearances. For further information go to www.vetjobs.com.

EMERGENCY AND FINANCIAL ASSISTANCE

Veterans Assistance Foundation: Operates programs designed to assist homeless or at risk of becoming homeless veterans maintain or improve their status in society by providing safe and secure environment through which they can access a wide array of human services. http://vafvets.org

VA Benefits: For information about education, home loans, disability, medical care, burial, life insurance, sexual trauma. 1-800-827-1000

VA Veterans Crisis Line: 800-273-8255 (press 1) www.veteranscrisisline.net

Swords to Plowshares: Their mission is to heal the wounds, to restore dignity, hope and self-sufficiency to all veterans in need, and to significantly reduce homelessness and poverty among veterans. Founded in 1974, Swords to Plowshares is a community-based, not-for-profit organization that provides counseling and case management, employment and training, housing and legal assistance to more than 1500 homeless and low-income veterans annually in the San Francisco Bay Area and beyond. They promote and protect the rights of veterans through advocacy, public education, and partnerships with local, state, and national entities. Swords to Plowshares is the only veteran's service agency in the U.S. that provides a full continuum of care. They help vets, as well as families of vets, in the following areas:

- Health & Social Services – drop-in center provides emergency shelter, mental health services and referrals to homeless veterans.

- Housing – residential programs provide housing, rehabilitation and counseling to veterans in need.

- Employment & Training – through direct training and job referrals Swords to Plowshares helps veterans re-enter the workforce.

- Veterans Academy – formerly homeless veterans can live in a supportive community.

- Legal – provides free attorney representation and advocacy to veterans seeking benefits.

For more information please visit the website at http://swords-to-plowshares. org/.

LEGAL RESOURCES

Lawyers for Warriors: This organization was created after a soldier was shot through the neck in Afghanistan and was paralyzed. While in the hospital, he was served with foreclosure papers. In cases such as this one, service members who are deployed often do not have someone to turn to for help. This organization is dedicated to remedying this problem. Lawyers for Warriors is a 501(c)3 organization which has a mission to provide pro bono legal services to members of the United States Armed Forces, especially those who are deployed to hostile fire zones. After identifying troops needing legal assistance, Lawyers for Warriors will pair the warrior with an attorney specializing in that area of law. Lawyers for Warriors also provides legal assistance to recently-returned veterans and their families. www.lawyersforwarriors.org

Lawyers Serving Warriors: Provides free legal services to warriors of OIF/OEF. www.lawyerservingwarriors.com

Legal Assistance: For the U.S. Armed Forces. http://legalassistance.law.af.mil

Legal Assistance Finder: http://legalassistance.law.af.mil/contect/locator.php

Legal ACE for Troops: Will provide a free will to any active duty service member of the U.S. Armed Forces, but will also provide more than 50 other discounted legal services to all active members and veterans of the military. http://legalacefortroops.com/

Operation Military Embrace: Coordinates legal assistance for those in the military who are accused of battlefield crimes. www.operationmilitaryembrace.com

National Veterans Legal Services Program: Provides legal assistance to all branches of the Armed Forces. www.nvlsp.org. 202-265-8305 and/or info@nvlsp.org

U.S. Air Force Legal Assistance: This website is intended for active duty, reserve component, and retired military members, their family members, and others eligible for legal assistance through the military. http://aflegalassistance.law.af.mil/lass/lass.html

U.S. Armed Forces Legal Assistance: Complete a form to locate active duty legal activities offering general legal services within the continental United States. http://legalassistance.law.af.mil/content/locator.php

U.S. Navy Judge Advocate General's Corps: Provides solutions, from a military perspective, to legal issues involving military operations, organization, and personnel, wherever and whenever such solutions are required, with primary focus on operations, accountability, Sailor legal readiness, and Navy legal readiness. www.jag.navy.mil

Stateside Legal: Has created a website to give legal help and/or advice for military members, veterans and their families. The goal is to help military families find their own solutions to common legal problems and find someone to help you if you need legal advice. If you are having trouble finding what you're looking for, check out the user guide for tips. http://statesidelegal.org/

The Center for Women Veterans: This organization assures women veterans receive benefits and services on a par with male veterans, encounter no discrimination in their attempt to access these services, and are treated with respect and dignity by VA service providers. They act as the primary advisor to the Secretary for Veterans' Affairs on all matters related to programs, issues, and initiatives for and affecting women veterans. http://www.va.gov/womenvet/

OTHER RESOURCES

Buddy to Buddy Program: Links trained vets to veterans struggling with reintegration. http://buddytobuddy.org

Civilian Deployment: Good information to stay updated on. http://www.dfas.mil/dfas/civilianemployees.html

Civilian Personnel Records: CPR houses the official personnel folders (OPF) and employee medical folders (EMF) of separated federal civilian employees. http://www.archives.gov

Divorce Care: Will help you find help and healing for the hurt of separation and divorce. Divorce Care is a friendly, caring group of people who will walk alongside you through one of life's most difficult experiences. Don't go through separation or divorce alone. Divorce Care has seminars and support groups that are led by people who understand what you are going through and want to help. You'll gain access to valuable Divorce Care resources to help you deal with the pain of the past and look forward to rebuilding your life. Divorce Care has a huge staff of recovery support groups meeting throughout the US, Canada and in other countries around the world. Please go to the website to find one close to you and for further information. www.divorcecare.com

Dryhootch of America: A nonprofit formed by combat veterans to help others returning home, officially opened its first veteran's center in Milwaukee on August 27, 2010. Rebuilding Together, a nonprofit group led the effort by partnering with The American Legion, Sears and Local Plumbers Union 75 to help make the veterans center a reality. Dryhootch of American mission is to give returning soldiers a peace of mind and any further assistance they may need to transition back to civilian life. For further information go to the Dryhootch of America Facebook page.

eMilitary.org: The homepage is provided to veterans to access the information they need and to help veterans network with other veterans. Provides forums and chat along with other assistance. Soon they will be providing other resources online. http://www.emilitary.org/usvet.php

Global Assessment Tool (GAT) for Soldiers: www.SFT.army.mil/; GAT for family members: www.SFT.army.mil/sftfamily.

Guardian Angels For Soldier's Pets: This organizations mission is supporting our military, veterans, and their beloved pets to ensure the pets are reunited with their owners following a deployment (combat or peace-keeping mission) in harm's way to fight the global war on terrorism or unforeseen emergency hardship impacting their ability to retain their pet's ownership rights. Please go to the website to get further information on eligibility. http://guardianangelsforsoldierspet.org

Honor Flight Network: A non-profit organization created solely to honor America's veterans for all their sacrifices. They will transport our heroes to Washington, D.C. to visit and reflect at their memorials. Top priority is given to the senior veterans—World War II survivors, along with those other veterans who may be terminally ill. For more information, go to http://www. honorflight.org.

Life Insurance: 800-669-8477

Iraqi and Afghanistan Veterans of American (IAVA): Connect with other veterans, get access to critical resources, and play a role in tackling issues that impact our community. http://iava.org/membership

Military One Source: Education, health, relocation, parenting, stress—you name it—Military OneSource is here to help you with just about any need. Available by phone or online, their free service is provided by the Department of Defense for active-duty, Guard, and Reserve service members and their families. The service is completely private and confidential, with few exceptions. http://www.militaryonesource.com/MOS.aspx

Military Personnel Records: The National Personnel Records Center, Military Personnel Records (NPRC-MPR) is the repository of millions of military personnel, health, and medical records of discharged and deceased veterans of all services during the 20th century. (Records prior to WW1 are in Washington, DC) NPRC (MPR) also stores medical treatment records of retirees from all services, as well as records for dependent and other persons treated at Naval medical facilities. http://www.archives.gov/st-louis/military-personnel/

MyArmyBenefits: MyArmyBenefits is your official Army benefits resource for the regular Army, Army National Guard, Army Reserve, family members and retirees. It is a one-stop shop for the latest, most up to date information on eligibility, benefits and locations where benefits services are provided. Visit http://myarmybenefits.us.army.mil/.

National Resource Directory: A revitalized Department of Labor online directory promises access to "thousands" of services and resources for wounded troops, veterans and their families. The National Resource Directory provides links to national, state and local sources that support "recovery, rehabilitation and community reintegration." The site offers information for vets seeking education, training and employment. It also provides help for employers who want to hire veterans, understand employment laws and make workplace accommodations for disabled vets. For more information go to http://www. nationalresourcedirectory.gov.

NCO Association USA: The Association was established in 1960 for all branches of Armed Forces, National Guard and Reserves. NCOA offers its members a wide range of benefits and services designed especially for enlisted service members and their families. NCO is partnered with various stores to provide huge discounts and other services for military families. There is a small membership fee to join. Go to http://www.ncoausa.org/ for further information.

Operation Homelink: Operation Homelink provides refurbished computers to the spouses or parents of junior enlisted (E1-E5) U.S. deployed service members, enabling email communication with their loved ones deployed overseas. To date, the nonprofit organization has partnered with corporate donors to link 3,200 deployed soldiers with their families using Internet-friendly computers. Regardless of where computers are sent, they are provided to units that are scheduled to deploy overseas in the next 90 days. Operation Homelink does not accept individual requests for computers. For more information, visit the Operation Homelink website at http://myarmyonesource.com/News/2010/02/OperationHomelink.

Soldiers Angels: Assistance for soldiers through their "Adopt a Soldier Program." http://www.soldiersangels.org

The Rucksack - Rewards for Vets: Where *IAVA* member veterans get access to exclusive tickets, giveaways and more. Signing up is free and easy. Open to all confirmed veterans of Iraq (OIF) and Afghanistan (OEF). www.rucksack.iava.org

*Veterans Network: This is a casual environment of information for the veterans and their families. *I found the site very enjoyable and I would not mind being on the show one day. Everyone should check this site out!* http://veteransnetwork. net/

Veterans License Plates: Provides information about the different military license plates that are offered. http://www.dmv.state.pa.us/militaryCenter/licensePlates.shtml

Veteran Resource: A VA newsletter offers resource for Iraq and Afghanistan veterans interested in learning more about benefits, health risks and current news. *The Operation Enduring Freedom/Operation Iraqi Freedom Review* can be accessed online at www.publichealth.va.gov/exposures/oefoif. Click on the "Resources and Materials" link in the upper right box to link to an electronic edition. Veterans also can order free hard-copy subscriptions at the site as well.

RESOURCES FOR SMALL BUSINESS

Business.gov: The U.S. government's official web site to help small businesses start and operate while staying compliant with laws and regulations. www.business.gov

Counselors to America's Small Business (SCORE): Is a non-profit association that provides FREE counseling and mentoring to entrepreneurs. www.score.org and/or 800-634-0245

National Federation of Independent Business (NFIB): Is a non-profit association that represents small and independent businesses in the United States. www.NFIB.com and/or 800-634-2669

Small Business Administration (SBA): An independent government agency that helps American Veterans starts, build and grow a business. www.sba.gov

DIVORCE IN THE MILITARY: A SPOUSE'S RIGHTS

Separation: Before you begin interviewing attorneys, spend a few days learning everything you can about military divorce. Search the Internet for branch specific divorce and military divorce. Don't sign anything without your attorney's approval. Your attorney should be experienced in military divorce and licensed to practice in the state where the divorce is filed.

Home of Record or Legal Residence: The home of record is the address used when the service member entered the military. The state of legal residence is where the service member intends to live after discharge. Military divorces must be filed in the home of record of the service member.

Uniformed Services Former Spouse Protection Act (USFSPA): All states allow military retirement pay to be recognized and divided as marital property. Different states use different formulas when dividing marital property. The spouse receives a percentage of "disposable" retired pay; this doesn't include disability pay or survivor benefit premiums paid by the service member for the spouse.

The USFSPA also addresses the spouse's continuing eligibility for commissary, exchange, and health-care benefits. If a couple divorces before the service member retires, the court may still award the spouse a share of future retired pay. Make sure your attorney understands the USFSPA.

Soldiers' and Sailors' Civil Relief Act (SSCRA): Congress protects service members from lawsuits, including divorces proceedings, especially when the service member is overseas. Courts can delay a divorce proceeding for as long as the service member is on active duty and for 60 days thereafter. The court may appoint an "ad litem" attorney to represent the service member in a temporary judgment. Make sure your attorney understands the SSCRA.

Separation Agreement: Even if you and your spouse have a separation agreement, you are still legally married. This is not a good time for either party to move in with a new significant other because this could be viewed as adultery by the court. (If the signed agreement states that you both agree to a no-fault divorce, this may remove the risk of being charged with adultery.) A spouse can continue to live in base housing and retain all military privileges during the separation.

Prenuptial or Postnuptial Agreement: If you both signed a prenuptial or postnuptial agreement relating to property settlement in the event of divorce, this agreement takes precedence over state and federal laws governing divorce in the military.

Divorce: Sailors, Marines and Soldiers wanting a fast, easy divorce will quickly find that the government expects them to remember their Core Values and act responsibly toward their spouses and children at all times. The military has severe penalties for any service member who deserts his or her family, up to and including court martial.

Quickie Divorce: Don't try to circumvent the system by going to Mexico or any other location outside of the United States for a quick divorce. The jurisdiction of a foreign court granting U.S. citizens a divorce is highly questionable and will not serve as a proper basis for payment of public funds. If the service member were to remarry and try to make the new spouse a military dependent (NAVMC 10922), he or she will have to show proof of divorce. The former spouse would still be legally married to the service member in the eyes of the military.

Adoption: If your spouse has a child from a previous marriage and you adopt the child, you are responsible for child support even after the divorce. (You divorce your spouse, not your children.) The law grants adopted children the same rights as biological children. Child support usually ends at age 18, but have your attorney clarify this in the divorce agreement.

Rules 20/20/20 and 20/20/15: In addition to half of the service member's disposable retirement pay, former spouses who qualify under the 20/20/20 rule may be permitted to retain their military ID and commissary, exchange, and healthcare benefits. 20/20/20 means that a spouse has been married to a service member for at least 20 years, the service member served at least 20 years, and there was at least a 20 year overlap of the marriage and military career. Because the state court decides how martial assets will be divided, a spouse married for only one or two years could be awarded a portion of the service members' pension. It is in the spouse's best interest to delay the final judgment until she or he meets the 20/20/20 or 20/20/15 rule. If the 20/20/20 spouse remarries, she or he will forfeit all military benefits, but if this new marriage ends due to divorce or death, the former spouse may have all military benefits reinstated.

Child Support and Alimony: MILPERSMAN Article 1754-030 states that whether it is a spouse or a spouse with children, or if there are no spousal benefits but child support, the alimony and child support entitlement can be determined by a simple formula. If you and your spouse have a separation agreement or court order, this formula will not apply.

Financial Need: If you are not receiving support and have been unable to contact your military member, call the Legal Assistance (JAG) or your chaplain. The chaplain will notify the service member's command officer about your situation. If your situation is critical, the Family Assistance Program can assist with grants for necessities. However, the service member will be in serious trouble for neglecting to provide for the family. Under DoD

Pay Manual Article, a service member must pay dependents, at minimum, his or her monthly basic allowance for subsistence (BAS).

SPECIAL INFORMATION

**OIF/OEF personnel who have sustained a TBI (concussion) while serving in Iraq or Afghanistan and sustained symptoms from the encounter may now qualify for Purple Heart Medals under new Army guidelines. The change, which was reported back in March 2011, means thousands of soldiers may qualify for the medal, which is awarded for wounds or injuries resulting from combat. Earlier attempts at adding concussions to the list of qualifying wounds was derided by those who thought conventional wounds only should be on the list but as traumatic brain injury has become more of a signature wound from roadside bombs and mental health issues, thinking has begun to change. Soldiers who suffer from concussions and were denied the medal are being encouraged to seek review of their cases. They can do so by calling 888-276-9472 or sending an email to hrc.tagd. awards@concus.army.mil.

**The VA has broadened its list of illnesses afflicting 1991 Persian Gulf War veterans. As of Aug 15th 2011, functional gastrointestinal disorders, such as irritable bowel syndrome or chronic constipation and diarrhea when lasting months or longer, are now considered eligible for presumptive service-connected disability care and compensation. Service members should make every effort to review their records for claims for these disorders if they were in the Gulf War and previously denied.

**Gulf War Veterans with certain ailments like Chronic Fatigue Syndrome, Fibromyalgia, functional gastrointestinal disorders and other previously undiagnosed illnesses can apply to have these ailments covered. The current deadline for when the condition must have "appeared" is on or before December 31, 2011. If you have any conditions that are "undiagnosed" and you did a tour in the Middle East, this could apply to you. The VA is working to extend the deadline to December 31, 2018. If this occurs, it will be great news for veterans and military members who develop symptoms after the 2011 cut-off. However, since there is no guarantee that the deadline will be extended, veterans suffering from undiagnosed conditions are encouraged to talk with their Veteran Service Officer about filing a disability claim for these conditions. http://www. military.com/veterans-report/gulf-war-claims-deadline?ESRC=vr.nl

**There is a new law in Colorado that offers a break for vets in their civilian careers. Colorado House Bill 11-1013, enacted on April 13, 2011 helps eligible vets who are licensed professionals, such as engineers, architects, doctors, plumbers and electricians. It applies to active-duty troops, members of the National Guard and Reserve and recently discharged vets who have served at least 120 days during "a war, emergency or contingency."

If you are eligible and hold a professional or occupational license with the state of Colorado, the state will do two things the next time you renew your license. First, it will waive the license renewal fee, and two; it will waive any continuing education credit requirements. This law applies to 53 professions. http://www.leg.state.co.us/CLICS/CLICS2011A/csl.nsf/fsbillcont3/B862E6856C0559DF87257816005837D9?open&file=1013_enr.pdf. *This is a great benefit to military families, thank you Colorado!!!*

As of September 2011, Veterans who served aboard U.S. Navy and Coast Guard ships operating on the waters of Vietnam between January 9, 1962 and May 7, 1975 may be eligible to receive Department of Veterans Affairs (VA) disability compensation for 14 medical conditions associated with presumptive exposure to Agent Orange. An updated list of U.S. Navy and Coast Guard ships confirmed to have operated on Vietnam's inland waterways, docked on shore, or had crewmembers sent ashore has been posted at the VA Public Health Agent Orange webpage to assist Vietnam Veterans in determining potential eligibility for compensation benefits. For questions about Agent Orange and the online of ships, veterans may call the VA Special Issues Helpline at 800-749-8387 and press 3. For more information you can go to: http://www.military.com/veterans-report/va-lists-ships-exposed-to-agent-orange?ESRC=vr.nl

As of the printing of this book, changes have been made to the Family Leave Act. Beginning October 31, 2011, federal employees will be entitled to take up to 12 weeks of unpaid leave to assist an active duty family member who is deployed overseas, or who is about to deploy. The new regulations issued by the Office of Personnel management amend the Family and Medical Leave Act. Employees will also be able to take leave to attend counseling, either for themselves, or for the service member or the service members' child, as long as the need for counseling is related to the deployment. A copy of the new regulations is available on the Office of Personnel Management website at http://www.gpo.gov/fdsys/pkg/FR-2011-09-30/html/2011-25310.htm.

Those denied Purple Heart should reapply. Active-duty and reserve-component soldiers, as well as veterans, who were denied Purple Heart awards for concussive or mild traumatic brain injuries, are encouraged to resubmit documentation for reconsideration of the medal. The injury must have occurred on or after Sept. 11, 2001. Active-duty and reserve-component soldiers must resubmit through their chains of command. Veterans should submit packages directly to Army Human Resources Command. They can obtain copies of their deployment orders from the Veteran's Inquiry Branch by Emailing veterans@conus.army.mil. Veterans will also need to submit their DD Form 214. More information on submission requirements is available at Army Human Resources Command. https://www.hrc.army.mil/

WEBSITES OF INTEREST

82nd Airborne Division Association - http://www.82ndassociation.org/Index.html

Air Force Aid Society – http://www.afas.org

American Division Veterans Association – http://www.americal.org/

Army Aviation Association of America – http://www.quad-a.org/

Association of Naval Aviation – http://www.anahq.org

Army Nurse Corps Association - http://e-anca.org/index.htm

Army Ranger Association - http://www.ranger.org/

Army Reserve Association – http://www.armyreserve.org

Association of the US Army – http://www.ausa.org

Coast Guard Chief Warrant and Warrant Officers Association - http://www.cwoauscg.org/

Coast Guard Foundation – http://www.coastguardfoundation.org/

Fleet Reserve Association – http://www.fra.org

Jewish War Veterans Association – http://www.jwv.org

Joe Foss Institute – http://www.joefoss.com/

Military Times – http://www.militarytimes.com

National Guard Association of the United States – http://www.ngaus.org/

Naval Enlisted Reserve Association – http://www.nea.org/

Naval Marine EOD Association – http://www.usn-usmceodassoc.org/look/links.html

Pearl Harbor Memorial Fund – http://www.trellon.com/project/pearl-harbor-memorial-fund

Professional Armed Forces Rodeo Association – http://www.pafra2000.com

Special Forces Association – http://www.specialforcesassociation.org/

Surface Navy Association - http://www.navysna.org/awards/index.html#walters

The Scottish-American Military Society – http://www.post1889.org

The Tailhook Association – http://www.tailhook.org/

The Retired Enlisted Association – http://www.trea.org/

U.S. Air Force Association - http://www.usafa.org

United States Coast Guard Academy Alumni Association – http://www.cgaalumni.org/S/1043/start.aspx

U.S. Coast Guard Chief Petty Officers Association – http://www.uscgcpoa.org/

U.S. Naval Academy Alumni Association – http://www.usna.com

Veterans Advocates of Ore-Ida – http://www.veteranadvocates.org

Women's Army Corps Veterans Association – http://www.armywomen.org

Women Organizing Women – http://www.vetwow.com/aboutus.htm

Service Member

EDUCATION FOR SERVICE MEMBERS AND SPOUSES

Military service provides access to a wide variety of educational benefits for military members and families (look in military spouse and youth & children for dependent educational information). Active-duty service members may qualify for more than $50,000 in education benefits, which can be used to obtain an undergraduate college degree, specific vocational training, or graduate and post-graduate degrees. Many of the educational programs available today are designed to fit your military lifestyle. Many universities have established special partnerships with the Armed Forces and have programs available on some military bases. There are great programs accessible to service members, spouses and dependents through independent study, distance learning, online courses and on base courses. There are many ways to obtain and pay for a formal education through scholarships, discounts and grants. Please review all your options.

The centerpiece of armed services educational benefits is the GI Bill which encompasses several Department of Veterans Affairs education programs including the Post-9/11 GI Bill, The Montgomery GI Bill for Active Duty and Veterans (MGIB-AD), Montgomery GI Bill for Selected Reserves (MGIB-SR). Reserve Education Assistance Program (REAP), Veterans Education Assistance Program (VEAP), Spouse and Dependents Education Assistance (DEA), and the Vocational Rehabilitation and Education (VR&E) program.

**You may be eligible for more than one educational benefit. Knowing when each is best for your situation can save you money and ensure you get the most out of your benefits. Finally, remember that each service has its own tuition assistance programs, college funds and other means that may be able to help you in ways beyond those of the "standard" benefits listed here (some of those are listed in the next section of this book). Talk with an Education Service Officer, Navy College counselor or military recruiter to find out more. And remember DO NOT sign off on any program before you review everything. A site may tell you that you cannot use both programs for educational assistance, but it will generally will mean you cannot at the same time. This does not mean you cannot use them at different times. Please be aware of these "catchy" comments.

Army Aviation Association (AAAA): The AAAA Scholarship Foundation, Inc., is a non-profit, tax-exempt corporation established to render financial assistance for the college-level education of members of the Army Aviation Association of America, Inc., (AAAA), and the spouses, unmarried siblings, unmarried children and unmarried grandchildren of current and deceased AAAA members. For further information about this scholarship and eligibility requirements go to http://www.quad-a.org/.

Army Master of Social Work (MSW) Program: The Army Medical Department (AMEDD) offers a variety of training opportunities for members of the Guard and Reserves to participate in graduate education alongside others in the AMEDD family. Among these educational opportunities is the Army Master of Social Work (MSW) Program. This program is 14 months long for Guard Soldiers who have undergraduate degrees from accredited colleges or universities. The MSU Program is nine months for Guard Soldiers who have completed a Bachelor of Social Work degree within five years of their program start date.

The objective of the internship phase is to enable new MSO graduates to complete state requirements to acquire their independent practitioner license. National Guard members who attend the MSU Program complete the internship phase at a Veterans Affairs hospital located in their home state. The program is also accredited by the Southern Association of Colleges and Schools. This enables graduates of the MSU Program to be eligible to take their license exam upon graduation.

The Army MSU Program is unlike any graduate social work program in that it equips its graduates to practice as social workers in a military community. Every course within this program is presented from a military perspective. It is essential that military social workers are able to provide competent and ethical social work support in a variety of settings.

So, if you have a passion for working with military families and would like to become a uniformed social worker in the Army National Guard, the Army MSU Program may be designed for you. This program will not only give you the opportunity to receive your graduate social work degree in 14 months, but will also equip and prepare you to take the Licensed Master of Social Work Exam prior to beginning your 24 month post-master's internship.

Army National Guard social work is an excellent opportunity to have a direct impact on both military and civilian communities. They work with soldiers and their families via education, prevention, intervention and ongoing career lifecycle support. For more information go to http://www.healthcare. goarmy.com.

Armed Forces Communications and Electronics Association: Is a registered 501c(3) non-profit organization dedicated to providing educational incentives, opportunities and assistance for people engaged in information management, communications and intelligence efforts and fostering excellence in education particularly in the "hard science" disciplines related to C4ISR. The mission of the foundation is to support development of engineers and technical personnel through selective training, scholarships, awards, prizes and grants for educational activities of unique and high value and professional educational programs.

The components of the AFCEA Educational Foundation's present efforts are: Scholarships, Fellowships and Grants Program, Awards for Excellence and Merit and the AFCEA Professional Development Center. For more information about the educational program and grants go to http://www.afcea. org/education/scholarships/mission.asp.

Army National Guard Tuition Assistance: Provides financial assistance for college or graduate school to members of the Army National Guard in each state. Amounts vary from $4,000-$4,999. http://www.military.com/education/ content/money-for-school/national-guard-tuition-assistance.html

Army Nurse Corps Association (ANCA): ANCA awards scholarships to U.S. citizen students attending accredited baccalaureate or graduate nursing or anesthesia nursing programs. This scholarship is in honor of Cpt. Joshua M. McClimans, AN, USAR, who was killed in a mortar attack in April 2011 while assigned to the Combat Support Hospital at Forward Operating Base Salerno in Afghanistan. For more information about this scholarship and eligibility requirements go to http://e-anca.org/ANCAEduc.htm.

Army Ranger Association: This scholarship program is memorial to selfless service and contributions made to our country by USARA members. These awards are given in their honor. This program provides an opportunity to provide financial assistance to qualified dependents of USARA members in furthering their education. The scholarship committee seeks to award scholarships to applicants displaying the potential for a degree in higher education, whether it is technical, university or professional. Each year the scholarship committee evaluates the scholarship applicants and selects the most outstanding submissions to be awarded to USARA Legacy Scholarship. For further information about this scholarship and eligibility requirements go to http://www.ranger.org/.

Bowfin Memorial Scholarship: For members of the Hawaii submarine force and personnel and their family members. Contact Patty Doty at 808-455-2597 or dcpcc@aol.com.

Concorde Career Colleges, Inc: Concorde has 15 campuses in seven states and offers 100% healthcare training for a variety of healthcare careers. Concorde offers 23 exciting programs in healthcare fields that are in demand like Vocational/Practical Nursing, Medical Assisting, Respiratory Therapy and more. View the website or call to get more information on training that is available for service members and their family members. 800-331-2397 and www.concorde4me.com.

Coast Guard Foundation: A non-profit organization dedicated to improving the lives of the men and women of the Coast Guard and their families. Founded more than 40 years ago, the Coast Guard Foundation provides education, support and relief for the brave men and women, who enforce maritime law, protect our homeland and preserve the environment. The Coast Guard Foundation aims to strengthen their service to our nation by encouraging them to be the best that they can be, on and off duty. http://www.coastguardfoundation.org/about

Coast Guard Mutual Assistance: Provides assistance, programs and educational programs. http://www.cgmahq.org/

82nd Airborne Division Association: Offers a scholarship to Former Troopers (within 2 years of their ETS date, some other restrictions may apply) and their dependent children. Spouses are not eligible. Applicant MUST be intent on pursuing a course toward a baccalaureate degree, and MUST gain at least 12 semester hours per semester toward that degree. Please go to the web site for further information and eligibility requirements at http://www.82ndassociation.org/Scholarships.html, you can also send inquiries to 82assnedfund@earthlink.net.

***eKnowlege:** Offers free SAT/ACT prep software for service members, veterans and their families. In alliance with the Department of Defense and supported by patriotic NFL players, eKnowledge is donating SAT/ACT PowerPrep Programs to military service members and their extended families.

The software comes in a single DVD and includes more than 11 hours of Virtual Classroom instruction and 3,000 files of supplemental test prep material. Thousands of interactive diagnostic tools, sample questions, practice tests and graphic teaching illustrations are indexed for easy use. The SAT and ACT sponsorship covers 100% of the total retail cost of the $200 program; there is a small fee of $13.84 per standard program (plus S/H) for the cost of materials, processing, worldwide distribution and customer service. To order online, go to: www.eknowledge.com/MIL to order by telephone, call: 951-256-4076 and reference Military.com. *This is such a great opportunity; love this organization!*

FCEA General Emmett Paige Scholarships: Provides scholarships to service members on active duty, veterans and their spouses. http://www.afcea.org/

Federal Employee Education & Assistance Fund (FEEA): Is the only non-profit organization devoted solely to helping civilian and postal employees. FEEA helps federal employees every day through three programs, Annual Scholarship Competitions, Emergency Assistance Programs and Child Care Subsidy Program. For more information on these programs go to http://www.feea.org/.

Federal Student Aid Programs (FSA): It doesn't matter whether you are active duty, reserve, veteran, retiree, using the GI Bill, or not—if you are going to college you should take advantage of the Federal Student Aid Programs. Many service members, even senior active duty members, apply for and receive direct loans and large grants.

As you know, colleges and universities charge fees for tuition, admissions applications, enrollment, books, technical support, labs, transcripts and anything else that they can. What you may not know is that if you don't use military tuition assistance, which is different from the GI Bill, you (not DoD or VA) are responsible for paying all of these additional fees. The schools hold you responsible for paying in most cases and the GI Bill is paid directly to you, the student, not the school.

NOTE: Each school's policies differ on how this money is collected, but in most cases you will be asked to sign a promissory note, apply for student aid, or both. That is why it is important for the service member or veteran to apply for **Federal Student Aid (FSA)**. FSA can help defer out-of-pocket expenses until GI Bill payments start coming in. In addition to low interest loans, FSA also offers grants that do not require repayment. You can see a list of available FSA options below. The key is to make sure you avoid long-term student debt and interest charges by paying off the FSA "Direct Loans" as soon as the GI Bill payments start hitting your bank account.

FSA ELIGIBILITY: You are eligible for FSA if you are **ALL** of the following.

- A high school graduate, or have a General Education Development (GED) certificate
- Working toward a degree or certificate
- Enrolled in an eligible school or program
- A U.S. citizen or eligible non-citizen (must have a valid Social Security Number)
- Registered with the Selective Service if required (you can use the paper or electronic FAFSA to register)

Once you have enrolled in college, you need to start the application process for FSA. You can apply for all of the available FSA by filling out the FAFSA for online http://www.fafsaonline.com/fafsa-form/. After you have submitted the **FREE** application for Federal Student Aid (FAFSA), your school will tell you which types of loans, grants and the total amounts you are qualified to receive. When you get this notification from the school, simply select the loans and grants you want and the school will finish the loan process.

TIP: Applying for FSA is easy if you use the FAFSA Pre-Application worksheet to guide you. Without the worksheet the FAFSA process can be complicated. You will need to gather your tax forms from previous years, including W-2's, bank statements and investment statements to complete the form.

Caution: FAFSA is a free application for federal student aid. However, there are some shady websites that offer to complete the FAFSA for you for a fee. Don't do it! The FAFSA form only takes a short time to complete. It is worth your time and saves money to complete it yourself.

Every accredited school that is recognized by the Education Department will be eligible for some form of FSA. But the search for the right school and program can be time-consuming. Let http://schools.military.com/schoolfinder/search-for-schools.do help you get free information on schools that fit your needs by filling out one simple form to find the schools that are eager to send you free information on how to get the funding you need to cover the cost of your education goals. For further information go to http://www.fafsa.ed.gov/.

GoArmyEd: Is a new Army National Guard online portal for the delivery of educational services and tuition assistance. https://www.goarmyed.com/login.aspx

Logistics Officer Association (LOA): Is comprised of over 3,200 military officers and civilians in logistics fields around the globe. The purpose of the Logistics Officer Association is to enhance the military logistics profession. LOA provides an open forum to promote quality logistical support and logistics officer professional development. LOA provides a great scholarship program that is intended to promote education for those who are members, children of active and corporate LOA members, and enlisted members of the armed forces. This program will allow applicants taking college classes to research and offer solutions to current logistics challenges within the Department of Defense or industry, high school students to explore and consider the implications of logistics in military operations, or other applicants to apply for scholarship awards based purely on a brief application. For more information about LOA and eligibility, rules and further guidelines go to http://www.loanational.org/.

Military Friendly Schools: This is a link to all the military friendly schools available to military families. They offer various discounts, online services and more to make your transition easier. www.militaryfriendlyschools.com

Montgomery G.I. Bill (MGIB): The MGIB provides a very generous tax-free entitlement to active duty service members, Guard/Reserve and veterans. More than $38,000 per eligible service member is available that can be used to pay for tuition, books, fees and living expenses while earning a college degree or certification from a technical school. The MGIB can also be used to professional licensing or certification and on-the-job training programs.

This entitlement is paid on a monthly basis. All active-duty service members are automatically enrolled in the MGIB unless they choose to "opt out" of this benefit. To "opt out" a soldier must do so during the first 3 days of active duty. The reason some service members do this is participation in the MGIB actually requires a contribution of $100 per month from the military pay for the first 12 months of service. Or a service member already has all the school he/she needs.

This seems like a lot of money to give but let's look at the difference down the road. For your $1,200 TOTAL commitment you could receive a benefit of up to $1,075 per month if enrolled as a full time student whether on active duty or within ten (10) years after the completion of your service. And you don't have to attend classes on a full time basis. You can receive a pro-rata share of this monthly stipend if you attend classes on a quarterly or half time basis. You more than make up the difference in the cost.

Service members can also get an extra $150 per month in MGIB benefits if he/she elects to contribute an additional $600 before leaving the service. This option is called the "GI Bill Buy-up." The Buy-up increases your total contribution to the Montgomery GI Bill Program to $1,800, however, it will increase your total GI benefits by as much as $5,400.

To qualify for the MGIB your service member must have completed high school or have the GED equivalency certificate and have completed at least two years on active duty prior to September 11, 2001. The MGIB is also extended to Guard and Reserve members. The Reserves GI Bill provides your soldier 36 months, up to 48 months if combined of benefits, which is worth more than $10,000 tax-free and can help pay for college tuition, books, fees, and vocational training expenses.

To qualify for the Reserve GI bill your service member must:
- Have a six (6) year enlistment obligation
- Completed their initial active duty
- Have a high school diploma or GED
- Remain in good standing

To access the Montgomery GI Bill benefits your service member must:
- Have served and separated before September 11, 2001
- Verify that the school where degree program is VA approved--call 888-442-4551
- Complete the application for VA educational benefits (VA Form 22-1990)
- Submit the completed form to your school's registrar's office

*__Military to Medicine:__ Offers an easy way for service members and military families to gain a career in health care that can move with you. Whether you have experience and/or education currently or just starting out this program can help you. Military to Medicine's online training is in partnership with The Claude Moore Health Education Program at http:// www.claudemoorefoundation.org/military.html and provides students with real-life job standards and role expectations. Both students and healthcare employers can feel confident that Military to Medicine course work demonstrates realistic, healthcare workplace skills. Military to Medicine is committed to participants' long-term career success. Before specific career courses begin, Military to Medicine assesses each student's interests and abilities, this information helps students set career goals and select career courses.

At the writing of this book, tuition for the initial assessment was $599; for the career-specific courses (front office medical assistant or medical records and health information assistant), the tuition was $1,850. The tuition includes the eBooks, eLearning materials and completion certificates, Scholarships are available. This program is available for military spouses, wounded warriors and their caregivers, veterans, National Guard, Reserve and their spouses and service members transitioning to civilian employment. For more information go to www.militarytomedicine.org.

Military Scholarship Finder: Will give you a list of hundreds of scholarships, grants and loans for military families to pursue their educational dreams. www.militaryscholarshipfinder.com

*National Student Loan Forgiveness: Military Mobilization Fact Sheet for Federal Family Education Loan B. If your National Guard or Reserve unit has been called to active duty, or if you are a regular, active-duty member of the Armed Forces who has been reassigned to another duty station, you may be eligible for benefits on any Federal Stafford, SLS, PLUS, and Consolidation loans you borrowed under the Federal Family Education Loan Program (FFELP) What this means is you may get part or all of it forgiven. This means you DO NOT have to pay the money back http://www2.ed.gov/fund/grants-college.html and http://www.nslp.org/pages/pdf/militarymobil.pdf **ALSO; While** you are deployed you need to have your student loans in "MILITARY DEFERMENT" not a regular deferment. This will keep any extra cost, fees and finance charges been added to your account while you are deployed.

Post-9/11 GI Bill: There were changes made to the G.I. Bill that went into effect on August 1, 2009. So if you are not familiar with these changes please review in more detail than what I will cover here briefly. All service members who have served three months or longer on active duty since September 11, 2001 are eligible for benefits under the new GI Bill. A couple of the things that I would like to point out are:

- Benefits are free and you have up to 15 years after active duty to utilize your benefits
- Benefits may be received for up to 36 months
- Service members with at least 36 months of service are entitled to
    - Tuition and fees, paid directly to a public institution of higher education, not to exceed the most expensive in state undergraduate tuition. Benefits may be paid for undergraduate and graduate coursework, as well as, distance learning, vocational, and technical training. However, the new GI Bill does not cover

apprenticeships, correspondence courses, flight training, and on the job training.

- Monthly housing allowance equal to your basic allowance for housing (BAH) amount payable to an E-5 with dependents (not available to active-duty service members)
- Annual books and supplies stipend of up to $1,000
- Spouses and dependents children may be able to use the benefit
- Service members who are currently utilizing or have not yet begun utilizing their MGIB benefits received a 20% raise in their benefits beginning August 1, 2008
- Officers who were ineligible for MGIB are now eligible with the Post 9/11 GI Bill
- Guard and Reserve members are eligible with as little as 30 days active duty--more active duty time equals higher percentage for the new GI Bill

Unlike the Montgomery GI Bill, a high school diploma is not required in order to qualify for the new Post-9/11 GI Bill. For more information on the new Post-9/11 GI Bill visit http://www.gibill.va.gov/s22.html and http://gibill.va.gov/benefits/post_911_gibill/index.html.

Reserve Officers Association of The US: This program is designed to assist deserving members of ROA, ROAL, their children, or grandchildren who wish to attend or who are now attending accredited U.S. colleges or universities. This scholarship is funded through the Henry J. Reilly Scholarship trust, which states that preference of its award will be given to those pursuing a military career. ROTC cadets, midshipmen and currently serving military graduate students are strongly encouraged to apply. This scholarship is granted to 30 applicants. For more information about ROA or this scholarship go to http://www.roa.org/.

Special Forces Association: The SFA Scholarship Fund was established to provide one-time scholarship grants to members, dependents and grandchildren of SFA members in good standing. For more information about this scholarship and eligibility requirements, go to http://www.specialforcesassociation.org/.

Servicemembers' Opportunity Colleges: This program is dedicated to helping service members and their families get college degrees, even as they move. Military students can take courses in their off-duty hours at or near military installations in the US, overseas, and on Navy ships. http://www.soc.aascu.org/

SOCAD: SOC Degree Network System Assist with Associates and Bachelor's Degrees for the Army. See site for further details. http://www.soc.aasu.org

Spouse Tuition Assistance Program (STAP)—For Air Force Spouses: If you are stationed overseas, you may be eligible for this assistance program. Other branches of service have their own versions. STAP provides enough funds to pay a portion of tuition costs and caps the maximum benefit to about $1,500 a years.

Education

Student Veterans of America (SVA): SVA mission is to help veterans overcome the challenges ranging from missing the sense of camaraderie to the lack of understanding by university faculty and peers. And when coupled with the visible and invisible wounds of war, college can seem unattainable. SVA goal and mission is to make sure all veterans succeed in higher education, achieve their academic goals, and gain meaningful employment. SVA will provide military veterans with the resources, support, and advocacy needed to succeed in higher education and following graduation. For further information and review go to http://www.studentveterans.org/about/.

The Billy Blanks Foundation: This foundation offers scholarships and support for after school programs. http://www.billyblanksfoundation.org/

The Freedom Alliance: Organizes donations and contributions for service members and also awards scholarships. http://www.freedomalliance.org/

The Armed Forces Military Tuition Assistance (TA) Program: Is available to all active-duty service members, and in most cases members of the Reserve. Each branch of the Armed Forces determines the maximum amount of tuition assistance benefit provided to their service member. The maximum benefit can be as much as $4,500 per year depending on the branch of service.

Tuition assistance is a benefit. It does not have to be repaid, unless your service member fails or drops out of the courses or program for which they are using the tuition assistance benefit.

Tuition assistance is usually paid directly to the institution rather than to the service member. Active duty members may elect to use their Montgomery GI Bill in addition to tuition assistance to cover more expensive programs. Tuition Assistance must be used in the year it is allotted or it is lost. So, use your tuition assistance first and then tap your Montgomery GI Bill if additional funds are needed to pay for your education.

The G.I. Go Fund: Provides transition assistance to ALL military veterans, with a focus on veterans from the Iraq and Afghanistan conflicts, by preparing veterans for the twenty-first century economy, securing education and health benefits, and providing aid and assistance to low income and homeless veterans. http://www.gigofund.org/

Troops to Teachers Program: Is a US Department of Education and Department of Defense Program that helps eligible military personnel begin a new career as teacher in public schools where their skills, knowledge and experience are most needed. http://usmilitary.about.com

*Tutoring: The Defense Department launched a **free**, online tutoring service for service members and their families. The site http://www.tutor.com/military offers round the clock professional tutors who can assist with homework, studying, test preparation, resume writing and more. *This site looks really interesting and cool. I wish I would have used it for my daughter last year.*

Veterans Upward Bound (VUB): Is a free U.S. Department of Education program designed to help refresh your academic skills and give you the confidence you need to successfully complete your choice of college degrees. For more information contact http://www.navub.org. The basic information that you should be aware of is this:

The VUB Program Services Include:
- Basic skills developments to help veterans successfully complete a high school equivalency program and gain admission to college education programs
- Short-term remedial or refresher classes for high school graduates that have put off pursuing a college education
- Assistance with applications to the college or university of choice
- Assistance with applying for financial aid
- Personalized counseling
- Academic advice and assistance
- Career counseling
- Assistance in getting veteran services from other available resources
- Exposure to cultural events, academic programs, and other educational activities not usually available to disadvantaged people

The VUB Program Improves:
- Mathematics
- Foreign Language
- Composition
- Laboratory Science
- Reading
- Literature
- Computer Basics
- Any other subjects you may need for success in education beyond high school
- Tutorial and Study Skills Assistance

To be Eligible for VUB you Must:
- Be a U.S. Military Veteran with 181 or more days active-duty service and discharged on/after January 31, 1955, under conditions other than dishonorable
- Meet the criteria for low-income according to guidelines published annually by the U.S. Department of Education, and/or a first-generation potential college graduate
- Demonstrate academic need for Veterans Upward Bound
- Meet other local eligibility criteria as noted in the local VUB project's Approved Grant Proposal, such as county of residence.
- Contact your local VUB program to see if you qualify. Visit the National Veterans Upward Bound Program website to find a program near you

Education

While in service, members have access to up to $4,500 a year in Tuition Assistance. Tuition Assistance is paid to the school on a per class basis. Service members can also use GI Bill benefits; however, make sure you look at all your options before signing anything. You will be surprised at what is offered to you while you are on active duty with other organizations. For more information and assistance contact http://www.navub.org.

Women Marines Association: This great organization that offers eight or more scholarships a year to women Marines and their dependents. For a list of these scholarships, eligibility and to download the applications go to http://www.womenmarines.org/scholarships.aspx.

SCHOLARSHIPS AND FINANCIAL AID

There are many sources for scholarships for service members their immediate family members and veterans that may help cover the costs of tuition, fees, books, and in some cases living expenses. You may be eligible for many scholarships and/or grants. If you are like many others you are wondering: "Where do I go?", "Whom do I ask?" and "What do I need to do to get these?" service members need to go to www.military.com/scholarships for more information about scholarships and grants that are available to them. As a military spouse you should visit www.military.com/spouse to find out more about scholarships and grants that may be available to you.

In addition to the benefits the government provides for you, you should also look off base for additional opportunities. Many military service organizations, such as **VFW's and American Legions and associations, corporate organizations, clubs and non-profits** (and don't forget to research your **public library**) have opportunities that are open to you in regards to your cultural backgrounds and/or area of study. Remember to start your search with a military scholarship finder. You will be surprised at what is there for you and your children.

One of the biggest things to remember is that if your service member has not used his/her **POST 9/11 Bill benefits service members may transfer them to their immediate dependents, under certain circumstances.** As of August 1, 2009, the Department of Defenses is making available the opportunity to transfer MGIB entitlements to spouses and eligible children. The details of this transferrable benefit are available at www.gibill.va.gov for up-to-date information.

I am not saying that all your expenses will be covered for your education. Use your Tuition Assistance Program first, then the Montgomery GI Bill and military scholarships and grants before applying for traditional federal financial aid.

Non-Traditional Scholarship: Is offered through The American Legion Auxiliary, getting a job or staying in today's workplace involves showing employers you have the skills and experience to get the job done. In many cases, returning to college is a must. This scholarship helps people who are a part of The Legion family pursue a college degree later in life or allow them to pick up where they left off when their studies were interrupted. Scholarship is giving to one annually per Auxiliary geographic division in the amount of $1,000. Criteria includes being a member of the Legion, Auxiliary, or Sons of the American Legion in good standing with dues paid for the two preceding years for calendar year in which the application is made. Must be pursuing training in a certified trade, professional, or technical program, or a two year/four year degree program. For more information and application go to http://www.alaforveterans.org/what_we_do/scholarships/Pages/Non-TraditionalStudentScholarship.aspx.

The Pat Tillman Scholarship: The Tillman Military Scholarship Program supports active duty service members, veterans and their families by removing financial barriers to completing a degree or certification program of their choice. The scholarships cover not only direct study-related expenses such as tuition and fees, but also other needs, including housing and childcare. The application period opens each spring, and a new class of Tillman Military Scholars is announced in June. More information on the application process for the upcoming academic year will be available on the website, www.pattillmanfoundation.org in January.

Reserve Educational Assistance Program (REAP): Is a Department of Defense/VA education benefit program designed to provide educational assistance to members of the Reserve and Guard components called or ordered to active duty in response to a war or national emergency (contingency operation) as declared by the President or Congress.

Chapter 1607 benefits cannot be used with other VA educational benefits. You must make an irrevocable election choosing which program you want your military service to count towards. However, if you are eligible for a Chapter 1606 kicker (college fund), you can still be paid that kicker while receiving Chapter 1607. REAP benefits are potentially payable from December 9, 2001 (90 days after September 11. 2001) for persons who were serving on a contingency operation on September 11, 2001 and who were in school on December 9, 2001. The Department of Defense will provide further guidance as to the retroactive nature of this program. For cost benefits, eligibility and how to apply go to http://www.military.com/education/content/gi-bill/reserve-education-assistance-program-reap.html and/or http://www.mass.gov/?pageID=elwdterminal&L=3&L0=Home&L1=Government&L2=Resources+for+Veterans&sid=Elwd&b=terminalcontent&f=dat_gibill_chapter1607&csid=Elwd.

Tuition Top-Up Program: Is a program that allows GI Bill participants' to use the GI Bill to supplement the tuition and fees not covered by tuition assistance. The amount of the benefit can be equal to the difference between the total cost of a college course and the amount of Tuition Assistance that is paid by the military for the course. Assistance by a military department and be eligible for MGIB AD benefits. To be eligible you must be a GI Bill participant, still on active duty, and must have served at least two full years. To get more information go to http://www.military.com/education/content/gi-bill/tuition-top-up-program.html?ESRC=mr.nl and/or http://www.gibill.com/benefits/tuition-top-up/.

Veterans Educational Assistance Program (VEAP): Is available if you elect to make contributions from your military pay to participate, which than would be matched by the government on a $2 for $1 basis. You may use these benefits for degree, certificate, correspondence, apprenticeship/on-the-job training programs and vocational flight training programs. In certain circumstances remedial, deficiency, and refresher training may also be available.

Benefit entitlement is one to 36 months depending on the number of monthly contributions. Service members have 10 years from your release from active duty to use VEAP benefits. If there is entitlement not used after the 10 year period, your portion remaining in the fund will be automatically refunded. For eligibility, how to apply and further information, go to http://www.military.com/education/content/gi-bill/veterans-educational-assistance-program-veap.html.

Veteran's Scholarship Fund, VFW Post 5855: This VFW Post out of Portage, Michigan offers a $500 grant to be awarded twice a year. This grant is open to **all Michigan veterans (only)** who are attending higher educational institutions. This is a onetime per person and grants will be sent to schools financial aid departments. For more information, eligibility requirements and to download the applications go to www.vfw5855.org. Or you can contact Mr. Al Mar at (269) 324-2371.

Resource Sites: Do your homework! These sites will help you research your options for higher education and vocational training.

- **Official Montgomery GI Bill web site:** www.GIBill.va.gov
- **Seamless Transition Web site for (OEF/OIF) Veterans:** www.Va.gov
- **American Association of State Colleges and Universities:** www.aascu.org
- **The U.S. Department of Education:** www.ed.gov/students
- **The Career College Association:** www.career.org
- **American Association of Community Colleges:** www.aacc.nche.edu/
- **Career OneStop:** www.acinet.org
- **College Search Engine:** www.collegesearchengine.net

***As of the printing of this book, Benedictine University through its "First Responder Program" is offering free tuition for **Illinois armed forces veterans,** active and Reserve, returning from service in Iraq and Afghanistan. Illinois veterans who participate in this program will be able to pursue an associate of arts in business administration or a Bachelor of Arts in management degree at no tuition cost. For more information, contact Autumn Lynumn at 630-829-6126 or Heena I. Jeelani at 630-829-1385 or visit http://www1.ben.edu/programs/adult_cohorts/first_responder_program.asp.*

OTHER EDUCATIONAL ASSISTANCE

Dr. Jack Callan Memorial Scholarship: Saint Leo University; spouse must have 9 credits minimum to qualify. Email Gloria.howell@saintleo.edu for more information.

Embarq Scholarship: Administered by the Low Country Chapter of the Military Officer's Association of America. Send information to C/O Harold Hirshman, Embarq Scholarship Committee, The Military Officers Association of 137 Chowan Creek Bluff, Beaufort, SC 29907.

Georgia's Hope Scholarship and Grant Program: Available only the Georgia residents who have demonstrated academic achievment. The scholarship provides assistance to students attending college in Georgia. Scholarships provided to HOPE scholars vary and depends on the type of education the applicant is persuing. For more information, go to http://www.gsfc.org/gsfcnew/contact.CFM.

Hearts and Hands Community Club Scholarship: For spouses within USAG Giessen. You can email heartsandhandscc@yahoo.com.

Officers Spouses' Club of San Diego, Inc. Scholarship: To dependent children or spouses of active duty, retired, or deceased military officers and enlisted personal. Applicants must reside in the greater San Diego area at time of application. For an application send a business size SASE to: NOWC, Navy Wives Clubs of American Scholarship Foundation, Scholarship Committee, P.O. Box 18-2104, Coronado, CA 92178.

Park University Military Family Scholarships: Used at home campus in Parkville, MO or at the Beaufort, SC Campus Center for non-military family members of active duty military personnel residing in the Beaufort area. 843-228-7052.

Protect and Serve Grant: A form of scholarship awarded to spouses of U.S. military from Peirce College, up to 25% on tuition fees. protetandserve@peirce.edu or 1-888-go-pierce X 9800.

Scholarship for Culinary Education: Les Dames d'Escoffier International, Atlanta Chapter. http://www.lesdamesatlanta.org/

Scholarships for Severely Injured Service Members and Their Dependents: http://www.dantes.doded.mil/sfd/index.asp?Flag=True

Spouse Fellowship: The FINRA Foundation Military Spouses Fellowship Program gives military spouses the opportunity to earn a career enhancing credential--the accredited financial counselor certificate--while providing financial counseling to the military community. Spouses of active duty, retired and reserve service members are eligible. http://www.saveandinvest.org/military/spousesFellowships/index.htm

THANKS USA: Spouses of military personnel can apply for one of nearly 1000 scholarships of up to $5000 each for college, vocational and technical schools. http://www.thanksusa.org/main/index.htm. 1-877-THX-USAS or shintz@scholarshipamerica.org

ADDITIONAL ONLINE GENERAL RESOURCES

American Association University Women: http://www.aauw.org/learn/fellows_directory/

College Board Scholarship Search: http://apps.collegeboard.com/cbsearch_ss/welcome.jsp

E-Student Loan.com: http://www.estudentloan.com/

Fast Web: http://www.fastweb.com/

Federal Student Financial Aid: http://studentaid.ed.gov/PORTALSWebApp/sudents/english/index.jsp

Scholarship Gateway: http://www.blackexcel.org/link4.htm

Scholarships.com: http://www.scholarships.com/

University of Maryland University College Scholarships: http://www.umuc.edu/financialaid/scholarships/02_programs.shtml

VA Education Assistance: http://www.gibill.va.gov/

BRANCH SPECIFIC EDUCATIONAL PROGRAMS

The U.S. Miltary believes that all of its service members should continue their education during their off-duty hours and they understand that helping you continue your education is mutually beneficial. It is understood the sacrifices sometimes made by military families as they relocate or lose their service members. The military has a number of programs in place to assist spouses and dependents further their education. There are some educational benefits that are available to all service members, but some are branch specific.

Service Members Opportunity Colleges (SOC): SOC is an organization of approximately 1800 colleges and universities that are working together to assist U.S. Military service members and their families continue their education and pursue degrees around military careers and life in the military.

ARMY
The Army offers the following Education Programs for its spouses and family members.

Army College Fund (MGIB Kicker): The U.S. Army and the federal government provide military education benefits programs for eligible service members, veterans and their military families seeking to continue their education. See website for more information and eligibility requirements. http://www.worldwidelearn.com/military/branch-education-benefits/army/army-college-fund.html

GoArmyEd Program for Global Education: The U.S. Army understands the importance of creating opportunities for active duty Army service members to continue their education. Service members earning undergraduate and graduate degrees today are the leaders of tomorrow. Various military education benefits are available to help active service members pursue a post-secondary education and earn an associate's, bachelors, or master's degree.

To equip service members with the right training and access to college courses, the Army created GoArmyEd, an online education portal. As a virtual entryway, GoArmyEd is the easiest way for active duty soldiers to complete both on-campus and online degree programs. By connecting soldiers with an Army education counselor, GoArmyEd helps soldiers realize their post-secondary education goals. Go to website or further information and eligibility requirements.   http://www.worldwidelearn.com/military/branch-education-benefits/army/goarmyed.html

SOCAD: Is **The Service Members Opportunity Colleges (SOC)** degree program for the Army. SOCAD consists of colleges that offer associate and bachelor's degree programs on or accessible to Army installations worldwide. SOCAD colleges form networks in which each college accepts credits from all the others. SOCAD guarantees that you and your adult family members can continue toward completion of your degree even though the Army may transfer you several times. There are also degrees available by distance learning that require no classroom residency. Visit the official website at http://www.soc.aascu.org/socad/Default.html.

Stateside Spouse Education Assistance Program (SEAP): Is provided through the **Army Emergency Relief (AER)** and is a need-based education assistance program designed to provide spouses of Army Soldiers and widowers of Army Soldiers who died while on active duty, and are residing in the United States, with financial assistance in pursuing educational goals.

The purpose of the program is to assist spouses/widowers in gaining the education required to allow them to qualify for increased occupational opportunities. Individuals who receive free tuition as a result of their employment will not receive tuition assistance from AER. However, they may apply for assistance for fees, supplies or books (no duplicates) for classes in which they are enrolled. SEAP is limited to $2500 maximum per academic year. See its website for more information at http://www.aerhq.org/education_spouseeducation_StateSide.asp or you can call 703-428-0000 for more information.

Spouse Education Assistance Program (EAP): If you are assigned to an Army base in Europe, Korea, Japan or Okinawa, Army Emergency Relief offers spouses a grant to assist with the costs associated with pursuing your education up to a maximum of $350 per term. Visit their website for more information at http://www.aerhq.org/education_spouseeducation.asp.

Loan Repayment Program (LRP): Is a program which helps Army service members repay student loans. http://www.military.com/Resources/ResourcesContent/0,13964,44245--,00.html and/or http://usmilitary.about.com/cs/joiningup/a/clrp.htm for more information and eligibility and rules regarding this resource.

Dependent Children Scholarships: Is a program administered by the Army Relief Society for Army service member dependents. http://www.aerhq.org

Tuition Assistance Program: Assists with the cost of tuition for off duty classes. Go to http://www.military.com/education/content/money-for-school/tuition-assistance-ta-program-overview.html for further information, rules and eligibility requirements.

AIR FORCE

The Air Force offers the following Education Programs for its spouses and family members.

AFA (Air Force Association) Spouse Scholarship: For a spouse of Air Force active duty, Air Guard, or Air Reserve. http://www.afa.org/aef/aid/spouse.asp

Air Force Tuition Assistance: Provides tuition assistance for off-duty education.http://www.worldwidelearn.com/military/branch-education-benefits/air-force/community-college-air-force.html

The College Loan Repayment Program: Assist Air Force service members repay student loans. http://www.allmilitary.com/gibill/airforce/clrp.html

Service Members Opportunity Colleges (SOC): These colleges and universities are dedicated to helping military families get college degrees. You can take courses in your off-duty hours at or near military installations in the United States, and overseas. Visit http://www.soc.aascu.org/ for more information.

General Henry H. Arnold Education Grant Program: Is the centerpiece of the **Air Force Society (AFAS)** education Programs and initiatives. This grant provides grants to selected sons and daughters of active duty, Title 10 AGR/Reserve, Title 32 AGR performing full-time active duty, retired, retired reserve and deceased Air Force members; spouses (stateside) of active duty members and Title 10 AGR/Reservists; and surviving spouses of deceased personnel for their undergraduate studies. The value and success of this program, is demonstrated in the 74,679 grants disbursed since the first awards were made for the 1988-1989 academic year. In recognition of escalating college costs, the-award amount for grants is now $2,000 for all qualifying applicants.

This grant program remains competitive in its need-based selection criteria, uniquely tailored to recognize the proper weighing of family income and education cost factors, and is administered by ACT Recognition Program Services. ACT, located in Iowa City IA, is an independent, not-for-profit organization with over 40 years' experience in providing support services to scholarship sponsors.

Awards for each academic year are announced in June each year. Use of funds is limited to tuition, books and fees, or other direct educational expenses. Please go to the website for further information at http://www.afas.org/Education/ArnoldEdGrant.cfm.

General George S. Brown Spouse Tuition Assistance Program (STAP): The purpose of the Spouse Tuition Assistance Program (STAP) is to provide partial tuition assistance for spouses of Active Duty airmen or officers, who accompany members to overseas locations and will be attending college programs. The focus of the program is on the completion of degree or certificate programs that provide increased occupational opportunities for spouses.

The program provides tuition assistance (TA) at a rate of 50% of unmet tuition charge per course, with a maximum of $1,500 per academic year and a term maximum, which is calculated by dividing the annual maximum ($1,500) by the number of terms within the academic year. For purposes of this program, "academic year" is defined as the 12-month period beginning August 1 through July 31 each year. For eligibility requirements, please review website at http://europe.ctcd.edu/students/services/afas_stap.php.

Other: A major educational benefit available to Air Force service members and their families that is not available to other branches of the U.S. Military is the Community College of the Air Force. This is a community college which provides online courses and distance learning for Air Force service members and their families and the degree programs are designed with them in mind.

COAST GUARD

The Coast Guard offers the following education programs for its spouses and family members.

Tuition Assistance Program: Up to $4,500 yearly, partially covering post-secondary education and fully covering high school level classes. http://www.military.com/education/content/money-for-school/tuition-assistance-ta-program-overview.html

SOCCOAST: Is the Service Members Opportunity Colleges (SOC) degree program for the Coast Guard. SOCCOAST consists of colleges that offer associate and bachelor's degree programs on or accessible to Navy and Marine installations worldwide and they form networks in which each college accepts credits from all the others.

SOCCOAST guarantees that you and your adult family members can continue toward completion of your degrees even though the Marine Corps may transfer you several times. There are also degrees available by distance learning that require no classroom residency. Go to http://www.soc.aascu.org/soccoast/Default.html for further information.

The Coast Guard Foundation: Provides for active duty enlisted members an annual Education Grant. This grant program is open to active duty enlisted personnel in pay grades E-3 to E-9 with two or more years of Coast Guard service. This $350 grant may be used in conjunction with the Coast Guard Tuition Assistance Program, or other non-funded relevant education items. http://coastguardfoundation.org/

Coast Guard Mutual Assistance (CGMA): Offers a Supplemental Education Grant (SEG) of up to $160 per year. You can use this grant for **ANY** family member's education expenses. However it does not cover tuition expenses. This grant can also be used to pay for ASVAB, CLEP, SAT, and other study guides. CGMA also offers several education related loans.

The Coast Guard also offers dependent spouses and Federal Coast Guard employees the opportunity to take CLEP, DANTES, and other tests at no cost. There are many advanced education programs available for both enlistees and officers. These are currently announced by way of ALCOAST, ALCGENL, and other general distribution messages from Coast Guard Headquarters.

To apply contact your local CG Mutual Assistance Representative or Education Officer at 800-881-2462 or visit http://www.cgmahq.org/ to learn more about the programs offered.

The Coast Guard Foundation Grant (CGFEF) and Vander Putten Education Grant (VPEG): Both help service members cover extraneous costs, like textbooks and other supplies. Learn more at http://www.cjfdn.org/.

Additional Education Assistance: The Coast Guard also offers dependent spouses and Federal Coast Guard employees the opportunity to take CLEP, DANTES, and other tests at **no cost**. Please visit the Coast Guard site for more information. http://www.military.com/education/content/money-for-school/coast-guard-education-programs.html

The Coast Guard has a program that allows the service member to get paid while finishing college. It is called the **Coast Guard College Student Pre-Commissioning Initiative (CGCSPCI).** It is similar to ROTC, the U.S. CGCSPCI is a military education benefit offered to eligible college students that provides military training and financial benefits during their last two years of college. The CGCSPCI allows you to earn a salary while completing college, develop your leadership skills, and receive navigation and marine science skills training. If you are accepted into the program, you must finish your bachelor's degree as well as all Coast Guard training requirements within two years. Training requirements include programs at the Coast Guard Academy and hands-on training with Coast Guard units. Once you finish your degree, you agree to serve for three years of active duty as a U.S. Coast Guard officer. Please review the website for more information, rules and requirements along with eligibility information. http://www.worldwidelearn.com/military/branch-education-benefits/coast-guard/pre-commissioning-initiative.html

MARINE CORPS/NAVY

Many of the educational benefits provided are similar for both the Navy and Marine Corps. The Navy-Marine Corps Relief Society also provides education benefits for eligible service members and their families.

The Tuition Assistance Program: Provides tuition assistance for Navy and Marine Corps service members to further their education during off duty hours.http://www.military.com/education/content/money-for-school/navy-tuition-assistance.html

The Spouse Tuition Aid Program: Assists spouses of Navy and Marine Corps service members who are overseas with their service member spouse with tuition costs. http://www.military.com/education/content/money-for-school/military-spouse-and-family-educational-assistance-programs.html

The Loan Repayment Program: Assist Navy service members in repaying student loans. http://www.cnrc.navy.mil/eincentives/N5311%20EB/EB/FAQ/LRP%20ADOBE.pdf

SOCMAR/SOCNAV: Is the Service Members Opportunity Colleges (SOC) degree program for the Marines. SOCMAR consists of colleges that offer associate and bachelor's degree programs on or accessible to navy and marine installations worldwide. SOCMAR colleges form networks in which each college accepts credits from all the others. SOCMAR guarantees that you and your adult family members can continue toward completion of your degree even though the Marine Corps may transfer you several times. There are also degrees available by distance learning that require no classroom residency. Go to http://www.soc.aascu.org/socmar/Default.html for more information.

NMCRS Gold Star Scholarship Program: Previously called the *Dependents of Deceased Service Member Scholarship Program*, the Gold Star Program provides academic grants for eligible children and un-remarried spouses of deceased Sailors and Marines. Awards are based on need and the amount is determined by NMCRS Headquarters Education Division.

- **For Children:** (use the application entitled Gold Star Scholarship for Children. Children of both active duty and retired are eligible.
  - The **USS STARK** Memorial Fund is a special program specifically for children of STARK crewmembers who died or were disabled as a result of the missile attack on the USS STARK in the Persian Gulf on May 17, 1987.
  - The **USS COLE** Memorial Fund is a special program specifically for the children of COLE crewmembers who died as a result of the terrorist attack on the USS COLE on October 12, 2000.
  - **The Pentagon Assistance Fund (PAF)** is a special program specifically for children of deceased Sailors and Marines who died as a result of the terrorist attack on the Pentagon on September 11, 2001. This program was also offered to children of active duty sailors and marines who died under hostile fire in

combat operations during Operation Enduring Freedom (OEF) until 1 June 2007. Applications for eligible children are posted on the Gold Star Program page http://www.nmcrs.org/goldstar.html in late November of each year. Application forms must be received at headquarters no later than March 1st each school year.

- **For Un-remarried Spouses:** Use the application entitled Gold Star Scholarship for Spouses
  - The **USS STARK** Memorial Fund and **Pentagon Assistance Fund** includes un-remarried spouses of crewmembers who died as a result of the missile attack on the USS STARK or those that died as a result of the terrorist attack on the Pentagon and from combat operations during OEF before 1 June 2007. Applications for un-remarried spouses are posted on the Gold Star Program page http://www.nmcrs.org/goldstar.html in late November. Application forms must be received at headquarters no later than two months prior to the start of school.

Joseph A. McAlinden Divers Scholarship: Is offered specifically to Navy and Marine Corps Divers, whether active duty or retired, and their eligible family members. This scholarship provides financial assistance for full-time undergraduate and graduate students, who must be participating in one of the following areas of study: Oceanography, Ocean Agriculture, or Aquaculture. The McAlinden Scholarship also assists with Department of the Navy approved advanced diver training, qualifications and certifications. The scholarship is need-based and ranges from $500 up to $3,000 per academic year, for the eligible students education. There is no deadline for this program; you may apply at any time. http://www.nmcrs.org/education.html

The Navy-Marine Corps Relief Society (NMCRS): The Admiral Mike Boorda Seaman-to-Admiral Educational Assistance Program offers grants and/or interest free loans of up to $2,000 a year to eligible active duty service members accepted to the following programs, Enlisted Commissioning Program, Marine Enlisted Commissioning Education Program and Medical Enlisted Commissioning Program. The program is also open to Midshipmen who have been released from active duty for immediate assignment to the Naval Reserve Officer Training Corps (NROTC) Program. Application is made through the Commanding Officer of the NROTC Unit, or by contacting NMCRS Headquarters. Go to http://www.militaryta.com/scholarships/admiral-mike-boorda-scholarship-program.shtml or http://www.scholarships4school.com/scholarships/admiral-mike-boorda-scholarship-program.html for more information and eligibility requirements and information. You can also view http://nmcrs.org/education.html and/or http://nmcrs.org/stap.html.

Spouse Tuition Aid Program (STAP): The Navy and Marine Corps Relief Society (NMCRS) offers STAP to active duty military spouses stationed in an overseas (OCONUS) location. Spouses may be a full or part-time students studying toward a vocational certificate or an undergraduate or graduate degree. This program was modified in 2009 to a need based no interest loan.

This is available to spouses residing with their active duty service member sponsor while stationed outside the United States. STAP no-interest loans are available for part/full time undergraduate and graduate studies. STAP offers significantly expanded eligibility with loans up to $3,000 per 12 month period. These modifications increase the number of qualified spouses and offer an excellent opportunity to complete an undergraduate or graduate degree when stationed overseas. Go to http://www.nmcrs.org/stap.html for more information.

The Navy Advanced Education Voucher Program (AEV): The AEV is a Navy program administered by the Naval Education and Training Command (NETC). The program is designed to provide eligible senior enlisted Navy service members with the opportunity to continue their education at the Navy's expense. The program is open to Navy service members who are an E7 or E8, and have demonstrated a desire to better themselves and the Navy. Senior Navy service members may apply for the program, and a review board selects program participants. Service members selected for the program agree to serve additional time on active duty after earning their degree, up to a maximum of three years. For further information, rules and eligibility requirements go to http://www.worldwidelearn.com/military/branch-education-benefits/navy/advanced-education-voucher.html.

Navy Graduate Education Voucher (GEV): Navy unrestricted line (URL) officers can apply to receive funding for Navy-relevant graduate education under the 2010 Graduate Education Voucher (GEV) program. The GEV program covers all required fees normally charged by the university relating directly to student application and enrollment, including mandatory health fees and health insurance, laboratory fees, vehicle registration and identification cards, and computer fees are reimbursable. Other reimbursable expenses include the cost of textbooks and course materials, and limited expenditures for transcript and entry fees, and final thesis productions.

GEV applicants must select a regionally accredited school and choose a specific course of study that meets specific officer community subspecialty requirements. The education plan is reviewed and approved for the Navy subspecialty code by the Naval Postgraduate School (NPS).

The GEV program is targeted at officers with demonstrated superior performance and upward career mobility who are transferring or have recently reported to shore duty, in order to allow sufficient time for completion of a graduate program. The GEV program is open to URL active duty list officers, pay grades 0-3 through 0-5. There are 80 planned quotas available for FY10 as follows. Surface Ware-28; Submarine-15; Aviation-35; Special Warfare/Special Operations (SPECWAR/SPECOPS)-2. Quotas by degree program and warfare areas are available in NANADMIN 052/10, and additional information can be found on the Navy College Program's GEV web page http://www.navy.mil/search/display.asp?story_id=37431.

Some restrictions apply and enrollment in the program carries a service obligation of three times the number of months of education completed, with a minimum of 24, and a maximum of 36 months obligation. Officers completing a degree using GEV should expect to serve one tour in a subspecialty billet not later than the second tour following graduation. For ships at sea, applications via naval message containing the required information will be accepted. If you are active duty, the Navy will pay up to 100% of your college tuition. The following limits apply: $250 per semester credit hour, 16 semester credit hours per year in addition to tuition the Navy will pay published fees that are mandatory, and charged for courses enrollment. Go to Navy Tuition Assistance Program Overview to get more details. http://www.military.com/education/content/money-for-school/tuition-assistance/tuition-assistance-ta-program-overview.html

The Navy College-at-Sea (NCPACE, for Navy and Marines): The NCPACE is an education benefits program that enables Navy and Marine service members stationed at sea to take college classes, and earn bachelor's and advanced college degrees. Some classes are available with classroom and instructor format, and others are offered as distance learning, technology delivered classes. Associates, bachelors, and graduate degrees are available through this military education benefits program. The Navy has developed the program with a group of colleges that are working together to provide the opportunity for Navy and Marine service members to continue their education while at sea. All of the colleges participating in the NCPACE program are members of the Service Members Opportunity College System (SOC). For further information, rules and eligibility requirements and benefits go to http://www.worldwidelearn.com/military/branch-education-benefits/navy/college-at-sea.html.

Navy Seaman to Admiral (STA-21): The Navy's Seaman to Admiral Program is a commissioning program in which Sailors keep their benefits, pay, and privileges while they receive a scholarship to attend college to earn their degree and their commission as a naval officer. Visit the STA-21 Navy Commissioning Program overview for more details at http://nrotc.ou.edu/sta-21.html.

VADM E.P. Travers Scholarship and Loan Program: To apply, you must be the spouse of an active duty service member or the dependent child of an active or retired member of the Navy or Marine Corps. You must also be a full time undergraduate student at an accredited college or university. This scholarship offers 1000 grants each academic year at $2000 each, students will be also be evaluated for an interest free student loan of up to $3000 and the loan repayment begins within 30 days of award and must be repaid by allotment within 24 months. Application deadline is 1 March of each year and late applications will not be considered for the scholarship; however they will be evaluated for a loan. Go to http://www.nmcrs.org/travers.html for more information.

Other Assistance: Navy (Marine Option) Reserve Officer Training Corps (NROTC) Scholarship: There is education benefit programs designed for high school and college students seeking help with the cost of a college education. The NROTC Scholarship program can provide high school and college students with most of the costs of a four year college education and provide them with a potential career as an officer in the Marine Corps Reserve. Please go to the website for more information, rules and eligibility requirements at http://www.worldwidelearn.com/military/branch-education-benefits/marine/nrotc-scholarship.html.

Marine Corps Scholarship Foundation: The Marine Corps Scholarship Foundation provides annual scholarships for undergraduate higher education to the eligible dependent children of Marines. It is a private, non-profit organization, staffed by volunteers and professional staff that raise funds for the Marine Corps scholarship by sponsoring a series of special events throughout the country. Scholarship benefits can be used for campus or online bachelor's degree or technical certificate programs at accredited educational institutions. For more information, rules and eligibility information go to http://www.worldwidelearn.com/military/ branch-education-benefits/marine/marine-corp-scholarship-foundation.html.

POPASMOKE Scholarships: The USMC Combat Helicopter Association in conjunction with the Marine Corps Scholarship Foundation announces the MGYSGT George T. Curtis, The LTCOL Hubert "Black Bart" Bartel and the PFC Mike Clausen Scholarship. Application forms will be available for download in January at www.mcsf.org.

Scholarships range annually from $500-$1,000 and you qualify if you are the child or grandchildren of members of the USMC/Combat Helicopter Association, the child or grandchild of a Marine on active duty, in the Reserve, retired or deceased, the child or grandchild of a Marine or Marine Reservist who has received an Honorable Discharge, Medical Discharge, or who was killed while in the service of our country, who is or was a member of the USMC/Combat Helicopter Association. AND IF YOU ARE: a senior in high school, a high school graduate, currently enrolled as an undergraduate in an accredited college or university, post high school accredited vocational/ technical school AND: your family income is TBD (consult MSCF Website). Please view website for further information and eligibility requirements and rules at http://www.popasmoke.com/scholarship.html.

The USMC Combat Helicopter Association is in the process of establishing the Capt. Stephen Pless Scholarship. Please check back to website for updates.

USS Tennessee Scholarship Fund: The scholarship provides grants of up to $2,000 for an academic year to eligible children, under the age of 23, of service members who are serving or have served aboard the USS Tennessee. Children of both active duty and retired USS Tennessee Sailors are eligible. The Tennessee application is posted on the USS Tennessee Scholarship program page in late November. Applications must be received at headquarters no later than March 1st each school year. http://www.nmcrs.org/spec-prgm.html

OTHER NAVY EDUCATION BENEFITS PROGRAMS

Alaska Sea Service Scholarship Fund: Applicant's Navy, Marine or Coast Guard sponsor must be a legal Alaskan resident. Applicant must be children or spouse of sponsor, who may be active duty, reserve, and retired, MIA or KIA. To request an application, send a 9x12 envelope with postage for 2 ounces to: C/O U.S. Navy League Council 55-151 Box 201510, Anchorage, AK 99520-1510.

Anchor Scholarship Foundation: For dependents of active duty or retired personnel who served in commands under the administrative control of

Commanders, Naval Surface Forces, US Atlantic or Pacific Fleets for a minimum of 6 years. http://www.anchorscholarship.com/ and the email is cnslschf@erols.com.

Blinded Veterans Association (BVA): Kathern F. Gruber Scholarship for spouses of legally blinded U.S. Forces veterans. Call 202-371-8880 for more information.

Bowfin Memorial Scholarship: For members of the Hawaii submarine force personnel and their family members. 808-455-2597 or email dcpcc@aol.com for more information.

FCEA General Emmett Paige Scholarships: Persons on active duty or veterans and either's spouses AFCEA=Armed Forces Communications & Electronics Association. http://www.afcea.org/. You can call 703-631-6149 or 800-336-4583 X 6149 or email scholarship@afcea.org.

Fleet Reserve Association (FRA): For dependents of members only. Members can be active duty, Reserve, or retired personnel of Navy, Marine Corps or Coast Guard. Go to the website and click on: About FRA, scroll down to scholarships. http://www.fra.org/ or call 800-FRA-1924.

Fleet Training Center Petty Officers Association Scholarship Fund: For spouses of a living or deceased, past or present staff members of the Fleet Training Center, Norfolk. Petty Officer Association, Fleet Training Center, P.O. Box 15245, Norfolk, VA 23511-6258.

Fold of Honor Foundation Scholarships: Is a legacy foundation designed to provide scholarships for dependents and spouses of service members that have been killed or disabled as a result of their military service. http://www.foldsofhonor.org/

Ladies Auxiliary of the FRA Scholarship: Visit http://www.la-fra.org/; the Ladies Auxiliary of the FRA Scholarship is awarded annually to the male or female candidate chosen from children or grandchildren of members of the FRA and LA FRA. Also offered is The Sam Rose Memorial Scholarship Fund: To be awarded to the male or female candidate chosen from the sons, daughters, grandsons, or granddaughters of deceased LA FRA and FRA members. And the Allie Mae Oden Memorial Scholarship: Awarded to a candidate chosen from the children or grandchildren of members of the FRA or LA FRA. Go to http://www.la-fra.org/scholarship.html and click on the link to learn more about these scholarships and eligibility requirements.

Marine Corps Air Station Officers Spouses Club (Parris Island): Contact Ellen DeWolfe 843-379-9654. http://www.mccs-sc.com/indexasp

The Navy College Fund: Also known as an MGIB Kicker, is available to those who sign up for the MGIB. If you are a high school graduate, score a 50 or better on the ASVAB, and qualify for certain Navy jobs or apprenticeships,

up enlistment, you can get more than $15,000 in addition to your MGIB money for your education. http://www.allmilitary.com/gibill/navy/ncf.html

Non-Commissioned Officers Association (NCOA) Scholarship Grant: For spouses of members of NCOA. http://www.ncoausa.org/ or call 210-653-6161

Parris Island Officers Spouse Club: Rebecca Varicak 843-522-1615. http://www.mccs-sc.com/index.asp

Parris Island Staff Non-Commissioned Officers Spouse Club: Joanne Bright 843-525-1756. http://www.mccs-sc.com/index.asp

Student Loan Repayment Program (LRP): If you are a college student or graduate who qualifies for the Loan Repayment Program, the Navy will pay, upon enlistment, up to $65,000 of your student loans for a college level education. Go to Navy Student Loan Repayment Program website for more information at http://www.cnrc.navy.mil/EIncentives/N5311%20EB/EB/FAQ/LRP%20ADOBE.pdf.

Surface Navy Association: Awards scholarships to members of the Surface Navy Association, their spouses, or children working toward their first undergraduate degree. http://www.navysna.org/ Email: navysna@aol.com Phone: 1-800-NAVY-SNA.

Navy College Assistance/Student Headstart (NAVY-CASH): You may apply for the navy CASH program if you are a motivated high school or college student who qualifies for the Nuclear Field. The program will allow you to receive full Navy pay and benefits while attending college for up to 12 months if you are accepted. http://www.allmilitary.com/gibill/navy/cash.html and http://www.cnrc.navy.mil/nucfield/college/enlisted_options.htm

Accelerate to Excellence Pilot Program: Commander, Navy Recruiting Command (CNRC) and Commander, Naval education and Training Command (NETC) are starting to see interest grow in a pilot program, launched May 1, 2007, that allows enlistees to obtain an associate's degree through a community or junior college as part of their initial rate training.

Called "Accelerate to Excellence," the program allows enlistees to enroll in community college while in the Delayed Entry Program (DEP) and get paid monthly stipend by the Navy. The enlistees are expected to eventually earn an associate's degree prior to reporting to their first permanent duty station. http://www.worldwidelearn.com/military/branch-education-benefits/navy/accelerate-to-excellence.html

ADDITIONAL PROGRAMS

Get Your Degree by Using Your Selected Reserve Education Benefits: As a Reservists or Guardsman, you are entitled to various education benefits to help you pay for school and get your degree. While some benefits apply while in a drilling status, others apply if you are ordered to active duty. http://www.gibill.va.gov/benefits/montgomery_gibill/selected_reserve.html and/or http://www.military.com/education/content/money-for-school/reserve-tuition-assistance.html

Guard Chaplains: Chaplains are leaders in the Guard, responsible for caring for the spiritual well-being of soldiers and their families. They provide advice in matters pertaining to religion, morals and morale. As a Guard Chaplain, you would lead a Unit Ministry Team (UMT), which consists of you and a trained Chaplain Assistant (an enlisted Soldier trained to support Chaplains during their missions and everyday activities). You will minister to Soldiers day to day, performing religious ceremonies, counseling soldiers during times of crisis and providing a spiritual compass. Chaplains are non-combatants so you would not carry a weapon. Your chaplain assistant will provide security. If you are an ordained minister, you can earn your commission and begin your ministry to Guard Soldiers as soon as you complete the Chaplain Officer Basic Leader Course (CH-BOLC). Learn more about Chaplain duties, eligibility requirements and training at http://www.nationalguard.com/careers/chaplain-corps/guard-chaplains.

If you join the National Guard prior to your ordination, you'll enter as a Chaplain Candidate. In addition to general officer eligibility, to qualify as a Chaplain Candidate, you'll need to obtain an ecclesiastical approval from your denomination or faith group. Find out more about the requirements and training for Chaplain Candidates. As a National Guard Chaplain, you will start as an officer, so you will earn excellent pay-especially for part-time service. The Guard helps honor your service and commitment with a number of incentives. Learn more about pay, incentives and other benefits. For more information about becoming a Chaplin for the Army National Guard go to http://www.nationalguard.com/careers/chaplain-corps?cid=gx8-2_missionready_chaplains and/or www.nationalguard.com/highercalling.

Guard/Reserve Education Benefits Overview: The military offers several programs to support your education goals including tuition assistance, the GI Bill, and other education programs. The following guide will help you make the most of these benefits. http://www.military.com/education/content/money-for-school/reserve-education-benefits-users-guide.html?ESRC=reservists.nl

Military Chaplains Association of USA (MCA): Are you preparing for ministry as a military chaplain? Each year, MCA provides financial assistance to several seminary students who are currently serving as chaplain candidates in the Air Force, Army, or Navy. Eligibility requirements are:

- Full time enrollment in an accredited seminary
- Ecclesiastical endorsement for future ministry as a military chaplain
- Appointment and active service as a "Chaplain Candidate" in one of the Armed Forces
- Completion of the MCA Chaplain Candidate Scholarship application
- Submission of all requirements

For further information and more about the MCA Association, go to http://mca-usa.org.

Montgomery GI Bill for Selected Reserve (MGIB-SR): Under the MGIB-SR program, drilling Reservists and Guardsman can receive up to 36 months of education benefits. As of October 1, 2009, a full-time student can get paid $333 per month to help pay for school. Eligibility consists of:

- Having your high school diploma or GED before completing Inactive Duty for Training (IADT)
- Completing IDAT
- Committing to a six-year enlistment obligation
- Remain in good standing in an active Selected Reserve unit

The MGIB (SR) applies to members of the Army Reserve, Navy Reserve, Air Force Reserve, Marines Reserve and Coast Guard Reserve along with the Army and Air National Guard. This benefit is available to service members who have served and separated before September 11, 2001.

US Army Reserve (USAR) Educational Benefits: In addition to the MGIB (SR), the USAR offers two additional education benefits. If you meet the USAR entrance eligibility requirement and enlist for six years, you can receive up to $22,000 in education benefits. If you enlist into a critical Military Occupational Specialty (MOS), you could also earn an additional $350 per month for up to 36 months.

Air Force Reserve Educational Benefits: As a drilling Air Force Reservist, you can earn college credits for taking job-related technical courses through the Community College of the Air Force. They are the only military college authorized to award associates' degrees.

Reserve Education Assistance Program (REAP): As a member of the Selected Reserves, if you are ordered to active duty for at least 90 consecutive days, then you could be eligible for REAP. Depending on your active duty tour length, you could receive up to $827.20 per month for up to 36 months.

Veterans and the Montgomery GI Bill for Active Duty - (MGIB-AD): As a veteran, if you served two years on active duty and then within one year of discharge enlist for four years into one of the Selected Reserves, you could be eligible for up to 36 months of MGIB (AD) education benefits.

Voluntary Education Programs: The Army, Navy, Marines and Coast Guard offer voluntary education opportunities through the Servicemembers Opportunity College (SOC). The SOC is a network of about 1,800 colleges working together by transferring credits from other colleges within the network. The courses may be taken either campus-resident or through distance learning. http://www.ala.usmc.mil/mccs/edu/voluntary.asp, http://www.defense.gov/specials/education/dod.html, and/or http://www.dantes.doded.mil/DANTES Homepage.html

Below is the SOC program for each branch:

- Army - SOCAD
- Navy - SOCNAV
- Marines - SOCMAR
- Coast Guard - SOCCOAST
- Air Force - The Air Force's uses its Community College of the Air Force as an affiliate program of the SOC program

Additionally, National Guard members have additional voluntary education opportunities available to them through each of their respective states. As a Selected Reserve member, now is the time to use your education benefits and pursue getting your degree. With the online option, it is easy.

State Education Benefits for Veterans: Although many education benefits for veterans are federal benefits administered through the U.S. Department of Veterans Affairs, each state also extends benefits to honor military service members. Some states make minor adjustments in the way that federal benefits are managed. Other benefits are entirely new and include fee waivers, tuition waivers, and more. Because each state is unique and this list of benefits is not exhaustive, you should contact your state's office for veterans if you're interested in finding out further information. http://www.worldwidelearn.com/military/state-veterans/index.html

USS Lake Champlain (CG-57) Scholarship: Provides assistance to spouses of members assigned to USS Lake Champlain on PCS orders since commissioning August 12, 1988. You can contact someone from the Scholarship Committee at 843-757-2806.

HEALTH

In this section I want everyone to realize there are more avenues of resources for your health than you are aware of. Many of the following organizations were started by veterans and/or military family members who have lived through war-related struggles; or they were started by people who knew veteran families and their unique struggles. Do not be afraid to call on any of these--they respect your privacy and many are CONFIDENTIAL. Remember, they have been in the exact same situations you go through on a daily basis and will be able to assist you. Some of these resources are even free of charge. Their main goal is for you to get the assistance that you deserve and need.

** An important update service members need to know is you can access, apply for and learn about your military benefits easier online with the Health Benefits Renewal Form (10-10EZR) at www.va.gov/healtheligibility or call VA at toll free 1-877-222-VETS. The online form is available at http://www.1010ez. med.va.gov/sec/vha/1010ez/Form/1010ezr/pdf.

ACT Today! (Autism Care and Treatment Today) for Military Families: ACT Today! (Autism Care and Treatment Today!), is a national non-profit organization whose mission is to raise awareness and provide treatment services to families who cannot afford the treatments and services their children require. Recognizing the extraordinary challenges military families experience (waging a battle on two fronts...one for their country and another for their children), ACT Today! for Military Families is a dedicated fund to assist military families impacted by autism and works to improve awareness and delivery of effective autism services, providing financial assistance to military families to help defray out-of-pocket costs associated with autism treatments and other quality of life programs. For more information please go to http://www. acttodayformilitaryfamilies.org/default.aspx.

Army Well-Being: www.army.mil/armylife/wellbeing

Army G-1 Suicide Prevention: www.armyg1.army.mil/hr/suicide/default.asp

Army Suicide Prevention Guidance: http://fhp.osd.mil/pdhrainfo/media/ suicide_Prevention_Training_Tip_Cards.pdf

American Red Cross (ARC) for Psychological First Aid: www.redcross.org/ services/disaster

Army National Guard Post Deployment Health Reassessments Website: www.virtualarmory.com/mobiledeploy/PDHRA

Army Post Deployment Health Reassessments Website: http://fhp.osd.mil/ pdhrainfo

***Army Family Health Care:** This site offers information about TRICARE, dental, life insurance, family members with special needs and more. This is a pretty informative website. *You will be surprised at what all they discuss.* Please review this site at http://www.goarmy.com/soldier-life/army-family-strong/ health-care/family-health-care.html.

Health Care Benefits: To locate your nearest VA medical facility, go online to http://www.va.gov/sta/guide/division.asp?divisionld or call 1-877-222-8387.

Hooah4Health: Citizen-soldiers, the U.S. Army hosts a comprehensive web site offering health information and support for reservists. The site contains tools and resources on everything from physical and mental health to deployment and family wellness issues. www.hooah4health.com

Mammography Helpline: 888-492-7844

Mental Health Self-Assessment Program: Military life, especially deployments or mobilizations, can present challenges to service members and their families that are both unique and difficult. Sometimes you can manage these and sometimes they get blown way out of control and we need help. It is best to keep an eye on these things and that is what this link is for. It is totally anonymous and voluntary self-assessments. The questions are designed so you can review your situation with regard to some of the more common mental health issues. The screening will not provide a diagnosis—for that you need to see a professional. It will however, tell you whether or not you have symptoms that are consistent with a condition or concern that would benefit from further evaluation or treatment and guidance as to where you might seek assistance. http://www.pdhealth.mil/mhsa.asp

Military Health System: http://www.ha.osd.mil

MyHealtheVet: On August 2, 2010, President Obama announced the "Blue Button" site that allows veterans to download their personal health information from their MyHealtheVet account. By having control of this information, the hope is that it will enable vets to share the data with health care providers, caregivers, or people they trust. You can download and/or review this information more at http://www.myhealth.va.gov/. http://www.va.gov/bluebutton/.

Military OneSource: A one-stop site for complete support of military and their families including free confidential counseling. http://www.militaryonesource.com

National Alliance on Mental Illness: Veterans resource center that offers links to many resources. Please review this site. http://www.nami.org/

National Association of American Veterans: Assist all veterans and families from WWII, Korean War, Vietnam, Desert Storm, Enduring Freedom, and Iraqi Freedom severely wounded by helping to access health benefits, improving communication and coordination and collaborating among health agencies, medical professional organizations, educational organizations and the public. http://www.naavets.org/

National Center for PTSD: 802-296-6300 and/or ncptsd@va.gov and the website is www.ptsd.va.gov. The VA PTSD Coach app (for smart phones) is www.ptsd.va.gov/public/pages/ptsdcoach.asp. And PTSD Foundation of America is 877-717-7873 or www.ptsdusa.net.

National Guard Psychological Health Program: National Guard members and their families should never weather emotional and behavioral challenges alone. That is why the National Guard Psychological Health Program is here for you, with Directors of Psychological help in every state, territory, and the District of Columbia to ensure you receives the care you deserve. On their new site, you'll find information and contacts to help you and your family build resiliency, including education to support overall wellness, support for family members and friends, and immediate access to help if you are experiencing troubling symptoms. Their library is home to numerous online resources on topics ranging from Post-Traumatic Stress Disorder to Traumatic Brain Injury and more. http://www.jointservicessupport.org/PHP/Default.aspx

National Resource Directory: Online resource for wounded, ill and injured service members, veterans and their families and those who support them. The directory provides information and contacts for those in the armed forces community to find support in a multitude of areas. http://www. nationalresourcedirectory.gov

National Suicide Prevention Life Line: www.suicidepreventionlifeline.org

Navy Bureau of Medicine and Surgery: The Navy Bureau of Medicine and Surgery (BUMED) is the headquarters command for Navy Medicine. Under the leadership of the Navy Surgeon General, Navy Medicine provides high-quality health care to beneficiaries in wartime and in peacetime. Highly trained Navy Medicine personnel deploy with Sailors and Marines worldwide providing critical mission support aboard ship, in the air, under the sea and on the battlefield. At the same time, Navy Medicine's military and civilian health care professionals are providing care for uniformed services' family members and retirees at military treatment facilities around the globe. Every day, no matter what the environment, Navy Medicine is ready to care for those in need, provide world-class care, anytime, anywhere. Today, BUMED is the site where the policies and direction for Navy Medicine are developed to ensure our Patient and Family Center Care vision carried out. http://www.med.navy. mil/BUMED/Pages/default.aspx

New Army Health Coordinator Program: This program will provide trained professionals to synchronize installation health and wellness programs. They are to not only address the physical but the emotional and spiritual needs of soldiers and their families. They plan to incorporate this into the Comprehensive Soldier Fitness Program. Seven installations now have health promotion coordinators and four more are being recruited. The new program brings a holistic approach to health and wellness...***Keep watch for this at your installation. I would like to know how this works out.*** http://www.military. com/military-report/new-army-health-coordinator-program

The North Dakota Legion Department: Offers its Courage Carries On Program to other state Legions for a minimal charge. Contact Jim Deremo, North Dakota Legion department service officer, at (701) 451-4646 or email jim.deremo@va.gov. To learn more about the Indiana National Guard's mobile crisis intervention teams, contact Lt. Col. Ross Waltemath at, (800) 237-2850, ext. 85450, or Capt. Elizabeth Williams, (317) 247-3300, ext. 85474.

Operation Second Chance: Committed to serving our wounded, injured and ill combat veterans, give support while recovering in a hospital. See site for more details. http://www.operationsecondchance.org/

*Operation We Are Here: This is a wonderful website offering twenty four different organizations that dedicate their time to training service dogs, home companion dogs and residential companion dogs to assist individuals who have a wide range of physical and cognitive disabilities for wounded warriors and veterans. Please take the time to review each organization as they differ in locations and abilities. *All are wonderful organizations. The website has other information about military families that will be of interest to you also.* http://www.operationwearehere.com/MilitaryServiceDogs.html.

The Post Deployment Health Reassessment Program: Is designed to encourage soldiers to get treatment for any injuries, physical or psychological, sustained in defending our country. If you were injured while deployed, you should take advantage of this benefit.

If you received a medical referral at your PDHRA screening, you are eligible to be placed on orders up to seven times to attend medical appointments. These medical appointments must be for the same medical issues you for which you were originally referred. If you are unsure if you have given a referral look at page 5, block 9 of your DD Form 2900; your referrals are listed here. You may request orders for appointments with any legitimate health care provider. If you want to request orders for a medical appointment, you must contact your unit at least three business days before the day of your appointment. Late requests will be denied. You can email as soon as you get an appointment with all pertinent information. Upon completion of your appointment, get letters from your doctor office verifying your attendance. You will not get paid until you show verification of attendance of attendance to your unit. If you travel more than 10 miles to your appointment, you may request travel reimbursement pay with form DTS or DD 1351-2 per unit SOP. You must request travel reimbursement through your unit and it must be requested within 20 days of your appointment, or you will not receive travel pay. And remember, if you collect mileage reimbursement from the VA, you CANNOT also claim mileage from the Army.

Additional special instructions for AGR Soldiers, Federal Technicians, and Soldiers on ADOS/AT orders are as follows:

**If you are on ADOS/AT orders when requesting your medical orders, clearly state that these are "travel only." Failure to do so will delay the processing of your request, and may result in you missing the deadline to be reimbursed.*

**If you are a Federal Technician you may either request travel-only orders as per ADOS/AT Soldier above, and remain on technician status, OR take military leave and be placed on ADSW/ADOS orders for the day. For more information, see "TAG's Technician Policy, 5 May 06."*

**If you are AGR, request all travel authorization through the AGR Office, PDGRA does not pay for AGR travel.*

Psychological Health Program: Need Help? Do you think you or someone you love might have PTSD? If so visit this website for helpful information and guidance. www.jointservicessupport.org/php/ and/or **National Center of Veterans Affairs** at www.ptsd.va.gov/index.asap

Real Warriors (Combating Psychological Health Care Stigma): SAMHSA is partnering with the Department of Defense's Centers of Excellence for Psychological Health and Traumatic Brain Injury (DCoE) on its Real Warriors Campaign. Real Warriors focuses on combating the stigma associated with seeking care and treatment for psychological health concerns. Using the campaign theme, "Real Warriors, Real Battles, Real Strength," the website features resources on psychological health issues, as well as video interviews with service members, their families, and others dealing with psychological health or traumatic brain injury issues. Every page of the site lists the Veterans Suicide Prevention Hotline (1-800-273-TALK, press 1 for veterans), which is a partnership between SAMHSA and the Department of Veterans Affairs. Please review the site for more important information about this subject. http://www.samhsa.gov/SAMHSAnewsLetter/Volume_17_Number_3/RealWarriors.aspx

SAVE: Suicide Awareness Voices Of Education: Mission is to prevent suicide through public awareness and education, eliminate stigma and serve as a resource to those touched by suicide. http://www.save.org

Service Women's Action Network (SWAN) National Peer Support Helpline: 888-729-2089 and/or peersupport@servicewomen.org, the website is www.servicewomen.org.

SOFAR: "Strategic Outreach to Families of all Reservists" provides free psychological support, psychotherapy, psychological education and prevention services to extended family of Reserve and National Guard deployed during the Global War on Terrorism from time of alert through the period of reunion and reintegration. http://www.sofarusa.org/index.html

Suicide-Prevention Resources: New suicide-prevention resources are available to help reduce suicides in the U.S. military and among veterans, including:

- **VA Suicide Prevention Lifeline/National Suicide Prevention Lifeline:** (800) 273-8255
- **Military OneSource Crisis Intervention Line:** (800) 342-9647
- **Wounded Soldier and Family Hotline:** (800) 984-8523
- **Tragedy Assistance Program:** (800) 959-8277

Telecommunications Device for the Deaf (TDD): 800-829-4833

United Concordia Dental Insurance: http://www.ucci.com

*United We Serve: Provides a safe haven for military service members, veterans and family members during time of difficulty and crisis, through Battle Buddy and family camp retreats. Each retreat offers hope and tools. Check site for more details. *This site looks really cool to me and I hope to be able to go and check it out.* http://www.unitedweservemil.org

Veterans & Families United: Assists with physical and mental issues with soldiers. http://www.veteransfamiliesunited.org/how_to_get_help.html

Veterans Support Center: Is a non-profit 501(c)3 organization that is **NOT** a government agency or affiliated with any government agency or government department. Veteran Support Center receives no Federal, State, or local tax aid. Please visit this website to see the resources that are available for you. Go to http://veteransupportcenter.org/.

The Warrior Combat Stress Reset Program: Aims to treat combat stress and PTSD symptoms before they worsen and cause dysfunction. Treatment is most effective soon after deployment, when it can prevent further deterioration of function. For symptoms and further information, visit its website at http://crdamc.amedd.army.mil/default.asp?page=randrreset and/or Telephone: (254) 288-4746.

Women Veterans of America (WVA): Women veterans face their own array of issues after they have finished active duty. WVA was created to be a resource for women veterans and for the families and friends who support them. On this site you can learn about women veteran's health issues, information on military sexual trauma, and the balancing of motherhood with service. The site will provide assistance with understanding military benefits and direct you towards organizations and resources advocating for women veterans. These resources are for current and past members of the military service. http://www.womenveteransofamerica.com/about

TRICARE RESOURCES

Transition Warrior Care: Ensures equitable, consistent, high-quality support and service for all branches of wounded warriors and their families, as well as transitioning members of the Armed Forces through effective outreach, interagency collaboration, policy and program oversight. http://warriorcare.dodlive.mil/about/

Toolkit: Helps Answer Service Members' Healthcare Questions: To assist with the continued care needed for returning veterans from Iraq and Afghanistan who suffer from major depression or post-traumatic stress disorder (PTSD) and other health conditions, TRICARE has created a toolkit for wounded, ill and injured service members. The toolkit is located at http://myarmyonesource.com/News/2010/02/TRICAREWII.

TRICARE: 1-877-TRICARE

TRICARE Benefit Information: www.healthnetfederalservices.com

TRICARE – South Region (Humana Military Healthcare Services Inc): 1-877-444-5445 and www.humana-military.com

TRICARE – West Region (TriWest Healthcare Alliance (TriWest)): 1-888-TRIWEST www.triwest.com

TRICARE – North Region: 1-877-TRICARE www.healthnetfederalservices.com

TRICARE–DentalInsurance: 1-800-866-8499 http:/TRICAREdentalprogram.com

TRICARE – Military Health Insurance: http://www.TRICARE.mil

TRICARE – My benefits: http://www.TRICARE.mil/mybenefit/

TRICARE – Online: http://www.TRICAREonline.com

TRICARE Assistance Program (TRIAP): A new program recently introduced by TRICARE, it is a way for service members and military families to reach out to a counselor or professional anytime you need help. For eligible TRICARE beneficiaries, this capability is as close as your computer. In a four-minute video, "Getting the help you need, when you need it," at www.TRICARE.mil/mentalhealth, service members and family members can reach out for help if they are struggling with feelings of stress, anxiety or depression.

To access information on TRIAP, go to www.TRICARE.mil/triap or go to your regional healthcare contractor's website. TRIAP is web-based videoconferencing that provides short-term, solution-focused, nonmedical counseling for situations resulting from commonly occurring life circumstances such as deployments, stress, relationships, personal loss and parent-child communications. All TRIAP services, available 24 hours a day, seven days a week and 365 days a year, are provided on a one-to-one basis, in the context of a confidential relationship with a licensed professional.

TRIAP services are available to active duty service members, active duty family members (children must be age 18 or older), beneficiaries using TRICARE Reserve Select, and beneficiaries covered under the Transition Assistance management Program. Beneficiaries do not need a referral or prior authorization to use TRIAP services.

If a beneficiary requests TRIAP services, they will receive an initial assessment with a licensed professional to determine if web-based counseling is an appropriate level of care. If video services are not possible or web-based counseling is an appropriate level of care, the licensed professional will refer the beneficiary to the correct organization to receive services.

If you can't access TRIAP services or you are not currently eligible, you may receive behavioral health support by telephone through Military OneSource at (800) 342-9647 or go to www.TRICARE.mil/mentalhealth to view other TRICARE behavioral health resources. TRIAP does not include medication management or financial counseling and is not for emergency situations. The Department of Defense and Veterans Affairs national suicide hotline is (800) 273-8255. In an emergency, beneficiaries should call 911.

TRICARE: Extended Care Health Option Helps Families with Special Need Issues: If a family member has special needs, a serious illness or sustains a serious injury, TRICARE has several programs in place to help. The TRICARE Extended Care Health Option (ECHO) provides assistance for active duty family members with physical or mental disabilities. The ECHO covers up to $36,000 per fiscal year in addition to regular TRICARE benefits to cover claims for care of a disabled family member. Some of the services ECHO can be used for include training, rehabilitation, special education (including applied behavioral analysis for the treatment of autism spectrum disorders), institutional care and, under certain circumstances, transportation to and from institutions or facilities. The benefit also includes ECHO Home Health Care, which provides skilled nursing care and other services for severely disabled beneficiaries and respite care for caregivers. To read more, visit http://www.myarmyonesource.com/news/2009/12/SpecialNeeds.

TRICARE Expands Vaccine Program: TRICARE officials are expanding the number of preventive vaccines covered at retail network pharmacies. The expanded program covers immunizations for measles, mumps, shingles and many other preventable diseases. To see the expanded list of vaccines available from authorized TRICARE retail pharmacies visit the TRICARE Vaccines webpage at www.TRICARE.mil/vaccines. Be sure to check ahead before making a trip to the pharmacy to make sure it is part of the TRICARE network and authorized to offer the vaccines. Ensuring that the pharmacy has the needed vaccine in stock is also recommended.

**As of September 2011, for Gulf War Veterans with certain ailments like: Chronic Fatigue Syndrome, Fibromyalgia, functional gastrointestinal disorders and other hard to diagnose or undiagnosed illnesses, the current deadline for when the condition must have "appeared" is on or before December 31, 2011. If you have any conditions that are "undiagnosed" and you did a tour in the Middle East, this could apply to you. The VA is working to extend the deadline to December 31, 2018. If this occurs, it will be great news for veterans and military members who develop symptoms after the 2011 cut-off. However, since there is no guarantee that the deadline will be extended, veterans suffering from undiagnosed conditions are encouraged to talk with their Veteran Service Officer about filing a disability claim for these conditions. http://www.military.com/veterans-report/gulf-war-claims-deadline?ESRC=vr.nl

MORE WEBSITES

Courage Carries On: www.couragecarrieson.org

Navy Suicide Prevention: www.suicide.navy.mil

Marine Corps: www.usmc-mccs.org/suicideprevent

Tragedy Assistance Program: www.taps.org/

The American Legion: www.legion.org

Returning Veterans Project: www.returningveterans.org

Health

GENERAL MILITARY RESOURCES

The resources listed in this chapter are available to all branches/status and their dependents. Please take the time to review these because I know you will be amazed at what is available for you and your families.

Adobe Reader: Free .pdf document reader download. http://www.adobe.com/products/acrobat/readstep2.html

America Supports You: Is a 501(c)3 out of the state of Texas; they promote public awareness and support for our U.S. military service members and veterans, as well as their families. Remain proactive supporters of these men and women in the U.S. military, in your community, across Texas and the USA. They provide Military Family Support, by assisting currently deployed military personnel and their families with financial assistance to meet the emergency needs that arise from deployments. They host various family support activities, Welcome Home Rally's, and Return to Duty Rally's for military. They also support and host patriotic events, parades on all military holidays; Armed Forces Day, Memorial Day, Flag Day, Independence Day and Veterans Day. Host/Sponsor annual America Supports You Texas Cookout honoring our military, veterans and their families. Host/sponsor annual Armed Forces Day, "Celebrating Freedom & Honoring Service" Banquet. And host/sponsor annual Washington, D.C. Veterans Tour, honoring Texas Veterans. For more information and emergency assistance help go to http:// americasupportsyoutexas.org/about.php.

AmeriForce Publishing Inc.: Publisher of military magazines and books. http://www.ameriforce.net

*Animal and Pet Rescue Effort: To learn more about the animal and pet rescue efforts related to the wars in Iraq and Afghanistan go to these websites at:
- Operation Baghdad Pups: www.spcai.org/baghdad0pups.html
- Guardian Angels for Soldier's Pet: www.guardianangelsforsoldierspet.org
- Humane Society International: www.hsi.org
- Afghan Stray Animal League: www.afghanstrayanimals.org.

I have a soft spot for animals, so I thank all the volunteers and efforts from everyone at these organizations.

Armed Forces Services Corporation: This organization began in 1879 as part of a nonprofit established to care for surviving spouses from The Battle of Little Big Horn. Today they've grown to provide management consult and program delivery to many of the most vital government programs serving the military community. They focus on strategic planning, operational services such as adjudication support and broader case management functions, quality-of-life programs serving the military life-cycle- including healthcare, resiliency, suicides, family strength, education, employment and financial/ legal support. When an AFSC member or a survivor needs to file a claim for benefits, they will have the support of experienced AFSC employees to help navigate the somewhat challenging maze of government bureaucracy. Living AFSC members can be assisted with Veterans Affairs and with their disability claims. http://www.afsc-usa.com

Armed Forces Relief Trust: Mission is to assist all branches of the military with aid through societies by providing a single vehicle to accept donations that will benefit the men and women of our Armed Forces and their families. Examples include assistance with airline tickets to come home for a funeral, tutoring for children, medical assistance, tuition for college and more. http:// www.afrtrust.org

*Armed Services YMCA: Has hooked up with your local YMCA to provide free membership to spouses and dependents of active duty deployed soldiers. Soldiers will get three months free before deployment and 3 months free post deployment. *This is a great opportunity for military families and a great assistance to my family when my husband was deployed. Double check in your state before you go, I have heard that some states (Texas for one) have backed out of helping military families. What a shame! (Also some YMCA's have respite care for kids during deployments.)* http://www.asymca.org

Army and Air Force Exchange Service–AAFES: This is a mini mall on base that sells items from toiletries to TV's and furniture with **NO TAXES**, depending on the base. The store size can vary. You can also order a catalog to come to your house and order online. http://www.aafes.com

Army and Air Force Mutual Aid Society: This site provides more than insurance for you and your family. Their mission is to serve members with low cost life insurance and assist their survivors in receiving the benefits they are entitled to from insurance claims and government benefits. They also provide other assistance, check out their site. http://www.aafmaa.com

Army Career and Alumni Program: Assistance for **ALL** branches of military in various ways. http://www.acap.army.mil

Armed Forces Legal Assistance: Explains the special legal rights of members of the military and includes contact information for legal-assistance offices at near by bases. http://legalassistance.law.af.mil

Army FRG (VFRG =Virtual Family Readiness Group): Family Readiness website and information. http://www.armyfrg.org

Army Family Team Building: http://www.myarmylifetoo.com

Army Newspapers – DOD: http://www.army.mil/newspapers/

*Army OneSource: Covers a variety of military information. *I enjoyed this site.* http://www.myarmyonesource.com

American Red Cross: The American Red Cross offers compassionate services for not only the community but also for military families. They provide grants and loans on case by case bases and will assist with emergency contact to your service member. http://www.redcross.org

Army Times-Military Newspaper: http://www.armytimes.com

Association of Military Banks of America: http://ambahq.org

*Association of the United States Army (Be an Author): The goal of the AUSA Book Program is to establish AUSA as a quality source of military books. To meet this goal, AUSA has established some guidelines for people interested in participating in the program. See site for more details; and *look at the wonderful opportunity for writers. I plan on sending something in myself soon.* http://www.ausa.org/resources/bookprogram/pages/beanauthor.aspx

AUSA Family Programs: AUSA coordinates a number of activities that support the needs and interest of family members. They will travel to educate military families about the programs that exist to ease the strain of military life. AUSA's site offers an extensive directory of internet resources for the use of military. http://www.ausa.org/resources/familyprograms/pages/default.aspx

Balfour Beatty Communities: The LifeWorks at Balfour Beatty Communities program is the perfect recipe offering fun and creative activities to promote wellness with healthy eating, fresh ideas and simple meals for active parents on the go and kids who want to enjoy a tasty treat. Balfour Beatty offers cooking classes, recipe swaps and holiday cookie exchange. Go to www. balfourbeattycommunities.com to see what's cooking in your community.

BBB Military Line: Focuses on information specifically for members of the military. www.bbb.org/military

Buy Veteran: Would you like to show your support? Find a veteran-owned business at www.buyveteran.com/ms. And look for the buy veteran badge wherever you buy stuff.

Cards for A Good Cause: You can order customized playing cards and a portion of every order goes to the Intrepid Fallen Heroes Fund. http://www. cards4agoodcause.com

Care4Hire: Is a data base that provides assistance to families in finding a quality babysitter, housekeeper, tutor, companion/eldercare, pet sitter and miscellaneous care such as a personal assistant, gardener, and party caregivers. Register to become a member than you will be given immediate access to babysitters through email and phone. In addition, helpful tools are available, including sample interview questions, a sample reference form and a sample contract. Care4hire.com also gives you advice, tips and information that will help you and your caregiver. www.care4hire.com

*Carolina Patriot Rovers Inc: Patriot Rovers is committed to rescuing, training, and deploying Psychiatric Service Dogs that will provide support 24/7 for veterans to enhance their lives. The dogs trained by this organization perform tasks and work as described by the final regulation under ADA. These tasks include but are not limited to: brace, get help, lights, doors, pull, dress, retrieve, reverse, (standard service dog training tasks) but also psychiatric service tasks, tactile stimulation, alert, interrupting, stabilizing, waking, initiate activity, initiate interpersonal interaction and much more. *Please visit this website and review this great organization.* http://www.patriotrovers.org.

Combat Veterans Motorcycle Association (CVMA): Is an association of Combat Veterans from all branches of the United States Armed Forces who ride motorcycles as a hobby. Their mission is to support and defend those who have defended our country and our freedoms. Their focus is to help veteran care facilities provide a warm meal, clothing, shelter, and guidance, or simply to say "Thank You" and "Welcome Home."

Their members comprised of full members (those with verified combat service) and supporter members (those who have non-combat military service, and have a sincere dedication to helping veterans). They have members from nearly all 50 states and living abroad. Many members continue to serve in our Armed Forces with several serving in combat areas at various times. CVMA sponsors and/or participates in many motorcycle-related charity events each year, and as a non-profit organization, donate to various veteran care facilities and veteran charities. Check out the website to click on your state for the organization closest to you and see the up and coming events. http://combatvet. org/

Commissary Locations: Find one near you at http://www.commissaries.com/locations.cfm.

Congress–American's Town Square: Find out where to write your elected officials about bills, etc. http://www.congress.org

Civilian Deployment: Good information to stay updated on, go to http://www.dfas.mil/dfas/civilianemployees.html.

Defense, U.S. Department of--DOD: http://www.defenselink.mil

Defense News: Military Times Media Group. http://www.defensenews.com

Department of Defense Issuances: Publications and forms. http://www.dtic.mil/whs/directives/

Department of Veterans Affairs SGLI: Visit this site for in-depth information about service members' group life insurance. www.insurance.va.gov/sglisite/default.htm

Divorce Care: Is a friendly, caring group of people who will walk alongside you through one of life's most difficult experiences. Don't go through separation or divorce alone. DivorceCare provides seminars and support groups that are led by people who understand what you are going through and want to help. You will gain access to valuable DivorceCare resources to help you deal with the pain of the past and help you to look forward to rebuilding your future. For more information go to their website at http://www.divorcecare.org/.

Exchange Store: Website for military exchange store for military families to shop. http://www.shopmyexchange.com/

GOVBenefits.gov: Helps citizens access government benefit eligibility information through a free, confidential, and easy-to-use online screening tool. After answering some basic questions, the user receives a customized report listing the benefit programs for which the user will be eligible. http://www.benefits.gov

Guidestar: Best site to learn information about a non-profit. http://www.2.guidestar.org

Honor Flight Network: Is a non-profit organization created solely to honor America's veterans for all their sacrifice. They will transport our heroes to Washington, D.C. to visit and reflect at their memorials. Top priority is given to the senior veterans—World War II survivors, along with those other veterans who may be terminally ill. For more information, go to http://www. honorflight.org/.

Iraq and Afghanistan Veterans Association (IAVA): IAVA is a 21st century veterans' organization dedicated to standing with the 2.3 million veterans of Iraq and Afghanistan from their first day home through the rest of their lives. Their mission is to improve the lives of our OIF/OEF veterans and their families through various resources. IAVA delivers services, resources and support through a three-pronged approach to generating transformative change in the lives of veterans and their families in four critical impact areas: Health, education, employment and community building. Please go to their website to view how they provide these services and much more empowerment at http://iava.org/content/iava-mission-and-history.

Kiplinger: Covers all personal finance topics, from saving and investing to insurance, taxes and financial planning. www.kiplinger.com

*Marc Wolfe: This is an artist who creates beautiful paintings and photos of not only the military but police, firefighters and comic heroes. Please take the time to visit his website at www.MarcWolfeArt.com. You can reach him by email at MarcWolfeArt@gmail.com and/or 517-204-9259. *From my home state of Michigan...Let him know I sent you!!*

Military Assistance Program (MAP): This program is through the VFW, for active duty, Guard, and Reserve military units. MAP offers grants to VFW Posts who participate in military unit's functions, such as sponsoring "Farewell and Welcome Home Activities," "Family Readiness Group" events, or other sponsorship ideas.

MAP also links with VFW's Operation Uplink and UnMet Needs programs to create an all-star team of military assistance. MAP and Operation Uplink have provided more than 200 computers to set up internet cafes where service member's families may e-mail their deployed loved ones. In addition, MAP has forged partnerships with various service providers, including www.vetjobs. com, aimed at providing the transitioning service member with relocation and employment assistance. For more information, call the MAP officer at 816-756-3390, ext 211 email: map@vfw.org Website: http://vfwwebcom.org/

*Military Benefits: Issued by Military.com and offers a vast amount of knowledge and resources for military families. http://www.militarybenefits.com

The Military Coalition: The Military Coalition is comprised of 34 organizations representing more than 5.5 million members of the uniformed services-active, reserve, retired, survivors, veterans and their families. http://www. themilitarycoalition.org/.

Military Connection: Vast resource network. http://militaryconnection.com

*Military.com: Great resource filled with military and veteran organizations. http://www.military.com

Military Financial: Provides financial information and ideas for military families. http://www.militaryfinancial.com/aboutus.aspx

Military 4 Life: Great resource network with links to lots of sites. http://www.military4life.com

Military Magazines: Offers variety of military magazines. http://www.operationwearehere.com/militarymagazines.html

The Military Homefront: Is a Department of Defense website for official military community and family policy program information, policy and guidance designed to help troops and their families, leaders and service providers. Whether you live the military lifestyle or support those who do, you'll find what you need. http://www.militaryhomefront.dod.mil

*Military OneSource: Whether it is help with child care, personal finances, and emotional support during deployments, relocation information, or resources needed for special circumstances, Military OneSource will have answers and information for you. *Military OneSource is a wonderful organization and all military families should be aware of it.* http://www.militaryonesource.com

Military Spot.com: Offers lots of information and an opportunity to be a guest writer for the website. http://www.militaryspot.com

*National Do Not Call List: Register your phone numbers to prevent unwanted sales calls. http://www.donotcall.gov

MyArmyLifeToo.com: Provides resources for when service member becomes activated. For those of you that are not aware of it, My Army Life Too and Army One Source combined into one website in the summer of 2009. http://www.myarmyonesource.com/default.aspx

Military Star Card: The new Military Star Card offered through the Army and Air Force Exchange Service will allow users to charge purchases at any store on or off base-that accepts MasterCard and you will earn points for purchases. The current military star credit card, which is run solely by AAFES, can only be used at military exchange stores. The new MasterCard is in partnership with Chase Card Services, a division of JP Morgan Chase & CO., and works like a regular credit card.

The interest rate for the rewards card is currently at 10.24% and AAFES sets the rate for both the rewards card and the military star card at 4.99% above the prime interest rate. Customers can earn points on the new card in two ways; buy purchases made at military exchanges will mean two points for every dollar spent. Purchases made at other stores, on or off base, will count for one point. The points can be redeemed for options such as cash back, airline tickets or exchange gift cards.

National Association of Insurance Commissioners' Military Site: This site focuses on special insurance considerations for members of the military and includes contact information for state insurance regulators. www.naic.org/consumer.Militaryinsurance.htm

North American Securities Administrators Association: This site includes links to state securities regulators, tips on avoiding scams and other valuable information for investors. www.nasaa.org

Office of Personnel Management: Provides contact information and resources for veterans and dependents in a variety of areas. For example job placement, scholarships and much more. http://www.opm.gov

Open Office: Free office software. http://www.openoffice.org

Operation Homelink: Provides refurbished computers to the spouse or parents of junior enlisted (E1-E5) deployed soldiers. See website for more information. http://www.opertionhomelink.org

*Operation Once in a Lifetime: This organization's mission is to make the dreams of service members and their families come true by providing free financial and moral support. Operation Once in a Lifetime was created by a service member to help other service members; created on the basis that "a service member knows what a service member needs," And a service member does not need to worry about providing beds for his kids, worrying if his electricity will still be on when he goes home or if his house will be foreclosed on when serving his/her country. A service member needs a program that will provide free financial assistance regardless of his rank, race, branch of service, physical condition or his deployment status. A service member needs a program that can help make a life altering contribution when he/she is in their greatest need. Operation Once in a Lifetime hopes to be that organization for you. *This is a wonderful organization; I wish I would have heard about them earlier in my past positions. Michigan soldiers could use this organization. I will be passing this information on to the Family Assistance Coordinators.* Please go to www.operationonceinalifetime.com.

Operation Special Delivery: Provides many online resources for Doulas and moms to be. Doulas.com will make finding a doula much easier and speed the process of connecting moms-to-be with OSD doulas. Operation Special Delivery will continue to maintain the integrity of its program and of the doula profession by serving as many military families who desire our services. *This is a great organization and it is too hard to explain in a small clip what they do. Please go to the site and review.* http://www.operationspecialdelivery.com/

*Operation We Are Here: This is a wonderful website that offers information and links to resources for military families and veterans about retreats, books, youth links, links for parents of service members, emotional support, marriage, and much more. Please review the site at http://www.operationwearehere.com.

Order of Daedalians: The Order of Daedalians honors, as its Founding Members, all WWI aviators who were commissioned as officers and rated as military pilots no later than the Armistice on 11 November 1918. It perpetuates their names as the first to fly our country's airplanes in time of war. The Order's membership of commissioned, warrant and flight officer military pilots and WASP's, with its worldwide network of Daedalian Flights and its comprehensive awards program, supports the military services and other aerospace activities.

The Awards and Scholarship Programs of the Order and Foundation encourage patriotism, integrity, and good character in our nation's youth; military careers as commissioned pilots; safety of flight, and excellence in the performance of military duties. The Daedalian Foundation's Scholarship program also promotes study in aerospace disciplines. For more information about this wonderful organization or eligibility requirements go to http://www. daedalians.org/.

Red Cross: Are your older kids ready to start babysitting? American Red Cross babysitters training gives tweens and teens the care-giving, safety, and first aid training they need. Get more information at www.redcross.org and you can also get the babysitter checklist at www.militaryonesource.com.

ReserveAid: Is a nonprofit organization committed to providing financial support to the families of Reserve Service Members from all services, which have been called to active duty and are experiencing financial difficulty. The goal is to alleviate the emotional and financial burdens placed on the men and women called to serve by supporting their families at home. www.reserveaid. org

Social Security Administration: http://www.ssa.gov

Soldiers Angels: "May no soldier go unloved" is the motivation behind Soldiers Angels. These volunteers work to show care and concern for veterans, the wounded, deployed and their families. Soldiers Angels provides care packages and letters to service members, First Response Backpacks to wounded service members directly at the combat support hospitals overseas and stateside. They will provide emergency aid to military families in need and have partnered with the Department of Defense to provide voice-controlled/adaptive laptops to over 6,000 severely-wounded service members, and well as other technology that supports rehabilitation.

They have provided flights to soldiers on leave or in emergency situations, and to their families wanting to be with them upon return from overseas; they work daily to provide assistance and honor military families of those who paid the ultimate price for freedom and safety. You can visit their website at http:// soldiersangels.org/about-us.html.

*Soldiers and Sailors Civil Relief Act: VERY IMPORTANT: All soldiers and spouses should understand and memorize these laws. http://www.defenselink. mil/specials/relief_act_revision

Strength for Service: To God and country. http://www.strengthforservice.org

*The American Legion's Family Support Network: Provides immediate assistance to service personnel and families whose lives have been directly affected by Operation Iraqi Freedom and America's war on terror. Since Sept. 11, 2001, the nation's active-duty military has been on high alert, and National Guard and reserve units are being mobilized in record numbers. As a result, the families of these men and women often find themselves unable to meet normal monthly expenses, and assistance is needed for a variety of everyday chores. These tasks include grocery shopping, child care, mowing the grass, fixing the family car and other routine household jobs.

To address these issues, The American Legion has a nationwide toll-free telephone number, (800) 504-4098, for service members and their family members to call for assistance. Applicants can apply online by clicking the assistance form at the top of the page. Calls are referred to The American Legion department, or state in which the call originated. Departments relay the collected information to a local American Legion post. The local post then contacts the service member or family to see how assistance can be provided locally. Since the creation of the Family Support Network during the first Persian Gulf War, thousands of posts have responded to meet these families' needs. *They are a wonderful organization, I have used their services in the past to assist military families and they are great!!* http://www.legion.org/familysupport

*The Military Family Network: *This is a great website loaded with resources for military families.* http://www.emilitary.org/

*The Military Working Dog Vest Project: Mission is to protect the working dogs overseas with special cooling vests, protective padding for paws and dog goggles called "doggles", ear protection for when they travel by helicopters, grooming tools and collapsible water bowls and toys. *This is a wonderful organization and it touched my heart when I read about them. These working dogs are heroes too!* http://www.supportmilitaryworkingdogs.org/

The National Governors Association Listing: States have independently started to recognize the difficulties that service members and their families endure in order to fulfill mission requirements. Since 2001, States have enhanced their support to service members, providing military families special support that is for their soldier that lives in their state.

This website lists a state-by-state programs and benefits on matters dealing with education, taxes, family support, finances, licensing, registrations and protections, recognitions and employment support, etc. In most counties they will have a Department of Military Affairs, trust fund that is for the people living in the county.

I am not going to list all those here as it would take up too much space. Just go to your **Department of Military Affairs Office** and they can assist you with a contact number and name.

Sittercity: This site provides access to hundreds of local quality babysitters and nannies in your neighborhood, at no cost to you. You can review detailed sitter profiles featuring their experience, background checks, references, reviews and photos. Membership is available at no cost to all Army, Marines, Navy and Air Force families (active and Reserve Guard). In addition to quality local babysitters and nannies, you can also find elder care providers, dog walkers, housekeepers and tutors. Go to www.sittercity. com/dod for more information.

The Securities and Exchange Commission's Military Site: Tracks enforcement actions regarding military sales practices and affinity fraud, and provides general investor education. www.sec.gov/investor/military. shtml

Tillman Troops: Does a variety of things for military families and soldiers. Please check out their site. http://tillmantroops.org

*United Service Organization: This is a wonderful organization that is all over the world helping military families with various things. *They were a comfort not only to me and my daughter, but also for my husband during his many travels abroad. Please check out their website, they deserve a handshake when you come across them.* http://www.uso.org

United We Serve: Provides a safe haven for all military branches, veterans and family members during times of difficulty and crisis. http://www. unitedweservemil.org/about-us

*Unmet Needs (Veterans of Foreign Wars): Was created to provide emergency financial support to families of military personnel. Funds from donations are available to the five branches of service (Army, Navy, Air Force, Marines and Coast Guard), as well as members of the Reserves and National Guard. Funds awarded by the program are offered in the form of grants, not loans, so recipients don't need to repay them. *Wonderful organization, they assisted my family in 2006 with an issue with our roof. I have also used this organization to assist military families in the past. Great organization!!!* http://www.vfw.org/Assistance/National-Military-Services/

United States Military Academies: List of United States Military Schools and Academies. http://en.wikipedia.org/wiki/List_of_United_States_military_schools_and_academies

*USA Cares: *USA Cares* exists to help bear the burdens of service by providing post-9/11 military families with financial and advocacy support in their time of need. Assistance is provided to all branches of service, all components, and all ranks while protecting the privacy and dignity of those military families and veterans who request our help. *Wonderful organization, I have used this company to assist many military families. They are a great organization!!* http://usacares.org/

USAA Mobile App: Car accidents are scary enough, and USAA has provided an Mobile App to help reduce the stress. With this one-stop app, available for iPhone and Android, you can report your loss, click on a schematic of a car to illustrate the damage, and quickly confirm your coverage. You can also take and upload photos of the damage to your car and any other vehicles involved, as well as skid marks, road debris or other evidence of the accident, all while at the accident scene. You can download the free USAA Mobile App for your phone at Apple iTunes or Android Market.

White House: http://www.whitehouse.gov

Yellow Ribbon America: Show your support with a yellow ribbon. http://wp.yellowribbonamerica.org/

USMC League: Is a wonderful organization for Marines and their families. Please go to the website to view more information out them and their specific programs which are Wounded Marine Program, Youth Physical Fitness Program, Young Marines of the Marine Corps League, Scholarship Program, Marine Military Expositions Program, Legislative Program, Veterans Service Officer Program, Veterans Affairs Voluntary Service Program (VAVS), Marine Corps League Auxiliary, Military Order of Devil Dogs, Toys for Tots, and various annual conventions. http://www.mcleague.com/mdp/index.php?module=ContentExpress&func=display&ceid=1

BUSINESS ASSISTANCE

Better Business Bureau: To help you check out businesses in your town. www.bbb.org

Business Assistance: For veteran business owners there are many basic assistance needs that you can get for free. For example, business startup, business-plan writing, basic contracting, marketing, networking, business development, growth, and similar types of help can all be found at no cost. Veteran programs continue to multiply, and a few free and low cost programs include:

- Veterans Business Outreach Centers www.usa.gov/vetcenter
- SBA Office of Veterans Business Development www.sba.gov/vets
- Entrepreneurship Bootcamp for Veterans with Disabilities www.whitman.syr.edu/ebv
- Women Veterans Igniting the Spirit of Entrepreneurship www.whitman.syr.edu/vwise
- National Center for the Veteran Institute for Procurement www.nationalvip.org
- Center for Veterans Enterprise www.vetbiz.gov
- Southwest Veterans' Business Resource Center www.wherecommunitiesserveveterans.org
- Inc./Joining Forces Military Entrepreneurs www.inc.com/militaryentrepreneurs
- National Veteran-Owned Business Association www.navoba.com

- Veteran and Military Business Owners Association www.vamboa. org
- Veterans Business Network www.veteransbusinessnetwork.com
- Veteran Franchises www.veteranfranchises.com
- Military.com www.military.com/benefits/veteran-benefits/veterans-in-business

Also, every government agency has an office specifically established to help small businesses get work with their agency. These are usually called the Office of Small and Disadvantaged Business Utilization www.osdbu.gov/members.html or simply the Office of Small Business Programs. All have veteran business programs; some have more in-depth programs than others but they all offer valuable information and host free or inexpensive veterans outreach events.

SBA Patriot Express: The SBA "Patriot Express" loan program helps the military community open their own small business. SBA loans up to $500,000 and may be used for business startup, expansion, equipment purchase, working capital, inventory or business occupied real estate purchase. Interest rates generally are 2.25% to 2.75% above the prime rate, based upon the amount and maturity of the loan. Veterans' business development officers man SBA district offices in every state. They can provide lists of area Patriot Express lenders as well as additional small business advice and resources.

In addition, the Veterans Business Outreach Program provides entrepreneurial development services such as business training, counseling and mentoring to eligible veterans owning or considering starting a small business. Check into your local SBA and see what all they have to provide for you and your family. Patriot Express Loans are available to veterans, service-disabled veterans, active-duty military eligible for the military's Transition Assistance Program, Reservists and National Guard members, current spouses of any of these groups, and surviving spouses of members or veterans who died during service or from a service-connected disability. http://www.sba.gov/content/patriot-express.

HEALTH AND WELL BEING

Comprehensive Soldier Fitness: http://csf.army.mil

*The Sanctuary: Provides advocacy, support and innovative, experiential recreational and wellness programs and reintegration retreats, projects and services for military family members and veterans. *This program looks wonderful; I would love to check it out sometime.* http://sanctuaryvf.org

A Warrior's Wish Foundation: The Warrior Wish Foundation enhances the lives of United States Military veterans and their families who are battling a life-limiting illness. Through the fantastic financial support of generous donors, the financial contributions of Veterans' Service Organizations, our volunteer network and our wonderful corporate partnerships, we are able to grant the wishes of those who have served this great nation of ours. A wish may be as simple as a new hearing aid or scooter chair, or as involved as one last family vacation or reunion. http://awarriorwish.org

HOUSING AND FINANCE ASSISTANCE

Armed Forces Foundation: Is dedicated to providing comfort and solace to members of the military community through financial support, career counseling, housing assistance and recreational therapy programs. They provide assistance to active duty and retired personnel, National Guard, Reserve Components, and their loved ones. http://www.armedforcesfoundation.org/about.php

*Army Emergency Relief Fund (AER): Is a private non-profit organization with a mission to help soldiers and their dependents. AER is the Army's own emergency financial assistance organization and is dedicated to "helping the army take care of its own." AER provides commanders a valuable asset in accomplishing their basic command responsibility for the morale and welfare of soldiers. AER funds are made available to commanders having AER sections to provide emergency financial assistance to soldiers, active and retired, and their dependents when there is a valid need. AER funds can be provided in the form of grants or no interest loans. Various Red Cross sites can provide assistance with AER Financial Assistance. http://www.aerhq.org/ Army Emergency Relief Headquarters is in Alexandria, VA. Phone number is 703-428-0000, toll free: 866-878-6378, fax: 703-325-7183. DSN: 328-0000 DSN FAX: 221-7183.

AER CONTACT LIST:
- AER: aer@aerhq.org use for any general questions/comments concerning AER organization.
- Assistance: assistance@aerhq.org use for any questions/comments concerning procedures and/or policy on obtaining AER financial assistance.
- Bankruptcy: bankruptcy@aerhq.org service member may use this email for questions about the status of their chapter 7 or chapter 13.
- Education: education@aerhq.org use for all questions concerning scholarship funds and spouses education assistance program. Use for questions concerning eligibility, awards, programs deadlines, and change of school.
- Hardship: hardship@earhq.org service members with a current AER loan may use this email to obtain more information about a hardship request.
- Repayment-Allotments: repayments-allotments@aerhq.org contact them for any questions/comments concerning repayment of AER loans and/or repayment allotments for active duty retire pay.
- Samaritan: samaritan@aerhq.org use for any matters related to the Samaritan Program. This includes questions regarding completion of assistance cases, campaign submissions, and corrections to errors that have been processed to HQAER.
- Training: training@aerhq.org use for any questions concerning AERO/AAERO training, either on site or through HQAER.

- Webmaster: Bernard@aerhq.org use for questions specific only to their website.

Assistance to Veterans with non-VA Guaranteed Home Loans: For veterans or service members who may have obtained a conventional or sub-prime loan, VA has a network of eight Regional Loan Centers and two special servicing centers that can offer advice and guidance. Borrowers may visit VA's website at www.benefits.va.gov/homeloans or call toll-free (877) 827-3702 to speak with a VA Loan Technician. However, unlike when a veteran has a VA-guaranteed home loan, VA does not have the legal authority to intervene on the borrower's behalf. It is imperative that a borrower contacts his/her servicer as quickly as possible.

Auxiliary Emergency Fund: Provided through the American Legion is a emergency financial assistance offered to members who have been apart of the American Legion for 3 years and are current of their dues. Grants can be used towards home repairs due to environmental hazards, food, shelter, utilities and/or educational training due to life changes such as death of a spouse, divorce or separation which necessitate the auxiliary member to become the primary source of income for her family. You can access the application and further rules and regulations and online at www.legion-aux.org and/or through your local legion office.

Clear Point Credit Counseling Solutions: Offers budget, housing and debt counseling. You can reach a financial specialist at www.clearpointCCS.org/military, or meet in person at their offices near military bases in Illinois, Maryland, Missouri, North Carolina, Tennessee, Virginia and Washington.

Defense Credit Union Council: Includes contact information for credit unions on base, and other financial information for service members. www.dcuc.org

Defense Finance and Accounting Service (DFAS): DFAS provides information on military entitlements, as well as general information on pay rates, per diem, taxes, etc. http://www.dfas.mil

Department of Labor: Department of Labor homepage provides a variety of information on many issues and concerns. http://www.dol.gov/

Disputing Credit Reports: This site is for your use. http://www.ftc.gov/bcp/edu/pubs/consumer/credit/cre21.shtm and http://credit.about.com/od/creditreportscoring/a/disputereport.htm Further news for you is the Amendments to the fair credit reporting act which allow you to place an "active duty alert" in your credit report. This requires creditors to verify your identity before granting credit in your name. Visit the FTC website for more information and read the information carefully.

GovLoans.gov: This site is for your insight into Federal loan information, brought to you through a partnership between Federal agencies and GovBenefits.

General

gov/ the official government benefits website. http://www.govloans.gov/

Investor Protection Trust: This site is packed with information about investing and protecting your money, including resources specifically for the military. www.investorprotection.org

Home Alarms: Provides free home alarm systems for military families. Eligibility is for family members of currently deployed service members or service members who will be deploying soon and have been issued orders. Protect our Troops will provide, free alarm system for home, free upgrades for your current alarm system or a home alarm fee reimbursement. For more information, rules and eligibility go to www.protectourtroops.org.

Homeowner Assistance Program: http://hap.usace.army.mil

Home Loan Assistance: When a VA-guaranteed home loan becomes delinquent, VA provides supplemental servicing assistance to help cure the default. The servicer has the primary responsibility of servicing the loan to resolve the default. However, in cases where the servicer is unable to help the veteran borrower, Loan Guaranty has Loan Technicians in eight Regional Loan Centers and two special servicing centers who take an active role in interceding with the servicer to explore all options to avoid foreclosure. Veterans with VA – guaranteed home loans can call (877) 827-3702 to reach the nearest Loan Guaranty office where loan specialists are prepared to discuss potential ways to help save the loan. For more information go to www.benefits.va.gov/homeloans.

If VA is not able to help a veteran borrower retain his/her home (whether a VA-guaranteed loan or not), the HOPE NOW Alliance may be of assistance. HOPE NOW is a joint alliance consisting of servicers, counselors, and investors whose main goal is to assist distressed borrowers retain their homes and avoid foreclosure. They have expertise in financial counseling, as well as programs that provide assistance to homeowners who have the willingness and ability to keep their homes but are facing financial difficulty as a result of the crisis in the mortgage market. The HOPE NOW Alliance can be reached at (888) 995-HOPE (888-995-4673) or by visiting www.hopenow.com.

For Veterans or service members who may have obtained a conventional or sub-prime loan, VA has a network of eight Regional Loan Centers and two special servicing centers that can offer advice and guidance. Borrowers may visit VA's website at www.benefits.va.gov/homeloans or call toll-free (877) 827-3702 to speak with a VA Loan Technician. However, unlike when a veteran has a VA-guaranteed home loan, VA does not have the legal authority to intervene on the borrower's behalf. It is imperative that a borrower contacts his/her servicer as quickly as possible.

Veterans with conventional home loans now have new options for refinancing to a VA-guaranteed home loan. These new options are available as a result of the Veterans' Benefits Improvement Act of 2008. Veterans who wish to refinance their subprime or conventional mortgage may now do so for up to 100 percent of the value of the property, which is up from the previous limit of 90%.

Additionally, Congress raised VA's maximum loan guaranty for these types of refinancing loans. Loan limits were effectively raised from $144,000 to $417,000. High cost counties have even higher maximum loan limits. VA County Loan Limits can be found at www.benefits.va.gov/homeloans. These changes will allow more qualified veterans to refinance through VA, allowing for savings on interest costs and avoiding foreclosure. A VA refinancing loan may help a veteran who is facing a big payment increase.

Most programs are best used before you miss a mortgage payment. If you need to renegotiate a mortgage or consider a short sale, you may get help at www.makinghomeaffordable.gov.

To get information on how to pursue a short sale on a VA loan, go to www.lgy/com-psale.html. There are tight guidelines, but significant help for those who bought before housing prices plunged. www.hap.usace.army.mil/homepage.asp

Military Housing Assistance Fund: A non-profit organization helping military families with home ownership. I am listing a couple different sites for your review. http://www.ehow.com/list_6728959_military-housing-assistance-programs.html http://www.va.gov and http://usmhaf.org/

MYPAY: This is the official pay web site. This site allows military personnel financial management of pay information, leave and earnings statements, W-2's and more. http://maypaydfas.mil/mypay.aspx

MyMoney: U.S. Financial Literacy and Education Commission. Offers financial guide information and resources from budgeting, taxes, homeownership, credit and avoiding scams. http://www.mymoney.gov

Military Pay: Includes information about military and retired pay, benefits and savings. www.dfas.mil/militarypay.html

MyPay Military Loans: *New to me!! I am not a fan of pay day loans but I am aware some people use them. So I placed it here for your attention.* http://www.mypayloanservices.com

Military Loans: There are some banks out there that understand the financial and family issues of the military lifestyle, and can answer your need for loan products at rates competitive with most banks and credit unions. As long as you are serving full-time in the United States Air Force, Army, Coast Guard, Marine Corps or Navy, any rank, you can get the loans you need at fair interest rates and repayment terms.

These companies understand there are cases where being military may mean you aren't eligible for more traditional loans. When you apply for a loan, he lender analyzes our application and grants you a loan based on your credit history, level of duty, and financial needs. Traditional credit scores may not accurately reflect a military service members true credit worthiness; the traditional loan model may not take into account the common aspects of a military lifestyle that could otherwise create a lower credit score such as frequent moves, deployments overseas, and financial situations unique to military service members. These elements can create an inaccurately low credit score with the three major bureaus. Through Pioneer Lending there are 6 types of loans available to military families.

- **The Disaster Relief Loan:** Funds for military families in times of disaster (hurricane Katrina for instance).
- Career Service Loan: Personal loans for military service members with a maximum of $6,500.
- **Leadership VIP Loan:** A maximum personal loan provides for maximum funding of $7,500 and once again at competitive rates of interest for service members.
- **Senior Leadership VIP Loan:** This personal loan offers funding up to a maximum of $10,000, at competitive rates of interest, for senior service members.
- **Officers Loans:** Loans at competitive interest rates for officers and for senior military service members.
- **The Bereavement Loan:** This 90-day interest free military personal loan, with guaranteed approval for those military serving members having family emergencies.

In addition to the Bereavement Loan, know that the VA wants to help in your time of need by quickly paying surviving spouses who are eligible to receive the deceased veterans VA compensation or pension benefit, for the month of the veteran's death. This benefit is only payable to surviving spouses of veterans who were receiving VA compensation or pension benefits at the time of the veteran's death. Because VA does not always know if a veteran is survived by a spouse, some surviving spouses have not received the month-of-death benefit to which they are entitled.

If you are surviving spouses of a veteran who was receiving VBAS benefits at the time of death and believe you may be eligible for the month of death benefit, please go to www.va.gov and provide the information requested. VA has also established a special Survivors' Call Center for spouses who believe they may be entitled to this retroactive month-of-death benefit for a deceased veteran.

You can also contact the Survivors Call Center toll free at 1-800-49-8838. VA will determine your eligibility. And, if you are a member of the United States Armed Forces, in any branch of the service, on any armed force base located anywhere in the world and you need cash in a hurry, online military loans are available to you also. http://www.pioneermilitaryloans.com

Other websites offering military loans are:
- http://www.militaryhub.com/
- http://www.mili-loans.com
- Omni Financial at http://www.militaryloans.com/

Military Money: Offers advice on all aspects of personal finance for military families, plus links to information about discount and support programs. www.militarymoney.com

*National Student Loan Forgiveness: Military Mobilization Fact Sheet for Federal Family Education Loan B. If your National Guard or Reserve unit has been called to active duty, or if you are a regular, active-duty member of the Armed Forces who has been reassigned to another duty station, you may be eligible for benefits on any Federal Stafford, SLS, PLUS, and Consolidation loans you borrowed under the Federal Family Education Loan Program (FFELP) What this mean is you may get part or all of it forgiven. This means you DO NOT have to pay the money back.http://studentaid.ed.gov/students/attachments/siteresources/loanforgivnessV4.pdf and http://www.nslp.org/pages/pdf/militarymobil.pdf ALSO, while you are deployed you need to have your student loans in "MILITARY DEFERMENT" not a regular deferment. This will keep any extra cost, fees and finance charges been added to your account while you are deployed.

OTHER Assistance for Delinquent Veteran Borrowers: If VA is not able to help a veteran borrower retain his/her home (whether a VA-guaranteed loan or not), the HOPE NOW Alliance may be of assistance. HOPE NOW is a joint alliance consisting of servicers, counselors, and investors whose main goal is to assist distressed borrowers retain their homes and avoid foreclosure. They have expertise in financial counseling, as well as programs that take advantage of relief measures that VA cannot. HOPE NOW provides outreach, counseling and assistance to homeowners who have the willingness and ability to keep their homes but are facing financial difficulty as a result of the crisis in the mortgage market. The HOPE NOW Alliance can be reached at (888) 995-4673 or by visiting www.hopenow.com. For more information about VA Loans go to www.benefits.va.gov/homeloans.

Overseas Housing Allowance Query: The overseas housing allowance compensates members for the majority of housing expenses. Comprised of three components: rental ceiling, utility/recurring maintenance allowance, and move-in housing allowance (MIHA). http://www.defensetravel.dod.mil/site/oha.cfm

Per Diem Rates: A direct link to the Department of Defense per diem, travel, transportation allowance Committee website. http://www.defensetravel.dod.mil/site/erdiemcalc.cfm

Pioneer Services: As the military division of MidCountry Bank, Pioneer Services offers financial assistance to active duty and retired military. From personal loans to VA home loans, they offer all ranks and branches the credit they deserve. For example, Pioneer offers no-hassle signature loans up to $10,000, VA home loans in all 50 states (refinance or new purchase), free award winning financial education (in-office/online) for more information or to apply visit www.pioneermilitaryloans.com or call 1-(880) for-loan.

Save and Invest: Alerts military families to active scams, includes advice on saving and investing, and provides resources for checking out advisors. www.saveandinvest.org

The Military Club: Provides instant credit for household items for military families. http://www.themilitaryclub.com/default.asp

TSP: Features details about the Thrift Savings Plan for military personnel. www.tsp.gov

US Department of Defense-Homeowners Assistance Guide: http://hapusace.army.mil/eligibility.html

VA Refinancing of a non-VA Guaranteed Home Loan: Veterans with conventional home loans now have new options for refinancing to a VA-guaranteed home loan. These new options are available as a result of the Veterans Benefits Improvement Act of 2008.

Veterans who wish to refinance their subprime or conventional mortgage may now do so for up to 100% of the value of the property, which is up from the previous limit of 90%. VA county Loan Limits can be found at www.benefits.va.gov/homeloans. These changes will allow more qualified veterans to refinance through VA, allowing for savings on interest costs and avoiding foreclosure. A VA refinancing loan may help a veteran who is facing a big payment increase.

Veteran Loan Center: Information on VA loans. http://www.veteranloancenter.com

VetFran Program: The Veterans Transition Franchise Initiative was established in 1991 and is a voluntary effort of International Franchise Association (IFA) member companies to encourage franchise ownership by offering financial incentives to honorably discharged veterans. More than 400 franchisors currently participate in the program, and more than 1,700 veterans have acquired a franchise business through the program.

The mission of VetFran Program is to become the leader in alliance with transitioning military personnel and current veterans to help them achieve their dreams and goals by being in business for themselves. VetFran offers a 25% discount on the initial base territory purchase and special vendor incentives for those who qualify. For current program benefits and requirements, contact The Dwyer Group Department of Veteran Entrepreneurship at (800) 396-6151 and visit http://www.leadingtheserviceindustry.com/vetfran.asp and/or http://veteranfranchisebusiness.com/vetfran_Program.html for further information and a list of franchise companies participating in the VetFran Program.

*VFW Military Assistance (MAP): A quality of life initiative that focuses on easing the financial emergencies of deploying service members and supporting them and their family through the hardships of deployments. They offer grants for emergency situation and at different locations assistance with job search and scholarships for children. *Wonderful organization, I have worked with them in the past.* http://www.vfw.org/Assistance/Family-Assistance/

NATIONAL GUARD AND RESERVES

*EANGUS: "The Enlisted Association of the National Guard of the United States" has established the "We Care for America Foundation", otherwise known as the National Guard Soldiers and Airmen Emergency Relief Fund. It is intended for members of the National Guard, but applicants to the fund do not have to be members of EANGUS for eligibility in the program. It's a onetime grant with the maximum grant awarded $500 paid directly to bill. EANGUS also provides scholarships, awards, patriotism awareness, veteran's drugs programs and emergency relief for families. For more information please go to http://www.membersconnections.com/olc/pub/LCNG/cpages/about_eangus/we_care_for_america.jsp . Or call 703-519-3846. *I used this organization back in 05-06. They were very professional and considerate to my family situation. Great organization!*

GX-The Guard Experience Magazine Online: http://www.gxonline.com

Joint Service Support Portal (JSS): The National Guard Bureau has put together the JSS Portal to help Guardsmen and their family members get information on an abundance of support programs. The new portal provides easy access to programs offered at the state and unit level, including the Yellow Ribbon Reintegration Program, Employer Support of the Guard and Reserve (ESGR), National Guard Family Program, Psychological Health Program, Sexual Assault Prevention and Response Program and Warrior Support Program. Anyone clicking on the portal's predecessor, Guardfamily.org will be rerouted to the new site. It is their plan to not only offer information about programs list but to update it with other resources and programs before, during and after deployments. You can go to www.jointservicessupport.org to see everything that is offered.

Military Avenue: http://militaryavenue.com

*National Guard Association of the United States (NGAUS): http://www.ngaus.org

*National Guard Bureau: http://www.ngb.army.mil

*National Guard Bureau-Family Program: This is the National Guard Bureau Family Programs website. It provides a variety of information on programs, benefits, resources and more. http://www.jointservicessupport.org and the online community is http://www.guardfamily.org

TRAVEL

Travel is one of the great benefits in being part of the military community. As a member of the military community, service members and their families are eligible for several travel benefits that can save you a great deal of money on vacations if you plan it ahead of time and review all your options. For example, there are thousands of bases around the world and in the U.S. that offer temporary housing for military families (cost is based on your service member's rank), you can fly free on Space Available (Space-A) military flights (depending on service members status), and many airlines, hotels, resorts, travel companies, and tour groups offer military discounts. Remember, just asking for a "military discount" can often save you money. This is one of the best benefits for military families and retired veterans. It is amazing the places you can go to that are safe, clean and within budget. You must review all these sites—you will be amazed!!

Armed Forces Recreation Center (AFRC): Military discount lodging and travel. Armed Forces Recreation Center is a full service resort hotels are joint

Service Facilities that provide quality, wholesome, affordable, family-oriented vacation recreation opportunities to service members, their families and other authorized patrons (including official travelers) of the total defense force. Authorized users include active duty military, retirees, currently employed and retired Department of Defense civilians, reservists, delayed entry recruits and family members.

- http://www.afvclub.com
- http://old.armymwr.com/portal/travel/recreationcenters/
- http://www.armymwr.com/travel/recreationcenters
- http://www.military.com/travel/content1/0,,ML-afrc,00.html

Easy Military Travel: Easy Military Travel, can assist with all your travel needs. Provides assistance with vacations, emergency travel, or just flying with a friend. The company finances 100% of your travel all with no money down. The site is a travel now and pay later. http://www.easymilitarytravel.com/index.php

Guide to Military Travel: Provides information about all types of military lodging, cruises, flights and much more. http://www.guidetomilitarytravel.com

Veterans Holidays Travel: Discount prices and great locations for military families. www.veteranshollidays.com

Legion Family Travel: Top vacation destinations with discount prices for lodging, car rental, cruises and lots more. www.legionfamilytravel.com

Installation Lodging Contact Information: Listed links and contact information about installation lodging and recreation facilities:
- **ARMY: (800)462-7691** http://www.armymwr.com/portal/travel/
- **AIRFORCE: (888)235-6343** http://dtic.mil/perdiem/af_lodgi.html
- **NAVY: (800)628-9466** http://www.navy-lodge.com/

Military Lodging Information:
- **Air Force Inns:** 1-(888)- AF-LODGE http://www-p.afsv.af.mil/LD
- **Army Central Reservation Center:** http://www.armymwr.com/portal/travel/lodging/
  In US: 1-800-GO-ARMY1
  In Germany: 01-30-81-7065
  In Korea: 00-78-11-893-0828
  In Italy: 16-78-70555
- **Navy Lodges worldwide:**1-800-NVAY-INN or 1-301-654-1795 http://www.navy-lodge.com/
  Marine Corps Lodging: http://usmc-mccs.org/lodging/index.cfm

Military To Go: Travel savings for military families and the soldier. http://militarytogo.com/index.php

Military Travel: (for Space -A -Travel and lodging) http://www.military.com/travel/travelprivileges/0,13396,,00.html

Military Travel Store: This is a *"fly now pay later"* so be careful. Provides assistance with travel needs. http://www.militarytravelstore.com

Recreational Facilities: This is a list of parks, campground, camping and other forms of recreational vacation locations.

> **Hotel Lodging:**
> - **Armed Force Recreation Centers-Europe** - http://www.afrceurope.com/
> - **Hale Koa Hotel, Hawaii** – http://www.halekoa.com
> - **Shades of Green** – http://www.armymwr.com/shades/index.html
> - **Armed Forces Vacation Club** – http://www.armymwr.com/portal/travel/lodging/patronlinks/sav.asp
> - **The New Sanno Hotel, Japan** – http://www.thenewsanno.com/home.html
> - **Keystone, Colorado Rocky Mountain Blue** – http://www.rockymountainblue.com/

This is a site for campgrounds and more: http://www.4militaryfamilies.com/militaryvacationspots.htm

For further information and list of locations go to http://www.88thservices.com/recoffsites.htm, http://www.military.com/Travel/Content1/0,,military_recreations,00.html and http://www.militarycampgrounds.us/state-listing. Make sure you review all the sites as each one has something different to offer.

SATO Vacations Europe: Discount military travel. http://www.europe.satovacations.com

*SPACE A TRAVEL (Space Available Travel): A specific travel program that allows **authorized** passengers to occupy DoD aircraft seats that are surplus after all space-required passengers have been accommodated. Space-available travel is allowed on a no mission interference basis ONLY. In order to maintain the equity and integrity of the space-available system, seats may not be reserved or "blocked" for use at en route stops along mission routes.

Space A travel is a privilege, **NOT an entitlement,** which accrues to service members as an avenue of respite from the rigors of uniformed service duty. Retired service members are given the privilege in recognition of a career of such rigorous duty and because they are eligible for recall to active duty. The underlying criteria for extending the privilege to other categories of passengers is their support to the mission being performed by uniformed services and to the enhancement of active duty service members quality of life.

The information and rules are quite in-depth and too much for me to put in this book. Please go to the web site and read up on this wonderful program. In December 2010, my daughter and I took a ride over to Europe to meet my husband in Ramstein, Germany and then we all traveled to Austria,

Luxembourg, Italy and Switzerland. This is a free program and you only pay a small fee for luggage and a meal. Total round trip for us was $150! We never could have done that without the availability of Space-A. I highly recommend taking the time involved with Space A travel. It was well worth it; we created memories for a lifetime and it helped relax my husband and take his mind off his deployment.

Visit these websites for more information on Space-A flights:

- www.amc.af.mil/amctravel/index.asp
- www.amc.af.mil/questions/topic.asp?id=380
- www.spacea.info
- www.militaryhops.com
- www.militarytravelstore.com

Get a copy of this book: *Military Space-A Air Travel Guide*. It's available through this section of the Military Living website or may be available in your base exchange: www.militaryliving.com

Other sites that will be useful for your Space A Travel are:

- **Baseops.net**: Flight planning information for military space available travel. http://www.baseops.net/spaceatravel/
- **Field Column Advice for Space A Travel (Army Wife Network):** Tips and advice on Space A Travel. www.armywifenetwork.com
- **John D's Military Space-A-Travel Pages:** Provides a variety of information about Space-A-Travel. http://www.spacea.net/
- **Military Hops:** Is a site dedicated to being a premier index of information about Space Available (Space A) Military Flights that qualified people can travel on. The sites goal is that if the information you seek on this subject is on the World Wide Web then you can find it from here. www.militaryhops.com.
- **Military Living:** Site includes Space A tools like Online Space A signup (via take a hop), AMC Form 140 for Space A signup, Space A travel for spouses of deployed military, and FAQ. http://militaryliving. com/spacea/index.html.
- **Take a Hop:** Is a private website supporting eligible DoD space-available travelers with easy sign ups. www.takeahop.com
- **The Space A Experience Demystified:** Download an information guide to traveling Space A brought to you by My Military Concierge and Army Wife Network. www.mymilitaryconcierge.com

U.S. Army MWR: Discount travel for **ALL** branches of military and families. http://www.armymwr.com/travel/offdutytravel/default.aspx

*Temporary Base Housing: (http://dodlodging.net) Get a copy of the book **Temporary Military Lodging Around the World**, which is available through the publisher-Military Living (www.militaryliving.com). Most exchanges also carry this book. *It will be your best friend when traveling; it was a great help to my family when we were in Europe in 2010.*

Outdoor Recreation: If you enjoy camping and outdoor activities, look for this book from Military Living: **Military RV, Camping, and Outdoor Recreation Around the World**. You must make reservations in order to use such housing/lodging. Rates are based on space available and your service member's rank. Use http://dodlodging.net to contact bases and try to make reservations as early as possible. There will be stipulations if you are traveling Space-A overseas. You can use these facilities when moving from base to base as well as when moving overseas. Check out www.temporarymilitarylodging. net for more information on temporary military/outdoor recreational housing.

SATO: One of the major travel agencies servicing the military is SATO Travel (www.satotravel.com). They handle much of the military's R&R travel. Many bases have travel offices called "The Information, Tickets, and Travel Offices (ITT)" and they function as full-service travel agencies. All profits from these one-stop shops go back into base recreational services. www.mwr.navy.mil/mwrprogms/itt.html

For listings in each state for the Army's Information, Ticket, and Reservation Offices go to www.armymwr.biz/docs/ITRDirectory.pdf. Be sure to check out these websites, which specialize in military travel discounts for active duty military personnel, their families, and veterans:

- www.militarytravelstore.com
- www.militaryhop.com
- www.militarytravel.com
- www.vettravel.com
- www.militarytraveldiscounts.com
- www.militaryfares.com
- www.military.com (entertainment section)
- www.army.com/travel

DISCOUNTS

There are many organizations, companies, and businesses that wish to say "thank you" for your service member's tour of duty. This is extended to all branches of military that are active, retired, Reserve and National Guard. Discount range differs from each place but is very helpful all the same. Make sure you share this information so these companies can get more of our business and while you are there be sure to stop by and say thank you!

ADA Nationwide Road Assistance: Legion Auto Club offers emergency roadside assistance for your vehicle and mobility device for the whole family at an exclusive rate for Legionnaires. Visit www.legionautoclub.com or call 800-720-3132.

Agentsource: Up to 40% off standard real estate closing costs for active duty men and women moving in the United States or Canada. www.agentsource. com

All Sate: Offers military personnel a $250 credit towards the appraisal of a residential property.

American Airlines: Discount varies, requires valid military ID card.

American Legion Wireless: Service members can get connected with a free cell phone from American Legion Wireless and discounts on services (not all programs and discounts available in all areas. For new purchases only) 866-318-5461.

American Video Productions: 10% off to active duty, retired, families of military and dependents. Call and ask for the discount. http://www.americanvideoproductions.net/

*Amtrak: Provides a 10% military discount to **all** branches of active duty military and their families. This is for the lowest available rail fare on most Amtrak trains and includes travel on the Auto Train as well. You must present your **vaild, current** military ID card at time of purchase. http://www.amtrak.com/military *I hope to get the pleasure of enjoying a train ride someday.*

Anna's Linens: 10% off any purchase with valid military ID (in store only).

*Apparel Clothing Stores: Aeropostale, Barnhill's, The Buckle, Dress Barn, Express Clothing Store, Extreme Outfitters, The Finish Line, FootAction, Footlocker, Gadzooks, Goody's, Hot Topic, Journey Shoes, Jos. A. Bank, Jockey, Kohl's, Lady Footlocker, Lerner, Nautica, New York & Company, Nike, Pac Sun, Payless Shoes, Rack Room Shoes, Suncoast, Timberland Outlets (active duty only), The Finish Line, The Buckle, Wilson's Leather offer in-store discounts that vary.

Armed Forces Eyewear: A resource for military families who need eyewear; eyeglasses, sunglasses or contact lenses. They attempt to bring the lowest prices possible to military families worldwide. www.AFeyewear.com

*Armed Forces Recreation Center (AFRC): Military discounted lodging in five locations;

- Edelweiss, Germany
- Dragon Hill Lodge, Korea
- Hale Koa Hotel, Hawaii
- Shades of Green, Florida
- Cape Henry Inn and Beach Club, Virginia Beach

The Armed Forces Recreation Center operates full-service resort hotels and are Joint Service Facilities that provide quality, wholesome, affordable, family-oriented vacation recreation opportunities to service members, their families and other authorized patrons (including official travelers) of the total defense force. Authorized users include active duty military, retirees, currently employed and retired Department of Defense civilians, reservists, delayed entry recruits, and family members.

Sites for you to review are:
- http://www.afvclub.com
- http://old.armymwr.com/portal/travel/recreationcenters/
- http://www.armymwr.com/travel/recreationcenters
- http://www.military.com/travel/content1/0,,ML-afrc,00.html

Armed Forces Vacation Club: This is a wonderful opportunity for military families to have a great vacation at great prices. You can book weekly rental lodgings for $349 per week per unit at great locations all over. These rentals provide clean, recreational facilities, resort amenities, full kitchen, washer and dryers and kids activities. Make your reservations and check out the sites at www.afvclub.com and/or 800-724-9988.

***Auto Location Discounts:** AutoZone, Big 10 Tires, Checker Auto Parts, Discount Tire, Geico, Jiffy Lube, Kragen Auto Parts, Meineke, Midas, NAPA Auto Parts, O'Reilly Auto Parts all offer various discounts to military ID holders.

The Apple Store: United States Armed Forces Discount: Look for the red "save" tag on the lower right side of the Apple EPP store. Apple has extended an exclusive EPP promotion offering some great deals for our EPP partners on the iPod and the new Intel based iMac for immediate distribution.

***Bowling-AMF Free Bowling:** This summer, your children 16 and under can bowl for free at your local AMF. Register your children to get weekly coupons via email for two free games per child per day all summer long. Children love bowling; it's fun, active, social and local and–best of all–it's FREE! http://freebowling.amf.com/

Bowling-Kids Bowl Free (Canada and US): Two free games of bowling every day. All summer long. Bowling centers, schools, and other organizations work together to launch a super summer activity option for kids and families across the country. www.kidsbowlfree.com

Brads Deals: Is a website that shows over 200 stores offering military discounts to active, reserve, and retired members of the U.S. Military and their immediate family members. Two things to remember, first some stores offer discounts only at the owner's discretion and other discounts vary by state. Second, many stores that give a military discount don't advertise it.

It is always worth asking and carrying your **CURRENT** military ID card. http://www.bradsdeals.com/blog/2010/09/22/160-stores-with-military-discounts/

*Birdies for the Brave (PGA Tour & Champions Tour events): Offers complimentary admission for active, retired, and Reserve military along with their dependents at select PGA TOUR & Champions Tour events. Many tournaments also offer discounted admission for Veterans. http://www.birdiesforthebrave.com/tickets.aspx

BNB for Vets (Veterans Day Bed & Breakfasts): B&Bs and Inns are providing free rooms on November 10, in observance of Veterans Day, November 11, to honor servicemen and women currently serving or who have previously served their country. The program was started in 2009 by the West Virginia B&B Association (formerly called MABB) and has expanded to include over 40 states and provinces and more than 300 Inns. Click here to see properties that are participating in the program. www.bnbsforvets.org

BOASTY-Boaters of America Say Thank You: This organization says thank you to the men and women of the United States Armed Forces both active and retired by taking them boating. If you are a veteran and would like to sign up for a free boat ride go to www.boasty.org.

*Build A Sign: Friends and family of the military can receive a free banner or jumbo card in support of troops at home and abroad. Check out the website and choose the free design you would like to customize. www.buildasign.com/troops

*Car Rental: Service members and their families can save money when renting a vehicle. Discounts will vary between the companies. *My family has had wonderful assistance from Enterprise over the years.*

- **Enterprise Auto Rental:** 800-227-7368
- **Budget:** 800-455-2848
- **Avis:** 800-225-7094
- **Alamo:** 800-462-5266
- **Hertz:** 800-654-2200

*Cell Phone Discounts: All federal employees and military families can get a 15% discount on their personal cell phones by calling their carrier and mentioning the "Federal Telecommunications Act of 1996 discount to Federal Employees Past and Present." You will need to know the service members supervisor's name, phone number and work address in the event they wish to verify service members status. *I currently get the military discount through AT&T and I did not have to send any information. AT&T has always been a great company to our family.*

- Sprint 877-812-1223
- T-Mobile 866-646-4688
- Nextel 800-639-6111
- Verizon 800-865-1825
- ATT 800-331-0500

*Computers 4 Soldiers: Provides refurbished laptops & desktop computers to military families for only $200-$250. Every system comes ready to use and preloaded with MS Windows XP, office productivity software and antivirus protection for **ALL** branches of military and veterans along with family members. *I have used this organization and I am VERY impressed. Shipped on a timely manner, packaged to protect and everything works great. I recommended this organization to all my military families.* http:// www.computersforsoldiers.org/

Computer Zone: Discount and free software & computers for military families. http://www.freecomputerzone.com/downloads/military.html

Coupons to Troops: Is your source for information on a greatly needed way Americans have shown their support for our military families who are stationed overseas, by simply mailing their unwanted and expired manufacturer's coupons. Military families are limited to doing their shopping for groceries and household items at the commissaries and post exchanges on base, where prices are much more expensive (in some cases) than you would find in our stores in the U.S. Both the commissaries and post exchanges allow the use of manufacturer's coupons up to 6 months past their expiration date. In other words, a coupon with the expiration date of January 31st can be used overseas until July 31st. Military families who are stationed overseas do not have easy access to the Sunday newspapers like we do here, so they are very appreciative of any coupons that are sent their way. www. couponstotroops.com

Coups for Troops: Being strong supporters of the U.S. military, this site is hoping to make military families lives easier while stationed abroad. Commissaries overseas accept expired coupons up to six months old. Families can help military families by mailing their unused coupons that are then organized and sent on to contacts at military bases overseas. www. coupsfortroops.com and www.wivesoffaith.org/ministries/coups-for-troops

*Crafts—Some Free, Some Inexpensive Events (Michaels): Michaels' new program, "The Knack" lets your kids explore their creativity through a wealth of great ideas, projects and crafts designed just for them. And to enhance kids' creative experience, Michaels offers fun in-store events and activities for kids and their families to enjoy. *Not all stores participate so check with your local store.* www.michaels.com

*Crafts, Wood—Free Kids Workshops (Home Depot): Kids workshops are free "How-To Clinics" designed for children ages 5-12. The workshops are offered on the first Saturday of each month between 9:00 a.m. and noon at all The Home Depot stores. *Make sure your local store is still participating in this program.* www.homedepot.com

*Crafts, Wood—Free Build and Grow Clinics (Lowes): Free clinics are offered on the second and fourth Saturdays of the month between 10:00 and 11:00 a.m. Project information and internet sign-up registration available at this link. *Check with your local store to make sure they still participate in this program.* www.lowesbuildandgrow.com

CVS Caremark: Offers a discount prescription drug program so service members and dependents can save. 888-414-3141

Dish Network: Service members can save on dish network satellite services for home, business, or post. (For new purchase only) 866-534-4669.

EyeMed Vision Care: Provides discounts on the purchase of eye examinations and eye wear materials. Service members and their families can save on eyeglasses purchased at network locations. 1-800-793-8626. Locations include JC Penney, Pearle Vision, Lenscrafters, Optical and Sears.

*Firehouse Subs and Hawks Cay Resort "Heroes Welcome:: Firehouse Subs and Hawks Cay Resort in the Florida Keys will honor military, fire rescue, police and medical personnel with the Heroes Welcome Program. Starting Aug. 15 through Oct 31, 2011. Heroes can enjoy reduced room rates starting at $99 per night, plus additional activity discounts. *I am listing this past the deadline given to me because most places will extend the timelines.* www.experience.hawkscay. com/heroes-welcome

*1-800-Flowers.com: 888-755-7474, service members receive discounts through 1-800-flowers.com, the world's #1 online florist. *I have ordered from here several times, flowers are always beautiful and a great price.* http://1-800-Flowers.com

4Nannies.com: Families of active duty military personnel, including active U.S. Coast Guard and activated members of the National Guard or Reserve, are eligible to receive a 20% discount on any 4nannies.com membership level. www.4nannies. com

Forget Me Not Jewelry: Offers a 30% discount. Online use code militarygen100 at www.forgetmenotjewelry.com

Freedom Furniture & Electronics: Shopping site with discounts for military families. http://ww.shopfreedom.com

Free Online Parenting Classes for Military Families: Amy McCready, author of "If I Have to Tell You One More Time..The Revolutionary Program That Gets Your Kids To Listen Without Nagging, Reminding or Yelling," is offering a limited number of free online parenting classes to military families. This comprehensive online parenting education program helps parents with discipline issues normally costs $199. To find out if there is space available and register for the free training, visit them online at www.PayitForwardParenting.com.

Frugal Girls: Offers discounts in the form of coupons to various items. www.frugalgirls.com

*GAP: Offers a 10% discount the 1st of every month (may vary by location; in stores only). Will need to have a valid, current military ID card.

GameFly: Has a military appreciation program that allows all military members (past and present) and their families a FREE 15 day membership. http://www.gamefly.com/ad/track/ldp001

Glasses USA: Discounts for eyewear. http://www.glassesusa.com

GEICO: 2%-15% discount in all states except Georgia, Indiana, Maine, Massachusetts, Michigan, Mississippi, New Jersey, New Mexico, Tennessee and Texas.

GM: Varies, always well below MSRP. You can sign in online at http://www.exclusivegmoffer.com/ip-gmpop/initPop.do?program=mpp.

Gold Canyon Candle Company: Has created a support-our-troops tribute candle to honor our troops serving proudly in the United States military and their families. 10% of the retail value from every tribute candle sold will be donated to Operation Homefront. (Operation Homefront provides emergency financial and other assistance to the families of our service members and wounded warriors.) www.goldcanyon.com

Greyhound: Active duty and retired military personal and their dependent family members get a 10% off the Greyhound walk-up (unrestricted) fare. Additionally, military personnel can travel on Greyhound for a maximum fare of $198 round trip anywhere in the continental United States. www.greyhound.com

Haber Vision: 50% discount on all sunglasses. Online at http://www.habervision.com/CodeResult.aspx?code=JB10222Q.

Health Clubs: In partnership with Joining Forces, IHRSA is asking health clubs around the country to serve military families and help encourage healthy living by giving free memberships to the families (age 13 and older, where applicable) of deployed reservists and National Guard members. Go to www. healthclubs.com/joiningforces to find participating clubs in your area.

*Here's to the Heroes: By Anheuser & Bush, members of ALL branches of military and up to (3) three dependents may enter Sea World, Bush Gardens or Sesame Place Parks for a day of free fun. *My husband and our family enjoyed the Anheuser & Bush factory this summer in St. Louis and I have to say it was a very enjoyable experience and we were impressed by how clean the factory and grounds were. All the horses were beautiful and we hope to go back again. Very enjoyable!* http://www.herosalute.com

Hewlett-Packard: Log on to their website and click on new user registration: Enter first and last name, user name, password and email address. Use Company code: 2727. Discounts vary and online only.

*Hickory Farms: Provides a 10% military discount on all items. Enter 892848 in code box on online order form. http://www.hickoryfarms.com/military

*The Home Depot Veterans Discount Program: Home Depot offers a year round 10% discount (up to a $500 maximum) in the U.S. stores to all active duty military personnel, reservists, retired or disabled veterans and their families. You will need to show your CURRENT military ID card at the cashier. *I shop at this store all the time, I get great service and a great discount.*

Honor Them Foundation: The Honor Them Foundation utilizes vacant timeshares and cancelled or un-booked cruises to send combat veterans and their families to five-star resorts or on cruises at no charge to them. www. honorthemfoundation.org

Inkshouse: Offers 20%-$50 or more, use cod Mil20. www.inkshouse.com

Istudysmart: Free shipping for military families, online only. www. Istudysmart.com

JEEP: Offers a $500 discount for active military, reserves and retired reserves or active after 20 years of service. Requires a valid military ID card.

*Legion Family Travel: This program provides military members and their extended families with specific rate packages negotiated for flights, rental cars, hotels, vacation packages and cruises. Visit www.legionfamilytravel. com or call 866-947-8630. *This site look really interesting!*

Life Line Screening: Service member discounts on potentially life-saving health screenings. 800-779-4965.

*Lodging Discounts: Many lodgings offer military discount at thousands of participating locations throughout the world. Some of the participations are:

- Baymont Inn&Suites: 800-980-1679
- Wingate: 877-202-8814
- Days Inn: 800-268-2195
- Howard Johnson: 800-769-0939
- Knights Inn: 866-854-1604
- Travel Lodge: 800-545-5545
- Ramada: 888-821-5779
- Wyndham Hotels and Resorts: 800-682-1071
- Super 8: 800-889-9706
- AmeriHost Inn: 800-996-2087

Call 877-670-7088 or the numbers listed for more information. You will need to provide valid, current military ID card and member ID number 61386 to receive discount.

*Lowe's: Home improvement retailer Lowe's has always been a great supporter of military families by offering 10% military discount for major holiday weekends of Memorial Day, Fourth of July and Veterans Day. They have expanded that discount to be available every day for active duty, National Guard and Reserve, retiree and disabled service members, and their families. *I give Lowe's a big thumbs up to offer this discount on a continued basis, they are a GREAT company and I have never had any problems receiving my discount. I give a big thank you to my store in Lansing, Michigan for their continued support and great staff.*

*Mary Kay Cosmetics: Military personnel and dependents receive 10% on online orders. Reference your service affiliation and status, and ask for additional free gift and bigger discounts by contacting website. http://www.armytimes.com/marketplace/discounts/products_and_services/mary_kay_cosmetics/692/ Be sure to ask your local representative for this discount. Some do offer it.

Military.com: Connects service members, military families and veterans to all the benefits of service-government benefits, scholarships, discounts, lifelong friends, mentors, great stories of military life or missions, and much more. www.military.com

Military Coupons & Discounts: http://www.militarycoupons.com

Military Discount on Gift Baskets: http://www.gourmetgiftbaskets.com

Military 4 Life: Military and federal employees are entitled to a computer discounts on various items. See site for more details. http://www.military4life. com/discounts/computers.shtml

Moving Companies:

- Allied Van Lines: 800-871-8864
- Atlas Moving Company: 800-211-5379
- Budget Truck Rental: 800-566-8422
- NorthAmerican Van Lines: 800-524-5533

Museum of the Great Plains in Lawton, MI: Every Monday, the museum will allow all active, reserve and guard duty service members and their immediate family (husbands, wives and children OR grandparents with grandchildren) to access the museum exhibits free of charge. Proof of military ID is required. For more information contact the museum at 580-581-3460.

Almost all museums across the nation offer free admission to military service members and their families in the summer. See website for more details. http://today.msnbc.msn.com/id/43134654/ns/today-travel/t/summertime-museum-discounts-military-families/

*****National Park Fees Waived:** National Park Service officials will waive admission fees on 17 selected dates throughout 2011 to encourage all Americans to visit a national park. With 394 national parks throughout the country, most Americans live within a few hours of a park, making them places for easy and affordable vacations any time of the year. Many national park concessions also will offer discounts on fee-free days, saving visitors money on food, lodging, tours and souvenirs. http://www.military.com/veterans-report/national-park-fees-waived?ESRC=vr.nl

Nickelodeon Hotels: Offering reduced rates and perks, online and in store. Go to www.nickhotel.com/military or/and 1- 877-NICK-111 and ask for the military family package.

Oakley: Oakley sunglasses have a government sales website that is normally not advertised. They offer sunglasses that meet military standards at about an average 50% savings. Service members need only to register and fax a copy of their military ID to Oakley to be eligible for their discount. https://secure.usstandardissue.com/, http://www.afeyewear.com/, and http://www.afeyewear.com/framesfc/Oakley-lamfpi-slb-l.html

Olan Mills: Professional portrait studio offers free baby portraits for parents who want to record their child's growth in pictures during their early years. Portraits can be taken every year on your child's birthday up to age 3, and one 8-by-10, one 5-by-7 and four wallet-sized prints are free. In additional you can get 20% off any additional portraits and the age limit is kids only age 1-3 years. http://www.olanmills.com/

*Old Navy: Offers a "Military Appreciation Day" on the 1st of every month. When you show your current (valid) U.S. Military ID card at checkout you receive a 10% discount on your purchase.

Operation Coupon Clipper: The American Legion Las Vegas Post 149 is helping America's military families meet the high costs of living overseas by providing them coupons. Commissaries in foreign overseas areas accept most types of coupons offered by food and product manufacturers up to six months after the expiration date stated on a coupon. Commissaries cannot accept coupons issued by commercial grocery stores or supermarkets. The Post has contacts with American Legion Posts and Auxiliaries overseas that will distribute the coupons to commissary shoppers in their community. http://nvf. org/pages/operation-coupon-clipper

Paradise Bakery: 40% off meals for military members with valid military ID card. This discount is not extended to family.

Paradise Limousine: $25 off for military service members and family. Coupon code is 1369 for service members.

*Products: The following is a list of companies that offer military discounts to all branches of military and in most cases retired veterans too, on products that you purchase. Most places do not advertise, and you will need your current military ID card. *I have received a discount from several of these locations and great service too.*

Apple Computers	At&T
Blockbuster	Bass Pro Shop
Bath and Body Works	Champs Sports
Coolmilitary.com	California Cryobank
Copeland's Sports	Dell
Dicks Sporting Goods	Discovery Channel Store
S.S.W. Shoe Warehouse	Dunhamn's Sports
DZ Web Design	El Molino Coffee Shop
Express Clothing Store	GNC
Great Party	Happy Harry's
IMAX	JC Penny Portrait
KB Toys	K-Mart

Michael's	Pampered Chef
Play It Again Sports	Pure Beauty
Rack Room Shoes	Sally Beauty Supply
Samsonite	Sea World
Sears Portrait Studio	Shoe Carnival
Spencer's Gifts	Sportsman's Warehouse

Also, many movie theatres will offer a 10% discount on movies after 5pm.

Purchasing Power: Military families and federal government families are pre-approved for the purchasing power program, which is an affordable way to get brand name computers, laptops, netbooks and more. Small payments over the course of a year make this a manageable option for lots of families. www.purchasingpower.com

*Restaurants: This is a list of restaurants that I am aware of and in some cases have used that offered military discount to all branches of military and retired veterans (but sometimes not family members). Discount will vary depending on the restaurant, and not all branches participate. Most will not advertise, you will need to ask and have a current military ID card. *The list is bigger, as I am sure places in states I do not live nor have I been to have restaurants that offer this. I am showing you a few places that I am familiar with. If there are places I have not listed, please send me names so that I can update my list for future updated copies.*

Applebee's	Arby's
A&W	Back Yard Burgers
Barnhill's	Burger King
Captain D's	Carl's Jr.
Champs Sports Bar	Chevy's Fresh Mex
Chipotle	Ci-Ci's Pizza
Chick-Fil-A	Cotton Patch
Dairy Queen	Denny's
Dunkin Donuts	Friendly Ice Cream Stores
Golden Corral	Hard Rock Café
IHOP	Java Café
KFC	Long John Silver
Longhorn Steakhouse	Maggie Moo's
McDonald's	Moe's
Mrs. Fields	Panda Express
Papa Murphy's	Pat & Oscar's
Pancho's Mexican Buffet	Pizza Hut
Quizno's	Outback Steak House
Raising Cane's Chicken	Red Robin
Shoney's	Sizzler

Sonic   Taco Bell
Texas Roadhouse   The Melting Pot
Wendy's   Whataburger

Restaurant Kids Eat Free (Frugal Living TV): On this website you will find a list of over 50 places where kids eat free or for very cheap! While the majority of the listings are places where kids eat free some of the restaurants charge a small amount–in most cases $.99 so they are not actually "free" but a very good deal nonetheless. You will also find that some of the restaurants where kids eat free have certain restrictions whether it be limited hours on a certain day, the number of kids eating free per purchasing adult or age restrictions. www.frugalliving.tv

Ripley's Believe It or Not: All eight Ripley's attractions offer a military discount. Tickets are only $3.99 for age's 6-adult and $1.99 for ages 2-5. Kids under age 2 are free.

*Sarge's List–(sell or donate your stuff): A brand new website that helps military members lighten their load during PCS, or every day, by selling or donating their stuff to other military families locally or globally. With over 500 installations worldwide, this FREE and made just-for-military community's website offers local PCS information as well as local classifieds for household goods, cars, real estate, pets, yard sales, military savings and more!

Sarge's List is different from other sites because if you sign up with a DOT MIL email, the site puts a paw stamp icon on the listings and communications so that you can identify who has been verified with a DOT MIL email. The site is fun, easy to use and has lots of neat functionality (save favorites, alert feature that sends you emails when listings are added that match what you are searching for, etc.). Heralded as the "Craigstlist for military," they are looking for local champions at each installation to post listings and share them via social networks to help spread the word about this valuable and free resource! They just added Afghanistan, Kuwait and Iraq to help our troops in the Middle East buy, sell and trade needed items. Check out *www.SargesList.com* and post and share with your network today! www.sargeslist.com. *This site is really interesting, take the time to check it out.*

*Sears: Will give 20% off your studio and online portrait purchases. Just show your current, valid ID card at the time of your session for this special military family discount. If ordering online, enter promotional code 48576 at checkout. www.searsportrait.com/cpi/en-US/offers/Military and/or go to **Sears commercial--**call a special number or visit a special website for exclusive members discounts. 214-392-5088. *I get great service and my discount.*

*SeaWorld, Bush Gardens and Sesame Place Here's to the Heroes: A military service member, accompanied by as many as three of their direct dependents, may enter Anheuser-Bush's SeaWorld, Busch Gardens or Sesame Place parks with FREE admission. This includes any active duty, activated or drilling Reservist, or National Guardsman. Get information and register online. www.commerce.4adventure.com/store/os_application.asp. *This is a great location for families, I enjoy it every time we visit. And a big thank you to all three parks for giving us this wonderful discount.*

Semper Finest Care Packages: With Semper Finest Care Packages, you don't have to worry about finding the time to go to the post office, completing a customs form, or what to send in a package. They take care of that for you. With a click of a button, you can show that you care and put a smile on your loved one's face. You can even join the "care package club" to have packages automatically shipped to your marine or loved one over the course of a deployment. Go to www.semperfinest.com for more information or to set up your account.

*Sea World: One-day complimentary admission for active duty service member and up to three direct dependents. Must have valid, current military ID card. www.herestotheheros.com

*Six Flags Mountain Magic: Service members receive special discounts on admission for special events and specific dates. Tickets must be purchased in advance at MWR and ITT 143 recreation offices, not at the park.

Tents for Troops: This site shows certain campgrounds and RV parks around the nation that would like to offer free camping for active military. Please visit the Camp Locations page to find a participating park near where you wish to spend some R&R. Active military will be required to present current active military I.D. at the time of check in. The offer is for all branches of active military and members of their immediate family **only**. Please call the park directly for reservations. Reservations are required. www.tentsfortroops.org

Texas Veteran Project (Texas): The following B&B's, Guest Cottages, Inns, and Hotels from Fayetteville and other communities within Central Texas have joined together to support returning Iraq and Afghanistan veterans and their spouses by donating 1 or 2 night stays at their establishments. Each proprietor is thankful for veterans' service to our country and feels honored to recognize the sacrifices of their time, talents, and in many cases, health. www.texasveteranproject.org

The Cove (Billy Graham Evangelistic Association-Asheville, NC): Offers full scholarships for active-duty military personnel and their spouses to attend a seminar at *The Cove*, located in Asheville, N.C. http://www.thecove.org/

The Rucksack - Rewards for Vets: Where *IAVA* member veterans get access to exclusive tickets, giveaways and more. Signing up is free and easy. Open to all confirmed veterans of Iraq (OIF) and Afghanistan (OEF). www.rucksack.iava.org

Travel and Leisure: These are ideas for you to keep in mind when you are traveling. Various companies in these areas will offer military discounts to all branches of military are retired veterans and their families. Many hotels, motels and airlines will also give discounts for military famlies, or specials for deployed families. Be sure to ask!

Other Places to Ask for Discounts:

Amtrak	Beach Family Resorts
Camp Jellystone	Car Rental Companies
Cedar Point	Cirque DU Soleil
Greyhound	MLB Hall of Fame
My Cruise Club	Professional Sports Teams
Ripley's Museums	Sandals Resorts

Thredup: As a military family that is constantly on the move around the country, finding reasonably priced clothes can be hard. ThredUP is an American online clothing swap; they help busy parents conveniently exchange outgrown clothes for the next size up. And they offer some great military benefits. Go to www. thredup.com/military for more information.

*Universal Studios:** Includes discounts and awesome packages. *My husband has been deployed a couple times since 2005 and on active duty most of his career. For as long as I can remember Universal Studio's, Sea World and Bush Gardens have honored military families with discounts is some way. What a great company, I cannot express how much that helped us enjoy a small vacation full of great memories!* http://www._universalstudioshollywood.com/vi_military.html.

US Army MWR: Discount travel for **ALL** branches of military and their families. http://www.armymwr.com/travel/offdutytravel/default.aspx

*Veterans Holidays:** Enjoy a week's stay for a price that most resorts charge for a single night. Call 877-772-2322 or visit www.veteransholidays.com for further details. *Cool site, check it out.*

*Veteran Tickets Foundation:** The mission is to give without prejudice Free tickets to all veterans, active duty military and their families as a way of saying Thank You! We team up with major sports teams, leagues, promoters, organizations, venues and everyday ticket holders to provide free and discounted tickets to the more than 26 million veterans and active duty military in the United States. www.vettix.org. *We have gotten tickets for various shows from here. Had a great time.*

*Walt Disney World Resort:** As a special salute to service members and their families, Walt Disney Resort is offering all military personnel 4 days of admission to all four of their theme parks at one special price of $138 each person. Tickets can be purchased at base ticket offices. *I enjoyed the park this past March and had great service and a wonderful time.* disneyworld.disney. go.com/special-offers/

*YMCA: The Department of Defense has contracted with the Armed Services YMCA to fund memberships at participating YMCA's throughout the United States and Puerto Rico. Check with your local YMCA for details for a free membership three months before deployment, during, and three months after service member comes home. This is for all branches and their families.

Most YMCA's will offer a discount for military families who are not deployed and programs for military children during deployments too. Check with your community YMCA today for more details. *I love our local YMCA in Lansing, Michigan. They continue to be very supportive of our troops and their families.*

ZOOLU: Zoolu, is an online store that provides thousands of name-brand and personalized items for babies, children and moms to all young families, with a particular focus on military families stationed overseas. From pacifiers to strollers, every item ships to APO/FPO addresses with FREE shipping on all orders over $75. Enter "MILSPOUSE" at checkout to receive 20% off your order. If ordering online, enter promotional code 48576 at checkout. www.shopzoolu.com

MILITARY DISCOUNT WEBSITES

BradsDeals: Is a site showing stores and services offering military discounts. www.bradsdeals.com

Canada - Canadian Forces Discounts: CF (Canadian Forces) Discounts is the National Website for Soldiers, Veterans and their families to find discounts and special offers anywhere in Canada by supportive businesses. www.cfdiscounts.ca

Canada - Canex Discount Program (CDP): The Canex Discount Program gives access, at discounted rates, to a wide range of commercial goods and services that benefit the military community. This program provides an online portal where members of the military community can obtain information about meaningful national and local discounts offered to them by Corporate Canada. www3.cfpsa. com/canexdiscounts

UK - Mil Assist: Mil Assist has been formed to bring special rates on all aspects of finances for the Military community, whether you are serving or not, a family member or friend of the Military or someone who was in the Military we can help you. We offer huge discounts and a unique VIP Package. www.milassist.co.uk

US - Army Times: Save on your purchases! In honor of your military service, you can find regular and name brand products at a special discount. www.armytimes. com

US - 4MilitaryFamilies.com: Has an easy-to-read format of discounts as you scroll down the page. www.4militaryfamilies.com

US - Military.com: Military.com's free membership connects service members, military families and veterans to all the benefits of service—government benefits, scholarships, discounts, lifelong friends, mentors, great stories of military life or missions, and much more. 700+ companies thank you for serving the country! www.military.com

US - Military and Veterans Discount Center: Join *MVDC* to find businesses that thank you for your service and appreciate the sacrifices you and your family have made for America. www.militaryandveteransdiscounts.com

US - MilitaryAvenue.com: Helps you find military-friendly businesses and resources for our mobile lifestyle in new communities by presenting information on businesses supporting our troops at both the national and local level. Goal: To create the Web's largest database of local military discounts. www.militaryavenue. com

US - MilitaryCoupons.com: Military friendly merchant list by category. www. militarycoupons.com

US - MilitaryFares.com (Airlines): Serving Military personnel and their spouses with special low airfares and with a special cancellation protection. www.militaryfares.com

US - MilitaryFinanceNetwork.com: A listing of the many military discounts that are available to service members and their family members. The best part is, some of these are available to active duty, veterans, family members, DOD civilians and the general public. Their goal is to help you make money and save money! www.militaryfinancenetwork.com

US - MilitarySpot.com: Discounts and deals for US military members. www. militaryspot.com

US - MyMilitaryMommy.com: *My Military Mommy* is a site that shows where to find the best sales, deals, coupons and military discounts all over the country! www.mymilitarymommy.com

Discounts

Military Spouse

There are many resources within the United States for military spouses; organizations to make your life easier in the ways of education, job search, emotional, spiritual and much more. Please take the time to really look over these sites. I think you will be amazed.

Career Sites

About.com: Has articles that will assist with creating resumes, cover letters and more. www.about.com

Army Command Job Swap Program: The U.S. Army Materiel Command (AMC) has launched its AMC Job Swap Program. The program was developed in an effort to alleviate challenges that AMC will face in filling critical positions during the dozens of Base Realignment and Closure moves happening throughout the command. There is no vacancy being filled in a swap. Instead, two permanent AMC civilian employees, in similar or like jobs, switch positions and organizations. AMC employees can express their interest in swapping through the use of Army Knowledge Online at https:// www.us.army.mil/suite/page/607469. For more information on the AMC Job Swap Program, contact Tracie Harris at (256) 450-9080.

CareerOneStop: Site offers career resources and workforce information to job seekers, students, businesses and workforce professionals to foster talent development in a global economy. Go to http://careeronestop.org, and www.careeronestop.org/militaryspouse.

Employer Partnership of the Armed Forces: Connects qualified reservists and veterans with civilian employers to achieve a mutually beneficial relationship. Reservists and National Guard members can take advantage of the program's online portal. Employer Partnership offers career support to soldiers, dependents and retirees along with resume tips and career development advice. There are over twenty program support managers located throughout the nation to assist service members with job placement and in some cases working one-on-one. For more information, visit the website at www.employerpartnership.org.

Hiring our Heroes: The U.S. Chamber of Commerce and the U.S. Department of Labor Veterans' Employment and Training Service (DOL VETS) launched this nationwide effort in March of 2011 to bring job fairs to military cities which are designed to help veterans and military spouses find meaningful employment, and to motivate companies to actively recruit veterans and military spouses.

Hiring our Heroes includes 100 job fairs where employers and potential job candidates can meet. In addition to connecting job-hunting military spouses with employment today, the goal is to raise solid awareness among civilian companies about military spouses and all they have to offer as employees. For more information about this program and to see if they are coming to your state or one close to you, you can go to http://www.uschamber.com/veterans/events.

Humana Military Healthcare Services (HMHS): Humana Military and the Army Spouse Employment Partnership are committed to recruiting military spouses for open positions. HMHS is committed to working proactively at encouraging military spouses to apply for open positions within their organization. Spouses from all branches of the military are encouraged to go to www.humana-military.com and click on "careers" at the bottom of the homepage.

Job Fairs: There are various job fairs that occur across the country whose participating companies are eager to hire military veterans or spouses. Sometimes there are websites with all the participating companies listed, you can send them an inquiry to see if they are hiring in your area. Just remember to BE PROFESSIONAL about what you sent and to whom. Your family support center will help you find the job fairs and their websites. Always remember to bring a professional resume and dress the part!

Job Sites: The Internet is a great tool for job searching. Some sites you may not have thought to look at are:

- Military Officers Association of America www.moaa.org
- Military Spouse Corporate Career Network www.msccn.org
- Federal Employment www.usajobs.com
- Non-profit Jobs www.idealist.org

While you are searching the Internet, don't forget to check out companies that have been identified as "military spouse-friendly employers" through programs such as Army Spouse Employment Partnership and Military Spouse Magazines' Top Military Spouse Friendly Employers. http://www.myarmyonesource.com/EducationCareersandLibraries/Spouses/MilitarySpouseEmploymentPartnership/default.aspx and http://www.milspouse.com/top10.aspx

Medical Transcriptionist: Another portable career choice for military spouses because of the nature of the work. Most of the data is submitted electronically, so you can work from anywhere. There are educational requirements associated with the field, but there are many schools that offer military spouse discounts for this field of study. www.aamt.org/scriptcontent/milspouses.cfm. For more information in this field, you can also go to www.militarytomedicine.org; they also offer free training in these areas (see below).

Military Franchising (JOBS): If you are looking to earn extra income on the side and operate a business out of your home, a home-based franchise may interest you. This website is a list of home-based franchise opportunities for military spouses and veterans. Click here to find "military-spouse friendly" home-based franchise opportunities that are looking for you! http://www.militaryfranchising.com/spouse/default.aspx

Military to Medicine: Is a partnership of Inova Health System. If you have healthcare experience, they can put you to work through their National Healthcare Career Network of hiring employers. If you need to acquire civilian healthcare credentials and/or if healthcare is a new career to you, Military to Medicine will provide online training for in-demand, entry-level healthcare jobs.

Military to Medicine serves transitioning service members, National Guard, Reserve, veterans, wounded warriors and their caregivers, and military spouses. Learn more at www.militarytomedicine.org.

*Military One Source: Education, health, relocation, parenting, stress—you name it—Military OneSource is here to help you with just about any need. Available by phone or online, their free service is provided by the Department of Defense for active-duty, Guard, and Reserve service members and their families. The service is completely private and confidential, with few exceptions. http://www.militaryonesource.com/MOS.aspx *This is a really great site with lots of useful information for military families.*

Military Spouse

MSBA: Military Spouse Business Association. http://www.milspousebiz. org/

Military Spouse Career Advancement Accounts (MyCAA): The Career Advancement Accounts Program provides assistance to military spouses seeking to gain the skills and credentials necessary to begin or advance their career. MyCAA covers the costs of training and education, enabling participants to earn a degree or credential in in-demand, portable fields in almost any community across the country.

MyCAA can be used to pay up to $2,000 in fees for one year, and may be renewed for one additional year, for a total three-year account amount of up to $4,000 per spouse. Unfortunately, DoD decided that only families of lower enlisted families were approved to use this program (E-1 through E-5 and O1-O2) And funding can be used only when obtaining an associate's degree, professional license or certification. Visit the website for further rules and restrictions. https://www.militaryonesource.com/MOS/FindInformation/Category/MilitarySpouseCareerAdvancementAccounts.aspx

Military Spouse Career Network: Gives options for employment possibilities. http://www.mscn.org

Military Spouse Job Search: Will assist military spouses with job searches and provide other useful information about working, relocations, networks and more. http://www.military.com/spouse

Military Spouse Preference (MSP) Program: The purpose of this program is to give military spouses a leg up in applying for jobs within the Department of Defense (DoD) by providing employment priority to those spouses who are accompanying their active duty service members on a PCS move. The hope is that military spouses' preference will lessen the impact that multiple military moves could potentially have on a spouse's career. This program is open to all branches of the military. Please review the website for the rules and regulations regarding this program. http://www.defenselink.mil/mapsite/spousefref.html

Milspouse: Is a support site to assist military spouses with their unique and challenging lifestyle. In the past Milspouse has assisted with careers such as nursing or education but they have greatly expanded and even assisted with home business information that works more easily within the military lifestyle. www.milspouse.org

*NEXStep: Employment Program for Military Spouses and DoD Civilians: A Department of Labor (DOL) funded program free assessment and training/educ   sources so military spouses and DoD Civilians can successfully   er, the workforce. *Great site, review it to get all information.* tecpro.com/instructor/ed/purchaseinfo/nexstep.htm

nel Management (OPM)–Federal Jobs for Veterans: ncipally those who are disabled or who served on active times, are entitled to preference for federal civil service jobs filled by open, competitive exams. Preference is also provided for widows/widowers not remarried, mothers of personnel who died in service, and spouses of service-connected disabled. This preference includes five or ten points added to passing scores on examinations. Individuals interested in federal information should contact the personnel officers of the federal agencies in which they wish to be employed. Or, contact any Office of Personnel Management (OPM) Service Center. The centers are listed in telephone books under U.S. Government, or you can visit the web site at http://www.opm.gov. Federal job opportunities can be found at http://www.usa.jobs.opm.gov. Also check out http://www.fedshirevets.gov.

Operation ReMax: Providing military spouses and others who have a military connection access to mentoring, ongoing education and coaching in the highly portable career field of real estate. http://operationremax.com/

Professional Associations: Expand your network by joining professional association tailored to your industry.

SBA Patriot Express: The SBA "Patriot Express" loan program helps the military community open their own small business. SBA loans up to $500,000 and may be used for business startup, expansion, equipment purchase, working capital, inventory or business occupied real estate purchase. Interest rates generally are 2.25% to 2.75% above the prime rate, based upon the amount and maturity of the loan. Veterans' business development officers man SBA district offices in every state. They can provide lists of area Patriot Express lenders as well as additional small business advice and resources.

In addition, the Veterans Business Outreach Program provides entrepreneurial development services such as business training, counseling and mentoring to eligible veterans owning or considering starting a small business. Check into your local SBA and see what all they have to provide for you and your family. Patriot Express Loans are available to veterans, service-disabled veterans, active-duty military eligible for the military's Transition Assistance Program, Reservists and National Guard members, current spouses of any of these groups, and surviving spouses of members or veterans who died during service or from a service-connected disability. http://www.sba.gov/content/patriot-express

Shaklee: Is a company that offers military spouses of all branches of military an opportunity to work from home. To find more information and find a Shaklee Independent Distributor near you, go to www.shaklee.com or call 1-800-SHAKLEE.

The GEO Group, INC: The GEO Group, Inc. is a leader in the delivery of private correctional and detention management, community re-entry services and behavioral and mental health services to government agencies around the globe. Their team of over 17,000 highly skilled professionals manages 118 correctional, detention and residential treatment facilities totaling approximately 81,000 beds. GEO is currently looking for: Correctional

Officers, Detention Officers, Safety Officers. To apply nationwide or view their benefits, visit www.jobs.geogroup.com.

USAJOBS: Features include USA Jobs online resumes, a personal career management home, an option to make resumes searchable by agency recruiters, and an option to create and store letters. For current federal employees, the site provides information about career and job opportunities, leadership, insurance, pay and leave, benefits, work life, retirement and other topics of interest. http://www.usajobs.opm.gov/

VetJobs: This website assists veterans, spouses and family members find quality jobs with employers worldwide. Vetjob is partially owned by VFW and has been endorsed by various other veterans' service organizations. Vetjob employment assistance section has all the tools and guidance needed to find jobs. It will start out with an career assessment, assistance on interviewing, writing resumes and other services. It also lists all legitimate job boards by occupation and location in the U.S. For employers, VetJobs is a flat-fee site that has the largest reach possible into the veteran job-candidate market. Additionally, VetJobs has been effective for those employers who need candidates with security clearances. For further information go to www.vetjobs.com.

OTHER EMPLOYMENT SOURCES

Sites to Join: Whether you are self-employed or looking to expand your employment there are networking associations that you can join to expand your pool of acquaintances. These associations will give you access to additional services and tools to aid in your job search. They have the potential to update and strengthen your leadership, presentation, communication skills and other various support.

- Home-based Working Moms www.hbwm.com
- American Telecommuting Association www.yourata.com
- National Association of Homebased Businesses www.usahomebusiness.com

Online Resources for Job Hunting:

- Military.com www.military.com/spouse
- National Military Family Association http://www.nmfa.org/PageServer?pagename=home_spousesemployment
- Military Spouse Job Search http://www.militaryspousejobsearch.org/msjs/app
- MilSpouse.org http://www.milspouse.org
- Military Spouse Career Network http://www.mscn.org
- Self Employed Web http://www.selfemployedweb.com/military-spouse-jobs.htm
- CareerBuilder http://www.CareerBuilder.com
- Monster.com http://www.monster.com

Online Resources for Networking and Mentorship:

- WAHM http://www.wahm.com
- DWSA http://www.dswa.org/
- WAHM Talk Radio http://www.wahmtalkradio.com
- Internet Based Moms http://www.internetbasedmoms.com
- Advertising Moms http://www.advertisingmoms.com/
- Telecommuting Moms http://www.telecommutingmoms.com/

Other: Companies pledging their support and on the list of military friendly employers list for military families include: The Home Depot, Sears Holdings Corp., Kmart, Lands End, Siemens, Goodwill, Cisco, Walmart, BestBuy, Better Business Bureau, YMCA and Indeed.com, to name a few.

Spouse employment issues have improved greatly; issues like reciprocity for certifications or licenses are currently under discussion in state governments. The Department of State has made progress in getting states to sign on to providing in-state tuition for service members and their dependents in the state where they are stationed. The State Liaison Office is pursuing alternative certification through the American Board for Certification of Teacher Excellence (ABCTE) Program that is portable from state to state (between participating states) and would allow spouses who achieve the certification to teach without a break in service. They are also going after states to adopt the Nurse Licensure Compact or to make similar provisions for military spouses who are transferring from one state to another. Many states have agreed to extend the in-state tuition benefits after the service member has PCS'ed. Many states have acknowledged that military spouses are being forced to move in support of their service member so they are beginning to provide unemployment benefits for military spouses.

Some states now assist spouses to become certified teachers through the "Spouses-to-Teachers" program. More information at http://www.spousestoteachers.com. More information on this and other initiatives of the Department of Defense State Liaison Office can be found at www.usa4militaryfamilies.dod.mil.

EDUCATION SCHOLARSHIPS AND GRANTS

American Military Retirees Association (AMRA): Is a wonderful organization that works on behalf of military retirees and their families to protect their rights and benefits under the law, and to lobby on their behalf in Washington, DC and elsewhere. Check out the website and learn more about their efforts and other resources they have available. Their latest in 2010 was the Associations Scholarship fund. Through the current generosity of AMRA members, the Association annually presents $35,000 in scholarships to AMRA members, their spouses and dependents, and their grandchildren. They hope to grow the program so they can award more scholarships in the future. Go to http://amra1973.org to learn more about this organization.

Air Force Aid Society Education Grant: The General Henry H. Arnold education grants program spouses (stateside) of active duty members, Title 10 ARG/Reservists and surviving spouses of deceased personnel. http://www. afas.org/education/arnoldedgrant.cfm

Air Force Aid Society Education Grant - The General George S. Brown Spouse Tuition Assistance Program (STAP): The purpose of the Spouse Tuition Assistance Program is to provide partial tuition assistance for spouses of Active Duty airmen or officers, who accompany members to overseas locations and will be attending college programs. The focus of the program is on the completion of degree or certificate programs that provide increased occupational opportunities for spouses.

The program provides tuition assistance (TA) at a rate of 50% of unmet tuition charges per course, with a maximum of $1,500 per academic year and term maximum, which is calculated by dividing the annual maximum ($1,500) by the number of terms within the academic year. For purposes of this program, "academic year" is defined as the 12-month period beginning August 1 through July 31 of each year. For eligibility requirements please go to http://europe.ctcd. edu/students/services/afas_stap.php.

Alaska Sea Service Scholarships: Is available for family members of Sea Service members with **Alaska residency only.** The Navy League and Naval Education and Training Command (NETC) announced on July 15, eligibility requirements for the Alaska Sea Services Scholarship for academic year 2012-2013. The program awards up to four $1,000 scholarships annually for undergraduate education to dependent children or spouses of personnel serving in the U.S. Navy, Marine Corps or Coast Guard (either active duty or reserve), retired from those services, or were serving at time of death or missing-in-action status and who also are legal residents of Alaska. Applicants will be ranked according to academic proficiency, character, leadership ability, community involvement and financial need.

The application deadline is March 1, 2012 for the FY-12 selection board, which convenes in April 2012. Applicants must show acceptance at an accredited college or university for full-time undergraduate study toward a Bachelor of Arts or a Bachelor of Science degree. No more than two scholarship awards may be given to any individual during pursuit of the four-year degree. The Alaska Sea Services Scholarship is one of 25 endowed scholarships available to sea services members through the Navy League Foundation. For complete information and an application to apply for the Alaska Sea Service Scholarship, visit http://www.navyleague.org/scholarship/ interested families may also contact Cheral Wintling at 850-452-3671 (DSN 922-3671), email cheral.wintling@navy.mil or contact Mike Carter at 703-312-1585, email mcarter@navyleague.org.

Anchor Scholarship Foundation: For dependents of active duty or retired personnel who served in commands under the administrative control of Commanders, Naval Surface Forces, US Atlantic or Pacific Fleets for a minimum of six years. http://www.anchorscholarship.com/

Army Aviation Association (AAAA): The AAAA Scholarship Foundation, Inc., is a non-profit, tax-exempt corporation established to render financial assistance for the college-level education of members of the Army Aviation Association of America, Inc., (AAAA), and the spouses, unmarried siblings, unmarried children and unmarried grandchildren of current and deceased AAAA members. For further information about this scholarship and eligibility requirements go to http://www.quad-a.org/.

Army Emergency Relief Spouse Education Assistance Program: http://www.aerhg.org/education_spouseeducation_assistance.asp

Army Nurse Corps Association (ANCA): ANCA awards scholarships to U.S. citizen students attending accredited baccalaureate or graduate nursing or anesthesia nursing programs. This scholarship is in honor of Cpt. Joshua M. McClimans, AN, USAR, who was killed in a mortar attack in April 2011 while assigned to the Combat Support Hospital at Forward Operating Base Salerno in Afghanistan. For more information about this scholarship and eligibility requirements go to http://e-anca.org/ANCAEduc.htm.

Army Ranger Association: This scholarship program is memorial to the selfless service and contributions made to our country by USARA members. These awards are given in their honor. This program provides financial assistance to qualified dependents of USARA members for furthering their education. The scholarship committee seeks to award scholarships to applicants displaying the potential for a degree in higher education, whether it is technical, university or professional. Each year the scholarship committee evaluates the scholarship applicants and selects the most outstanding submissions to be awarded to USARA Legacy Scholarship. For further information about this scholarship and eligibility requirements go to http://www.ranger.org/.

Army Reserve Association: Offers scholarships for dependents of service members. Please review the website at http://www.armyreserve.org for further information and eligibility.

Bowfin Memorial Scholarship: For members of the Hawaii submarine force personnel and their family members. Contact Patty Doty at (808) 455-2597 or by email at dcpcc@aol.com.

Blinded Veterans Association (BVA): Offers the Kathern F. Gruber Scholarship, for spouses of legally blinded U.S. Forces veterans. Call (202) 371-8880.

Children of Fallen Soldiers Relief Fund: Was founded as a means to providing college grants and financial assistance to surviving children and spouses of our U.S. military service members who have lost their lives in the Iraq and Afghanistan wars. The program will assists disabled service member families too. For further information or to apply for assistance, go to http://www.cfsrf.org/.

Coast Guard Mutual Assistance (CGMA): Offers a Supplemental Education Grant (SEG) of up to $160 per year. You can use this grant for **ANY** family member's education expenses. However it does not cover tuition expenses. This grant can also be used to pay for ASVAB, CLEP, SAT and other study guides. CGMA also offers several education related loans.

The Coast Guard also offers dependent spouses and Federal Coast Guard employees the opportunity to take CLEP, DANTES, and other tests at no cost. There are many advanced education programs available for both enlistees and officers. These are currently announced by way of ALCOAST, ALCGENL, and other general distribution messages from Coast Guard Headquarters.

To apply contact your local CG Mutual Assistance Representative or Education Officer or visit http://www.cgmahq.org/ to learn more about the programs offered.

Commissioned Officers Association of the USPHS Inc.: Offers thousands of dollars towards college scholarships for children and spouses of COA members. Please go to the site to review all requirements and eligibility at http://www.coausphs.org/education.cfm.

Concorde Career Colleges, Inc.: Concorde has 15 campuses in seven states and offers 100% healthcare training for a variety of healthcare careers. Concorde offers 23 exciting programs in healthcare fields that are in demand like Vocational/Practical Nursing, Medical Assisting, Respiratory Therapy and more. View the website or call to get more information on training that is available for service members and their family members. 800-331-2397 and www.concorde4me.com

Department of Defense/Department of Labor: Resource library for military spouse education, employment and relocation information. http://www.careeronestop.org/militaryspouse/

Department of Defense - Post 9/11 GI Bill Transferability: In addition to the education benefits offered by the Post 9/11 GI Bill, there is a special provision of the program that allows career service members to share their remaining GI Bill education benefits with immediate family members.

The key factor is whether or not the service member has used any of his/her GI Bill in the past; only unused benefits can be transferred. This means that if the member has used 12 months of his/her GI Bill, then there are only 24 months of benefits left to share. Service members must meet specific criteria to be eligible to transfer their GI Bill benefits. This includes having at least six years of service and an obligation to serve at least four more.

Go to http://www.veteransbenefitsgibill.com/2009/06/23/family-transfer-with-the-gi-bill-finalized/ and/or http://usmilitary.about.com/od/benefits/a/gibilltransfer.htm, or http://www.gibill.va.gov/post-911/post-911-gi-bill-summary/transfer-of-benefits.html.

Department Educational Assistance (DEA) Program: Provides education and training opportunities to eligible dependents of certain veterans. The program offers 45 months of education benefits. These benefits may be used for a degree and certificate programs, apprenticeship and on-the-job- training. If you are a spouse, you may take a correspondence course. Remedial, deficiency and refresher courses may be approved under certain circumstances. Spouses benefits end 10 years from the date VA finds you eligible or from the date of death of the veteran. Please go to the website for more information http://www.directoryofschools.com/Military/Dependents-Education-Assistance-Program.htm and http://www.military.com/education/content/money-for-school/dependents-educational-assistance-dea.html.

Dr. Jack Callan Memorial Scholarship: Saint Leo University. Spouse must have a 9-credit minimum to qualify. Contact, Gloria Howell at Gloria.howell@saintleo.eud.

eKnowlege: Offers free SAT/ACT prep software for service members, veterans and their families. In alliance with the Department of Defense and supported by patriotic NFL players, eKnowledge is donating SAT/ACT PowerPrep Programs to military service members and their extended families. The software comes in a single DVD and includes more than 11 hours of Virtual Classroom instruction and 3,000 files of supplemental test prep material. Thousands of interactive diagnostic tools, sample questions, practice tests and graphic teaching illustrations are indexed for easy use. The SAT and ACT sponsorship covers 100% of the total retail cost of the $200 program; there is a small fee of $13.84 per standard program (plus S/H) for the cost of materials, processing, worldwide distribution and customer service. To order online, go to: www.eknowledge.com/MIL To order by telephone, call: 951-256-4076 and reference Military.com

Embarq Scholarship: To receive the Embarq Scholarship (formerly Sprint) you must be a resident of North Carolina and reside in Embarq's local service territory. Thirty-four (34) scholarships valued at $300 each are offered and may be distributed in two (2) payments: fall semester, $150; and spring semester, $150. Scholarship checks will be issued jointly to the recipient and the college. For more information and eligibility criteria go to http://www.surry.edu/attending/financial/Embarq.pdf.

FCEA General Emmett Paige Scholarships: Available to those on active duty or veterans and spouses of the AFCEA (Armed Forces Communications & Electronic Association). http://www.afcea.org click on scholarships education foundation.

Financial Aid for Spouses of Service members: A very comprehensive listing of financial aid resources. http://www.dantes.doded.mil/dantesweb/library/doc/counselorsupport/FOSSM.pdf

Fleet Reserve Association (FRA): For dependents of members only. Members can be active duty, Reserve, or retired personnel of Navy, Marine Corps or Coast Guard. http://www.fra.org/

Fleet Training Center Petty Officers Association Scholarship Fund: For spouses of a living or deceased past or present staff member of the fleet training center, Norfolk. Contact 800-FRA-1924 for more information.

Fold of Honor Foundation Scholarship: Fold of Honor Foundation is a legacy foundation designed to provide scholarships for dependents and spouses of service members who have been killed or disabled as a result of their military service. http://www.foldsofhonor.org/

General George S. Brown Spouse Tuition Assistance Program (STAP): The purpose of the STAP is to provide partial tuition assistance for spouses of Active Duty airmen or officers, who accompany members to overseas locations and will be attending college programs. The focus of the program is on the completion of degree or certificate programs that provide increased occupational opportunities for spouses.

The program provides tuition assistance at a rate of 50% of unmet tuition charges per course, with a maximum of $1,500 per academic year and a term maximum, which is calculated by dividing the annual maximum by the number of terms within the academic year. For purposes of this program, "academic year" is defined as the 12-month period beginning August 1 through July 21 of each year. For more information go to http://www.afas.org/Education/STAP.cfm.

GEICO Offers Student Scholarships: GEICO is sponsoring two free registrations for women college students ages 18-35 to attend the Business and Professional Women's (BPW) Foundation's Policy and Action Day 2010. Students should submit their name, age, email, educational institution, major and two-three sentences about "What a Successful Workplace Means to Me" to policy@bpwfoundation.org. Deadline for submission is February 12, 2010. For more information about upcoming scholarships, visit the BPW Foundation's website. *This scholarship may be ongoing, so please check the website for this year's current information.*

Georgia's Hope Scholarship and Grant Program: For residents of Georgia who wish to further their education. For more information and eligibility requirements and application contact 800-505-GSFC or email gsfcinfo@gsfc.org. http://www.gsfc.org/gsfcnew/contact.CFM.

Hearts and Hands Community Club Scholarship: For spouses within USAG Giessen. (email) heartsandhandscc@yahoo.com

Joanne Holbrook Patton Military Spouse Scholarship: (Falls under the National Military Family Organization) http://www.militaryfamily.org click on education.

Ladies Auxiliary Of The FRA Scholarship: http://www.la-fra.org/

Joseph A. McAlinden Divers Scholarship: Is offered specifically to Navy and Marine Corps Divers, whether active duty or retired, and their eligible family members. This scholarship provides financial assistance for full-time undergraduate and graduate students who must be participating in one of the following areas of study: Oceanography, Ocean Agriculture or Aquaculture. The McAlinden Scholarship also assists with Department of the Navy approved advanced diver training, qualifications and certifications. The scholarship is need-based and ranges from $500 up to $3,000 per academic year for the eligible students education. There is no deadline for this program; you may apply at any time. http://www.nmcrs.org/education.html

Louis H. Schilt Memorial Scholarship: Offers scholarships to military spouses of service members injured in the line of duty who are interested in pursuing a career in graphic or web design. All required supplies, including state of the art Apple iMac computers and Adobe Creative Suite software, are provided to scholarship recipients at no cost. www.sessions.edu/scholarship/military/idex.asp

Marine Corps Air Station Officers Spouses Club (Parris Island): Contact Mary Ellen DeWolfe (843)379-9654.

Military.com: Scholarship Finder for Military Families
* http://aid.military.com/scholarship/search-for-scholarships.do
* www.military.com/education
* www.education4military.com/military-spouses.asp

Military Friendly Schools: This is a link to all the military friendly schools available to military families. They offer various discounts, online services and more to make your transition easier. www.militaryfriendlyschools.com

Military Scholarship Finder: Will give you a list of hundreds of scholarships, grants and loans for military families to pursue their educational goals. www.militaryscholarshipfinder.com

*Military to Medicine: Offers an easy way for service members and military families to gain a career in health care that can move with you. Whether you have experience and/or education currently or just starting out this program can help you. Military to Medicine's online training is in partnership with The Claude Moore Health Education Program and provides students with real-life job standards and role expectations. Both students and healthcare employers can feel confident that Military to Medicine course work demonstrates realistic, healthcare workplace skills. Military to Medicine is committed to participants' long-term career success. Before specific career courses begin, Military to Medicine assesses each student's interests and abilities, this information helps students set career goals and select career courses.

At the writing of this book, tuition for the initial assessment was $599, for the career-specific courses (front office medical assistant or medical records and health information assistant), the tuition was $1,850. The tuition includes the eBooks, eLearning materials and completion certificates, Scholarships are available. This program is available for military spouses, wounded warriors and their caregivers, veterans, National Guard, Reserve and their spouses and service members transitioning to civilian employment. For more information go to www.militarytomedicine.org.

MilSpouse.org Military Family Scholarships: Mission is to provide easy access to information, resources and opportunities related to education, training and employment for military spouses. http://www.careeronestop.org/militaryspouse/

Military Spouse Career Advancement Accounts (MyCAA): The Career Advancement Accounts Program provides assistance to military spouses seeking to gain the skills and credentials necessary to begin or advance their career. MyCAA covers the costs of training and education, enabling participants to earn a degree or credential in in-demand, portable fields in almost any community across the country. MyCAA can be used to pay up to $2,000 in fees for one year, and may be renewed for one additional year, for a total three-year account amount of up to $4,000 per spouse. Unfortunately, DoD decided that only families of lower enlisted families were approved to use this program (E-1 through E-5 and O1-02). Funding can be used only when obtaining an associate's degree, professional license or certification. Visit the website for further rules and restrictions. https://www.militaryonesource.com/MOS/FindInformation/Category/MilitarySpouseCareerAdvancementAccounts.aspx

NMCRS Gold Star Scholarship Program: Previously called the Dependents of Deceased Service Member Scholarship Program, the Gold Star Program provides academic grants for eligible children and un-remarried spouses of deceased Sailors and Marines. Awards are based on need and amounts are determined by NMCRS Headquarters Education Division.

- **For Children:** (use the application entitled Gold Star Scholarship for Children. Children of both active duty and retired are eligible.
  - The **USS STARK** Memorial Fund is a special program specifically for children of STARK crewmembers who died or were disabled as a result of the missile attack on the USS STARK in the Persian Gulf on May 17, 1987.
  - The **USS COLE** Memorial Fund is a special program specifically for the children of COLE crewmembers who died as a result of the terrorist attack on the USS COLE on October 12, 2000.
  - **The Pentagon Assistance Fund (PAF)** is a special program specifically for children of deceased Sailors and Marines who died as a result of the terrorist attack on the Pentagon on September 11, 2001. This program was also offered to children of active duty sailors and marines who died under hostile fire in combat operations during Operation Enduring Freedom (OEF) until 1 June 2007. Applications for eligible children are posted on the Gold Star Program page http://www.nmcrs.org/goldstar.html in late November of each year. Application forms must be received at headquarters no later than March 1st each school year.

- **For Un-remarried Spouses:** (use the application entitled Gold Star Scholarship for Spouses). The **USS STARK** Memorial Fund and **Pentagon Assistance Fund** includes un-remarried spouses of crewmembers who died as a result of the missile attack on the USS STARK or those who died as a result of the terrorist attack on the Pentagon and from combat operations during OEF before 1 June 2007. Applications for un-remarried spouses are posted on the Gold Star Program page http://www.nmcrs.org/goldstar.html in late November. Application forms must be received at headquarters no later than two months prior to the start of school.

Navy-Marine Corps Relief Society Education Programs: Offers USS Stark Memorial Fund, Travers Loan Program, Spouse TA Program for spouses accompanying their husbands or wives overseas; managed by local NMCRS offices. http://www.nmcrs.org/education.html and http://www.nmcrs.org/stap.html

Non-Commissioned Officers Association (NCOA) Scholarship Grant: For spouses of members of NCOA. http://www.ncoausa.org/

Non-Traditional Scholarship: Is offered through The American Legion Auxiliary. Getting a job or staying in today's workplace involves showing employers you have the skills and experience to get the job done. In many cases, returning to college is a must. This scholarship helps people who are a part of The Legion Family pursue a college degree later in life or allow them to pick up where they left off when their studies were interrupted. Scholarship is given to one recipient annually per Auxiliary geographic division in the amount of $1,000. Criteria includes being a member of the Legion, Auxiliary, or Sons of the American Legion in good standing with dues paid for the two preceding years for calendar year in which the application is made. Must be pursuing training in a certified trade, professional, or technical program, or a two year or four year degree program. For more information and application go to http://www.alaforveterans.org/what_we_do/scholarships/Pages/Non-TraditionalStudentScholarship.aspx

Officers Spouses' Club of San Diego, Inc. Scholarship: Provided for dependent children and spouses of active duty, retired, or deceased military officers and enlisted personnel. Applicants must reside in the greater San Diego area at time of application. Send a business sized SASE (self addressed stamped envelope) to: NOWC Navy Wives Clubs of American Scholarship Foundation, Scholarship Committee, P.O. Box 18-2104, Coronado, CA 92178 for an application and further information.

Overseas Spouse Education Assistance Program (OSEAP): Army Emergency Relief OSEAP is for spouses of active duty soldiers assigned and living in overseas commands only (Alaska, Hawaii, and Puerto Rico are **NOT** accepted for OSEAP). The spouse must also reside with the soldier at the assigned command. **Active duty military personnel are not eligible.** This scholarship is for first undergraduate degrees only. Assistance is not for any type of graduate degree level courses. Point of contact for OSEAP is Mrs. Angie Pratt, commercial phone number is 703-325-0313, DSN is (US) 221-0313, and toll free phone number is 866-878-6378 or email overseas@aerhq. org. For deadline information, other eligibility questions and copy of the application go to http://www.aerhq.org/education_spouse_Overseas.asp.

Links for other aid society sites are
- Air Force Society: www.afas.org
- Navy Marine Corps Society: www.nmcrs.org
- Coast Guard Mutual Aid: www.cgmahg.org

Parris Island Officer's Spouse Club: Contact Rebecca Varicak (843)522-1615.

Parris Island Staff Non-Commissioned Officers Spouse Club: Contact Joanne Bright at (843) 525-1756.

Park University Military Family Scholarships: Used at home campus in Parkville, MO or at the Beaufort, SC Campus in Parkville, MO or at the Beaufort. Contact 843-228-7052.

The Pat Tillman Scholarship: The Tillman Military Scholarship Program supports active duty service members, veterans and their families by removing financial barriers to completing a degree or certification program of their choice. The scholarships cover not only direct study-related expenses such as tuition and fees, but also other needs, including housing and childcare. The application period opens each spring, and a new class of Tillman Military Scholars is announced in June. More information on the application process for the upcoming academic year will be available on the website, www. pattillmanfoundation.org in January. http://www.pattillmanfoundation.org/tillman-military-scholars/apply/

Protect and Serve Grant: A form of scholarship awarded to spouses of U.S. Military from Peirce College, up to 25% on tuition fees. Email questions at protectandserve@peirce.edu. Or you can call 888-GO-PEIRCE ext 9800.

Salute to Spouses: Bryant & Stratton College online is offering a $6,000 scholarship to military spouses; recipients can use the scholarship in combination with MyCAA (see above). As long as your service member is active duty, you qualify. The web site will also provide articles on best careers for military spouses, helpful tips on how to get the most out of military financial aid for your education, weekly blogs written by military spouses covering topics you care about and forums where you can connect with other military spouses. Visit the website at www.salutetospouses.com

Scholarshiphelp.org: Site provides students with information to assist them in locating available scholarships as well as in skill building for future success. http://www.scholarshiphelp.org

Scholarships for Severely Injured Service Members and Their Dependents: http://www.dantes.doded.mil/sfd/index.asp?Flag=True

Scholarship for Culinary Education: Les Dames d'Escoffier International http://www.lesdamesatlanta.org/

Special Forces Association: The SFA Scholarship Fund was established to provide one-time scholarship grants to members, dependents and grandchildren of SFA members in good standing. For more information about this scholarship and eligibility requirements, go to http://www.specialforcesassociation.org/.

Spouse Fellowship—The FINRA Foundation Military Spouse Fellowship Program: This program gives military spouses the opportunity to earn a career-enhancing credential—the accredited financial counselor certificate while providing financial counseling to the military community. Spouses of active duty, retired and reserve service members are eligible. http://www. saveandinvest.org/military/spousefellowships/index.htm

Spouse Tuition Aid Program (STAP): The Navy and Marine Corps Relief Society (NMCRS) offers STAP to active duty military spouses stationed in an overseas (OCONUS) location. Spouses may be a full or part-time students studying toward a vocational certificate or an undergraduate or graduate degree.

This program was modified in 2009 to a need-based no-interest loan. This is available to spouses residing with their active duty service member sponsor, while stationed outside the United States. STAP no-interest loans are available for part/full time undergraduate and graduate studies. STAP offers significantly expanded eligibility with loans up to $3,000 per 12-month period. These modifications increase the number of qualified spouses and offer an excellent opportunity to complete an undergraduate or graduate degree when stationed overseas. Go to http://www.nmcrs.org/stap.html for more information.

State Provided Educational Benefits: Educational benefits for families, particularly children of deceased, MIA, POW, and disabled veterans may be available in some states. Military.com has developed an on-line general summary of educational benefits for veterans, surviving spouses and their dependents. www.military.com and/or http://www.military.com/benefits/content/survivor-benefits/surviving-spouse-and-family-education-benefits. html, http://www.military.com/benefits/content/survivor-benefits/survivors-resource-list.html

Stateside Spouse Education Assistance Program (SSEAP): This scholarship program assists Army spouses obtain a four-year undergraduate degree. Spouses of active duty soldiers, spouses of retired soldiers and widows/widowers of soldiers who died either on active duty or in a retired status are eligible. http://www.aerhq.org/education_spouseeducation_StateSide.asp

Surface Navy Association: Awards scholarships to members of the Surface Navy Association, their spouses or children working toward their first undergraduate degree. http://www.navysna.org/

Thanks USA Scholarship: Spouses of military personnel can apply for one of nearly 1000 scholarships of up to $5000 each for college. With this scholarship they will provide assistance for college, technical and vocational school scholarships for military families. http://thanksusa.org/main/index. html, shintz@scholarshipamerica.org and www.thanksusa.org

Tutoring: The Defense Department launched a free, online tutoring service for service members and their families. The site, http://www.tutor.com/military, offers round-the-clock professional tutors who can assist with homework, studying, test preparation, resume writing and more.

USS Lake Champlain (CG-57) Scholarship Foundation: Provides assistance to spouses of members assigned to USS Lake Champlain on PCS orders since commissioning Aug 1988. Contact (843) 757-2806.

VADM E.P. Travers Scholarship and Loan Program: To apply, you must be the spouse of an active duty service member or the dependent child of an active or retired member of the Navy or Marine Corps. You must also be a full-time undergraduate student at an accredited college or university. This scholarship offers 1000 grants each academic year at $2000 each. Students will be also be evaluated for an interest-free student loan of up to $3000; loan repayment begins within 30 days of award and must be repaid by allotment within 24 months. Application deadline is 1 March of each year and late applications will not be considered for the scholarship; however they will be evaluated for a loan. Go to http://www.nmcrs.org/travers.html for more information.

Women's Army Corps Veterans Association: This wonderful scholarship has been established to recognize relatives of Army Service Women. This scholarship is based upon academic achievement and leadership as expressed through co-curricular activities and community involvement. A $1,500 scholarship will be given annually. The recipient will be notified by mail or email. The check will be forwarded to the acceptance institution. For further information and eligibility requirements go to http://www.armywomen.org.

Yellow Ribbon Program: Learn about the Yellow Ribbon GI Education Enhancement Program, which allows approved degree granting institutions to enter into an agreement with VA to fund tuition expenses that exceed the highest public in-state undergraduate tuition rate. http://www.gibill.va.gov/GI_Info/CH33/Yellow_ribbon.htm-

ONLINE FINANCIAL RESOURCES

American Association University Women: http://www.aauw.org/learn. fellows_director/

College Board Scholarship Search: http://apps.collegeboard.com/cbsearch_ss/welcom.jsp

E-StudentLoan.com: http://www.estudentloan.com/

Fast Web: Provides assistance with scholarships, career planning, education and more. http://www.fastweb.com

Federal Student Financial Aid: http://studentaid.ed.gov/PORTALSWebApp/students/english/index.jsp

Scholarship Gateway: http://www.blackexcel.org/link4.htm

Scholarships.com: http://www.scholarships.com/

University of Maryland University College Scholarships: http://www.umuc.edu/financialaid/scholarships/02_programs.shtml

VA Education Assistance: http://www.gibill.va.gov/

OTHER MILITARY SPOUSE RESOURCES

Abandoned Military Spouses: U.S. Army officials have started an "Abandoned Spouses Hotline" in hopes of helping women left stranded, both intentionally and unintentionally, by their service members/husbands. This has become a rising problem in overseas countries like Korea. This is illegal and should not be tolerated. Please call the hotline if you or someone you know is in this situation at 505-730-3635 and leave a message in one of five different languages, English, Korean, Spanish, Russian or Tagalog. Officials are hoping to get the word out and military personnel realize they can no longer do this to their families. http://www.military.com/news/article/abandoned-spouses-hotline-program-may-become-a-model.html

After Deployment: Great resource to assist with medical issues that arise from deployments with soldiers and their families. http://www.afterdeployment.org

A Pink Heart: Support network for military families. http://www.apinkheart.org

*Army Wife Network: Vast area of support and resources. *I liked this site!* http://www.armywifenetwork.com/

*ASK the MILIES: This is a link for military wives to feel free and ask any question, get answers and read about others have experienced similar situations and emotions. They also provide links to some other military resources. *I think this website is really cute and I have asked a couple of questions myself and found the site informative.* http://www.askthemilies.com/

*CINCHouse: This site used to be attached with Operation Homefront but they have branched off on their own. This is a site that is geared towards military wives. It provides lots of information and is a site where you can correspond with other military spouses. *I have been on this site and I enjoy it and find it informative.* http://cinchouse.com

Ex-Partners of Service Members for Equality (EXPOSE): Provides information for spouses regarding separation and divorce from active duty, reserve or retired military service members. Expose informs spouses about their eligibility for a share of the military pension, which is not an entitlement, and explains the benefits and requirements of the Survivor Benefits Plan (SBP) which ends one year from the date of the divorce if appropriate action is not taken. EXPOSE provides an attorney referral service for members along with a quarterly newsletter for members to stay informed about potential changes to the laws affecting their rights, benefits, interests and future. For more information you can visit the website at http://www.ex-pose.org or call 703-941-5844.

Free-Ed.Net: Free education on the Internet, helpful information for finding the right school. http://www.free-ed.net

*Homefront Hugs: Is a wonderful non-profit organization located in the great state of Michigan. They provide unconditional support for military service members, wounded warriors and military families through writing cards, adopting a service member or their families and other creative ways. Please check out this website and show your support. *This is a new organization to me but from what I can tell they are a great group. I plan on taking a trip to Ann Arbor and speaking to them more about their program.* http://homefronthugs.com

Housing: Certain surviving spouses are entitled to VA home loan benefits similar to those enjoyed by veterans and active duty military members. Those who lose a military service member may be exempt from the VA funding fee. For more information and eligibility requirements go to http://www.military.com/finance/homebuying/surviving-spouses-may-qualify-for-va-loan-benefits.html?ESRC=family.nl.

Marine Wives: Informative site for Marine wives. http://marinewives.com

Mil Blogging: A daily snapshot of the top military blogs by county, and other cool stuff in the military blogosphere. Currently Milblogging has 3,147 blogs in 46 countries with 16,669 registered members. http://www.milblogging.com

Military and Family Life Consultant (MFLC) Program: (800) 646-5613, or visit the MFLC section of the MHN website: www.MHNGS.com/app/home.content

MilSpouse.com: This is a discussion site with many discounts and military updates. http://www. milspouse.com/military-discount-archives.aspx

MILSpouse: Military Spouse Resource Center, offers a vast amount of information. http://www.milspouse.org

Military Spouse Magazine: Is a wonderful magazine created for the military spouses. Provides helpful websites, creative ideas, resources and more. www.milspouse.com *I get this magazine, I do enjoy it. I would like to see more information for National Guard and Reserve Families.*

Military Significant Other Support: Support and information resources for military spouses and significant others of all branches around the world. http://www.militarysos.com

Military Spouse Association: Helping military spouses start their own business. *Looks like an interesting site. I plan on looking into this a bit more. I know many families this could help (myself included!).* http://www.milspousebiz.org

Military Spouse Help Site: http://www.miitaryspousehelp.com

My Military Life: A great site for military spouses with lots of help and resources. http://mymilitarylife.com

My Wingman Diana: Site for military wives that is enjoyable. http://mywingmandiana.military.com/4911/are-there-rules-to-being-a-military-wife/

National Resource Directory: A revitalized Department of Labor online directory promises access to "thousands" of services and resources for wounded troops, veterans and their families. The National Resource Directory provides links to national, state and local sources that support "recovery, rehabilitation and community reintegration." The site offers information for vets seeking education, training and employment. It also provides help for employers who want to hire veterans, understand employment laws and make workplace accommodations for disabled vets. http://www.nationalresourcedirectory.gov. *I love this website it is loaded with links to other sites.*

Operation MOM: A support group and a site full of resources for families of all branches of service. http://www.operationmom.org/

Operation We Are Here: This is a wonderful website that offers information and links to resources for military families and veterans for retreats, books, youth, parents of service members, emotional support, marriage, churches and much more. Please review the site at http://www.operationwearehere.com. *This is another website that I feel is really informative. Provides useful links to other sites.*

Project Sanctuary: Mission is to provide therapeutic, curative support and recreational activities to veterans, active duty military personnel, their spouses and children in a leisure environment. *I would love to go and check this place out. It sounds wonderful.* http://www.projectsanctury.us

The Military Spouse Preference Program: Affords spouses of active-duty service members and full-time Reserve or National Guardsmen moving to a new duty station priority consideration for competitive federal service positions nationwide. The program has many subprograms that apply to different placement categories. The Office of Personnel Management sets the requirements for civil service jobs. Eligible spouses must be ranked among the best qualified for the position and be within reach for the selection. For more information, contact your base Civilian Personnel Advisory Center and/ or http://www.military.com/spouse/job-search and http://www.military.com/spouse.

Uniformed Services Former Spouse's Protection Act: The name of this site speaks for itself. This is important information to know. http://www.military.com/benefits/retiree/uniformed-services-former-spouses-protection-act

FREE BOOKLETS

Need a Lift?: This free online handbook published by the American Legion is filled with scholarships, grants, fee waivers, student loans and the organizations that provide them. Cost is FREE http://www.needalift.org.

Funding Education Beyond High School: FREE at http://www.fsapubs.gov/

Managing the Price of College: FREE at http://www2.ed.gov/pubs/collegecosts/cover.html

MILITARY CHILDREN/YOUTH

I had trouble deciding how to broach this subject. I don't want to seem uncaring or over-bearing. I just simply want to let you know that you are not alone in how you (and your children) feel about your military life—your anger, frustration, sorrow and all the other feelings you get when you are married to the military. The military can be hard to bear, especially during deployments. My husband is a technician but also an aviator, so he works 8-hour days (sometimes longer) five days a week, but also has to fly many hours a month, day and night, for certification requirements. One weekend a month, two additional weeks a year he is gone—not to mention the countless schools that pop up at the most inconvenient times when you want to be a family. Then the deployments....I so understand!!

I want to share with you the many organizations that are available to help your children with military life; this is NOT to say that you cannot handle the stress or that you are not a good parent if you ask for help. These organizations are filled with people like me who are saying, "We understand and we want to help" in the event "you need or want it." So please look at these resources with an open heart and mind and feel comfortable using these services. Kids sometimes have a difficult time understanding why one parent keeps missing softball games, birthdays or field trips. When a service member joins the military, he/she understands what they signed up for; it's a way of life. Spouses marry the service member understanding what they are getting into (for the most part) and accept the missed dinners, holidays and events (not liking it, but trying to understand). But children have not been given a choice. Raising happy children in any family is a challenge in itself, but when you throw in the extra challenges of being a military child, it can sometimes seem impossible. I hope you find these resources helpful for you and your children.

CHILD CARE

Whether it is for full-time or part-time needs, or you are a stay at home mom and you need a few hours to yourself a couple of hours a week, these resources are available.

*YMCA: YMCAs across the country have a wonderful package for military families. Many offer free gym services to military families three months prior to deployment and three months after a service member comes home to his/ her family. They have daycare at facilities for a reasonable cost. You may also want to check into the various camps that are offered. *My family has used this wonderful benefit and I really appreciate how professional they were about getting us taken care of. Also our branch in Lansing, Michigan offers various programs for military families. They are a great group of people. They deserve many thanks! It is unfortunate, but I have learned in the past year that not all YMCA in various states offer this wonderful resource for military families, please check with your local branch.*

*Local Churches: I have found in most military towns the local churches are filled with generous and caring families that want to help military families. They have local fundraisers, offer free daycare, counseling and much more. Don't be afraid to approach your local church. They are a caring group of people, they are not judgmental.

Family Care-On Base Childcare (FCC): For those who cannot get into the CDC, your other option is FCC. Through the FCC Program, certified day care providers living in government housing provide flexible childcare options that include night, weekend, and hourly care.

National Association of Child Care Resource & Referral Agencies (NACCRRA): Our nation's leading voice for childcare. They work with more than 800 state and local childcare resources & referral agencies to ensure that families in every local community have access to high-quality, affordable childcare. Military will find discount childcare cost. Contact your local Family Assistance Coordinator, they can assist you with this service and provide contact information. *Priority is given to active duty families but (at least in Michigan) help has been given to soldiers on technicians' status who works at the armories.* http://www.naccrra.org

*Off-Base Childcare (R&R) and (NACCRRA): For those who cannot get your childcare needs met at the installation, or for those of you who do not live near one, this option is for you. Contact your local **Family Assistance Center** for contact information already on hand for your referrals or you can go to the website listed below.

The Department of Defense has entered into a partnership with the **National Association of Child Care Resources and Referral Agencies (NACCRRA)** to help service members and their families find affordable childcare in their community. Along with the locator services, NACCRRA also has some programs in place that subsidizes the cost of childcare for certain demographics.

I am aware that some military families have a difficult time finding childcare because they live too far away to tap into base resources, it is too expensive and they fear they won't be able to find reliable, safe childcare. NACCRRA can help you with this and take away the stress. They check out every facility and it has to reach certain standards set in place before they agree to let them be a part of the program. The programs differ from branch to branch, so you need to check out the web site and research the options open to your branch of service. www.naccrra.org/militaryprograms

*On Base Child Care: Most installations have **Child Development Center (CDC).** The centers generally provide care for children between the ages of six weeks and twelve years. Many centers also run a school age program known as **School Age Care (SAC) SAC** programs are offered for children ages 6-12 years before and/or after school and during holidays and summer vacations.

CDCs follow a priority ranking system that varies by facility, but top priority tends to go to military families stationed at the installation in the following order: single/dual active duty military; single/dual **DoD** civilian employees; active duty military with a working spouse and **DoD** civilian employees with a working spouse. The childcare costs at these facilities are subsidized, determined on a sliding scale based on the family's total income. The **CDCs** are a relatively affordable option. The facilities also open a little earlier and stay open a little later than comparable places off base to accommodate military schedules. *Be aware of possible waiting lists!*

Operation Child Care: Provides childcare services for the families of Reserve and National Guard members. http://childcareaware.org/

Zero to Three: Is a resource for the healthy development of infants and toddlers by supporting and strengthening families and communities and those who work in their behalf. http://www.zerotothree.org

EDUCATION AND RESOURCES

*eKnowledge: Partners DoD and NFL players are offering FREE SAT/ACT prep software for service members, veterans and their families. This single DVD includes more than 11 hours of virtual classroom instruction and 3,000 files of supplemental test prep material. Thousands of interactive diagnostic tools, sample questions, practice tests and graphic teaching illustrations are indexed for easy use. This software is free; the only cost is $13.84 for the standard program fee (plus the S/H) for the cost of materials, processing, worldwide distribution and customer service. To order online go to www.eknowledge.com/mil and/or www.eKowledge.com/powerpreppromo.aspx and by phone call 951-256-4076 (reference Military.com) *Great resource for military kids! I give this a thumb up! You can also get free SAT/ACT at* www.soarathome.com.

Military OneSource: I have been told that a truly free prep resource is available through http://www.militaryonesource.com in the library e-resource section. DoD MWR pays for study materials. Free for those who serve and their families. Army Veterans can access these resources through AKO in "my Library" under the "self service" tab. *I have not confirmed this resource; I do not have an AKO. So would someone check it out and let me know?*

Teens in Crisis: Resources, links, information for parents struggling with a troubled teen. http://www.teensncrisis.org/

*Test Prep Review: Source for free online practice tests in all areas of education from SAT/GRE and more. http://www.testprewiew.com *This site looks interesting and very helpful!*

The American Association of School Administrators Toolkit: This toolkit hopes to show the challenges and how to understand the challenges facing military families and the resources available to assist military children. The American Association of School Administrators (AASA) has released a toolkit on supporting the military child to help school leaders meet the needs of children whose parents are deployed or in transition. This is a free, online resource and is available on the AASA website at http://www.myarmyonesource.com/news/2009/12/Toolkit.

Military Child Educational Coalition: Provides professional development opportunities on working with military populations for school personnel and community members making them aware of the stressors that can be associated with a military deployment. http://www.militarychild.org

Military Children and School an Educator's Guide to Military Children During Deployment: This is a great site for information about how to help children of deployed service members. It does take some time to download the PDF file–includes coloring books, too! http://www2.ed.gov/about/offices/list/os/homefront/homefront.pdf

Military Friendly Schools: This is a link to all the military friendly schools available to military families. They offer various discounts, online services and more to make your transition easier. www.militaryfriendlyschools.com

Military Student.org: Site offers plenty of information for parents, students and teaching professionals about education issues for military children. http://militaryimpactedschoolsassociation.org

Military Student: Assistance for a military child in transition and deployment. http://www.militarystudent.dod.mil

Military Study Strong: Free tutoring for military children. http://www.myarmyonesource.com/

Military Teens on the Move-Tips and School Links: http://www.defenselink.mil/mtom/t3.htm.

Morgan's Kid World: This is a great site that offers assistance with homework from first grade up to college. Also, offers other educational resources for families. Please review the website for in-depth information at http://www.discover-net.net/~mlana/morENCY.html.

MyArmyOneSource: For children of active, wounded, reserve, National Guard and Army civilians (including survivors). Offers free resources and online 24/7 tutoring services for grades K-12+ in various subjects. Subjects include math, English, science project, spelling test, history, book reports and social studies. Go to www.myarmyonesource.com/cyss_tutor for more information.

National Association for Gifted Children (NAGC): http://www.nagc.org

National Guard Child and Youth Program: Offers educational and resources for military kids. http://www.guardfamily.org/youth/

Partners in Education: Army National Guard Soldiers are called into action during storms, fires, earthquakes and times of war. But did you know that they are also called upon to help your student's choose a career path, apply to college, and prepare for life outside the classroom.

The Partners in Education Program connects schools, teachers, and students with free Army National Guard educational resources, from classroom presentations to programs for at-risk youth. Through the Career Mentor volunteer database, educators and students can learn more about the diverse civilian occupations held by members of the National Guard.

The Partners in Education database is open to both current and retired National Guard members who can share their diverse career stories with students in their community. The database has more than 800 registered mentors from around the country. http://partnersineducation.com/

Project PASS (Partnership for All Student Success): Is a program offered for middle school and high school students. Project Pass is a new program for high schools that feature Junior ROTC. And the other program, called Junior Leadership Corps, was introduced for seventh and eighth grade students. Both programs offer potential life-changing options for students in need of structure and motivation. The intent is to introduce students to a program of leadership and character development using military-style techniques as early as seventh grade and allow them to continue throughout high school, if they choose. It is the hope of the program to give the students self-esteem and confidence and improve their grades and goals for their future and their families. For more information go to http://www.army.mil/article/53186/army-unveils-project-pass-junior-leadership-corps/.

*Rosetta Stone: This is a very expensive foreign language kit to purchase. I know I have this listed in another area of this book but I wanted to remind you that your soldier can get this FREE for your use at home. *We find it very useful for our daughter's education. This is a wonderful opportunity and I cannot say "thank you" enough for this opportunity.* Your service member will be able to download this from his/her AKO account.

SOAR: This is a student online achievement resource. You can get free ACT and SAT programs. http://www.soarathome.org/

State Provided Educational Benefits: Educational Benefits for families, particularly children of deceased, MIA, POW, and disabled veterans, may be available in some states. Military.com has developed an on-line general summary of educational benefits for veterans, surviving spouses and their dependents.

- www.military.com
- http://www.military.com/benefits/content/survivor-benefitssurviving-spouse-and-family-education-benefits.html
- http://www.military.com/benefits/content/survivor-benefits/survivors-resource-list.html

Specialized Training of Military Parents (STOMP): http://www.
stompproject.org

The Official Source of Education Information for the Department of
Defense and LIFELines Partner Organizations: http://militarystudent.org/

*Tutoring: The Defense Department launched a **free**, online tutoring service
for service members and their families. The site offers round the clock 24/7
professional tutors who can assist with homework (in all subjects), studying,
test preparation, resume writing and more. *This site looks really interesting
and cool. I wish I would have used it for my daughter last year.* http://www.
tutor.com/military

SCHOLARSHIPS

Alaska Sea Service Scholarships: Available for family members of Sea
Service members with **Alaska residency only.** The Navy League and
Naval Education and Training Command (NETC) announced eligibility
requirements for the Alaska Sea Services Scholarship for academic year 2012-
2013 on July 15. The program awards up to four $1,000 scholarships annually
for undergraduate education to dependent children or spouses of personnel
serving in the U.S. Navy, Marine Corps or Coast Guard (either active duty
or reserve), retired from those services, or were serving at time of death or
missing-in-action status and who also are legal residents of Alaska. Applicants
will be ranked according to academic proficiency, character, leadership ability,
community involvement and financial need.

The application deadline is March 1, 2012 for the FY-12 selection
board, which convenes in April 2012. Applicants must show acceptance at
an accredited college or university for full-time undergraduate study toward a
Bachelor of Arts or a Bachelor of Science degree. No more than two scholarship
awards may be given to any individual during pursuit of the four-year degree.
The Alaska Sea Services Scholarship is one of 25 endowed scholarships
available to sea services members through the Navy League Foundation. For
complete information and an application to apply for the Alaska Sea Service
Scholarship, visit http://www.navyleague.org/scholarship/ interested families
may also contact Cheral Wintling at 850-452-3671 (DSN 922-3671), email
cheral.wintling@navy.mil or contact Mike Carter at 703-312-1585, email
mcarter@navyleague.org.

American Military Retirees Association (AMRA): Is a wonderful
organization the works on behalf of military retirees and their families, to
protect their rights and benefits under the law, and to lobby on their behalf
in Washington, DC and elsewhere. Check out the website and learn more
about their efforts and other resources they have available. Their latest in 2010

was the Associations Scholarship fund. Through the current generosity of AMRA members, the Associations annually present $35,000 in scholarships to AMRA members, their spouses and dependents, and their grandchildren. They hope to grow the program so they can award more scholarships in the future. Go to http://amra1973.org to learn more about this organization.

Americorps National Educational Award Program: Provides educational assistance. http://www.americorps.gov

American Patriot Freedom Scholarship: The fourth annual Homefront America, American Patriot Freedom Scholarship program is now accepting applications from qualified military dependent children. Applications must be postmarked by April 24 of the year you are applying. http://www.homefrontamerica.org/oohrahhome.htm

American Legion Baseball & Scholarship: This state and national high school baseball competition is open to players from grades 10-12 recruited by a registered American Legion Team. This scholarship is available to seniors who are a member of a registered team. In 2008, The American Legion awarded $22,000 in scholarships to deserving players. Each Department Baseball Committee may select a player from their Department to receive this scholarship. Several scholarships will be awarded depending on the number of applicants and interest earned from the trust fund. Review the website for more information and rules. http://www.legion.org/scholarships

Americal Division Veterans Association: Please view website for eligibility and further information about this scholarship at http://www.americal.org/.

Anchor Scholarship Foundation: For dependents of active duty or retired personnel who served in commands under the administrative control of Commanders, Naval Surface Forces, US Atlantic or Pacific Fleets for a minimum of six years. You can call 843-757-2806 for further information and an application.

Army Aviation Association (AAAA): The AAAA Scholarship Foundation, Inc., is a non-profit, tax-exempt corporation established to render financial assistance for the college-level education of members of the Army Aviation Association of America, Inc., (AAAA), and the spouses, unmarried siblings, unmarried children and unmarried grandchildren of current and deceased AAAA members. For further information about this scholarship and eligibility requirements go to http://www.quad-a.org/.

Army Nurse Corps Association (ANCA): ANCA awards scholarships to U.S. citizen students attending accredited baccalaureate or graduate nursing or anesthesia nursing programs. This scholarship is in honor of Cpt. Joshua M.

McClimans, AN, USAR, who was killed in a mortar attack in April 2011 while assigned to the Combat Support Hospital at Forward Operating Base Salerno in Afghanistan. For more information about this scholarship and eligibility requirements go to http://e-anca.org/ANCAEduc.htm.

Army Ranger Association: This scholarship program is memorial to selfless service and contributions made to our country by USARA members. These awards are given in their honor. This program provides an opportunity to provide financial assistance to qualified dependents of USARA members in furthering their education. The scholarship committee seeks to award scholarships to applicants displaying the potential for a degree in higher education, whether it is technical, university or professional. Each year the scholarship committee evaluates the scholarship applicants and selects the most outstanding submissions to be awarded to USARA Legacy Scholarship. For further information about this scholarship and eligibility requirements go to http://www.ranger.org/.

Army Reserve Association: Offers scholarships for dependents of service members. Please review the website at http://www.armyreserve.org for further information and eligibility.

*ASVAB Career Exploration Program: This is a career planning and exploration program that combines a multiple-aptitude test with an interest self-assessment and a wide range of career exploration tools. And it's FREE to participating schools. This site also offers other tools for military children and parents. *I was really impressed with this site. I have emailed this material to my daughter's school and to the Army National Guard Family Programs Office in Michigan at Joint Force Headquarters to see if they are aware of it.* http://www.asvabprogram.com

Association of Naval Aviation: This scholarship is provided by The Philip H. Jones Family and the Association of Naval Aviation to honor the service and sacrifice of LCDR Philip H. Jones, USN (RET), who started his Naval Aviation career as an Aviation Pilot during WWII. This scholarship is provided for the sons and daughters of Naval Aviators and Navy, Marine Corps and Coast Guard Aircrewmen who died while on active duty serving in the United States Navy, Marine Corps or Coast Guard. Please review the website for further information and eligibility requirements and contact information at http://www.anahq.org/scholarship2011.htm.

The Billy Blanks Foundation: This foundation offers scholarships and support for after school programs. http://www.billyblanksfoundation.org/.

Boys State Endowment Fund (Through the American Legion): They have a scholarship called "The Voice of Democracy," the maximum award is $6,000. They also have the "The Patriot Pen" with a maximum award of $1,000. Both are great scholarships for kids and improve their skills in writing. Each year The American Legion will have a different theme. The theme for the 2011/2012 is "The Voice of Democracy" and "Is There Pride in Serving in our Military?" Please review the website for rules and regulations. http://www.michiganlegion.org/pdfs/endow_fund.pdf

Brewer & Wilson Scholarship: Offered through the Michigan American Legion, applicants must have a 2.5 minimum grade point average, financial need, and be a child, grandchild or great grandchild of an honorably discharged war veteran. Scholarship is $500. www.michiganlegion.org

Coast Guard Chief Warrant and Warrant Officers Association: Offers the CWO John A. Keller-CWOA Scholarship Grant and The Art and Eleanor Colona Scholarship Program. Go to http://www.cwoauscg.org/docs/2010-april-bylaws-edition.pdf for further information and eligibility requirements.

Children of Fallen Soldiers Relief Fund: Was founded as a means to providing college grants and financial assistance to surviving children and spouses of our U.S. military service members who have lost their lives in the Iraq and Afghanistan wars. The program will assists disabled service member families too. For further information or to apply for assistance, go to http://www.cfsrf.org/.

Child and Student Programs: MilitaryChild.org has Child and Student Programs providing information regarding student opportunities to participate in peer-to-peer programs to assist students who are relocating into and out of their schools, art and space camp opportunities, early literacy resources, and state and national transition information.

- Arts - The MCEC's promotion of the Arts by featuring great works of military children, including artwork, film, and written work. For more information regarding the Arts, contact Arts@MilitaryChild.org.
- Education Resource Center - A single, central site designed and updated by MCEC for school requirements and resources for all fifty states, DoDEA, and Washington D.C. For more information regarding the Education Resource Center, contact Ask Aunt Peggie.
- Early Literacy - Growing, Learning, Understanding Kits - The MCEC designed kits for developing early literacy skills in children from birth through second grade, and covering a range of themes and literacies. For more information regarding Early Literacy, contact EarlyLiteracy@MilitaryChild.org.
- Frances Hesselbein Student Leadership Program - Established by the Military Child Education Coalition (MCEC) in 2006 to identify exemplary young people through their participation in the MCEC

Student 2 Student (S2S) program. Contact S2S@MilitaryChild.org for questions.

- Space Camp Scholarship - MCEC's scholarship that sends active duty military students to space camp annually, including the application criteria and registration form. For more information regarding the Space Camp Scholarship, contact SpaceCamp@MilitaryChild.org.
- Student 2 Student and Junior Student 2 Student - A student-led program at the high school and middle school levels to support students who are transitioning to and from their school. For more information regarding Student 2 Student, contact S2S@MilitaryChild.org.

Children of Warriors Scholarship: Is offered to children of our fallen warriors so they can pursue higher education. This is provided by The American Legion Auxiliary to support the children of our warriors. These scholarships are awarded to 15 students annually who excel in academics and volunteer in their communities. Grants range from $1,500 to $2,500 and are offered for an undergraduate study at a four-year accredited college or university, and may be used for tuition, books, fees, and room and board.

Candidates for this award range from children down to step and great grandchildren of veterans who served in the Armed Forces during eligibility dates. And applicant must have completed 50 hours or more of community service during his/her high school years. For more information and eligibility criteria go to: http://www.alaforveterans.org/what_we_do/scholarships/Pages/NatPresScholECW.aspx.

College Board Scholarship Search: http://apps.collegeboard.com/cbsearch_ss/welcome.jsp.

CollegeNet Mach25 Scholarship Database: http://www.collegenet.com/mach25

Commissioned Officers Association of the USPHS Inc.: Offers thousands of dollars towards college scholarships for children and spouses of COA members. Please go to the site to review all requirements and eligibility at http://www.coausphs.org/education.cfm.

Connect Kids: Is a wonderful site that offers educational assistance and offers you other state websites for review. Just click on the state of your interest and see the websites for your review. http://www.kids.ct.gov/kids/cwp/view.asp?a=2574&Q=328116

CYFERnet: This is a Children, Youth and Families Education and Research Network. *Looks really cool!* http://www.cyfernet.org

Crisis Management Toolkit: The purpose of the DoDEA Crisis Management website is to help families, educators, and community members understand how schools will ensure that children and personnel are safe and secure in the event of a crisis. This site also provides other useful information for families; please take the time to review. http://www.dodea.edu

Sgt. Dakota Meyer Scholarship: This scholarship is in partnership with the Marine Corps Scholarship Foundation to help education the children of wounded Marines and Navy Corpsmen. http://www.dakotameyer.com/

Defense Commissary Agency (DeCA) 2010 Scholarship for Military Children: Only dependent, unmarried children, younger than age 21 (age 23 if enrolled as a full-time student at a college or university), of active duty personnel, Reserve, Guard and retired military members, and survivors of the Fallen may apply for a scholarship. Eligibility is determined using the Defense Enrollment Eligibility Reporting System database.

The applicant must be planning to attend, or already be attending, an accredited college or university full time in the fall of the year applying, or be enrolled in a program of studies designed to transfer directly into a four-year program. Applicants should prepare to submit an essay on the following topic: "You can travel back in time; however, you cannot change events. What point in history would you visit and why?"

Applications must be submitted to a commissary by close of business February 17. Each commissary with qualified applicants will have at least one scholarship awarded. To learn more, go to http://www.myarmyonesource.com/news/2009/12/DeCA2010Scholarship3.

Scholarship applications are now available in commissaries worldwide and online through a link at http://www.myarmyonesource.com/news/2009/12/DeCA2010Scholarship and directly at http://www.myarmyonesource.com/news/2009/12/DeCA2010Scholarship2.

Department of Defense - Post 9/11 GI Bill Transferability: In addition to the education benefits offered by the Post 9/11 GI Bill, there is a special provision of the program that allows career service members to share their remaining GI Bill education benefits with immediate family members. The key factor is whether or not the service member has used any of his/her GI Bill in the past; only unused benefits can be transferred. This means that if the member has used 12 months of his/her GI Bill, then there is only 24 months of benefits left to share. Service members must meet specific criteria to be eligible to transfer their GI Bill beneifts. This includes having at least six years of service and an obligation to serve at least four more. Go to http://www.veteransbenefitsgibill.com/2009/06/23/family-transfer-with-the-gi-bill-finalized/, http://usmilitary.about.com/od/benefits/a/gibilltransfer.htm, or http://www.gibill.va.gov/post-911/post-911-gi-bill-summary/transfer-of-benefits.html.

Department Educational Assistance (DEA) Program: Provides education and training opportunities to eligible dependents of certain veterans. The program offers 45 months of education benefits. These benefits may be used for a degree and certificate programs, apprenticeship, and on-the-job- training. If you are a spouse, you may take a correspondence course. Remedial, deficiency, and refresher courses may be approved under certain circumstances. Spouses benefits end 10 years from the date VA finds you eligible or from the date of death of the veteran.

If you are a son or daughter and wish to receive benefits for attending school or job training, you must be between the ages of 18-26. In certain instances, it is possible to begin before the age of 18 and to continue after the age of 26. Marriage is not a bar to this benefit. If you are in the Armed Forces, you may not receive this benefit while on active duty.

To pursue training after military service, your discharge must not be under dishonorable conditions. VA can extend your period of eligibility by the number of months and days equal to the time spent on active duty. This extension cannot go beyond your 31st birthday. Please go to the websites for more information: http://www.directoryofschools.com/Military/Dependents-Education-Assistance-Program.htm and http://www.military.com/education/content/money-for-school/dependents-educational-assistance-dea.html.

Department of Defense Districts and Schools on the Web: http://www.dodea.edu/

Department of Defense Education Activity (DODEA): DODEA's mission is to plan, direct, coordinate, and manage the education programs for eligible dependents of U.S. military personnel and civilian personnel of the DoD. DoDEA provides an exemplary education that inspires and prepares all students for success in a dynamic, global environment. Dependents of military personnel face unique challenges to their educational attainment. They move more frequently than typical students and are also subject to the stress that accompanies the potential deployment of parents to combat. DoDEA schools provide students with a uniform curriculum and standards that mitigate the stress of frequent moves and other DoD challenges faced by military dependents. http://www.dodea.edu/home/about.cfm

Eagle Scout of the Year: The American Legion honors the Eagle Scout of the Year at the national convention with a $10,000 scholarship. The three runners-up get $2,500. Further information is available from department adjutants or the Americanism and Children & Youth Division. www.michigan.org and/or http://www.legion.org/scholarships

*Educational Benefits for Children of Disabled or Deceased Veterans: This tuition grant program is administered by the Michigan (or your state) Higher Education Assistance Authority in the Michigan Department of

Treasury provides payment for the education of the children of a veteran who is totally disabled from service incurred causes, was killed in the line of duty, has died subsequently from a service-related disability, was totally disabled before death from a service-connected illness or injury, or who is listed by the federal government as missing in action in a foreign country. A student may be eligible for a tuition waiver of up to $2,800 annually for undergraduate study. Recipients must meet certain eligibility requirements. Information on eligibility and application forms are available at www.michigan.gov/studentaid or by calling toll-free 888-447-2687. *Check with your state for this same support.*

EScholar: Is a site for Apprenticeships, Cooperative, Fellowships, Grants, Internships and Scholarships. http://www.studentjobs.gov/e-scholar.asp

82nd Airborne Division Association: Offers a scholarship to Former Troopers (within 2 yrs their ETS date, some other restrictions may apply) and their dependent children. Spouses are not eligible. Applicant **MUST** be intent on pursuing a course toward a baccalaureate degree, and **MUST** gain at least **12 semester hours per semester** toward that degree. Please go to the web site for further information and eligibility requirements at http://www.82ndassociation.org/Scholarships.html, you can also send inquiries to 82assnedfund@earthlink.net.

FastWEB: Provides assistance with scholarships, career planning, education and more. http://www.fastweb.com

Federal Student Aid Gateway: Students.gov is an official U.S. government website designed for college students and their families. Their mission is to provide you with easy access to information and resources from the U.S. government; all the information you need, in one place, from all parts of the government. Through student.gov, you can link to government (and selected non-government) web sites to help you with all areas of your education and possible career choices. http://www.students.gov/STUGOVWebApp/aboutus.jsp

FinAid: http://www.finaid.org

FirstGov for Kids: U.S. Government interagency kids' portal. It provides links to Federal Kids' sites along with some of the best kids' sites from other organizations all grouped by subject, explore, learn, and have fun. http://kids.gov

FisherHouse Foundation: This is a wonderful organization that offers assistance through scholarships for the education of military children and other useful resources. http://www.militaryscholar.org

Fleet Reserve Association Scholarship Deadline: The FRA Education Foundation is reminding college-bound students to apply for its 25 plus scholarships before April 15 of the year you are applying. http://www.fra.org/

Fold of Honor Foundation Scholarship: Provides scholarships for dependents and spouses of service members that have been killed or disabled as a result of their military service. http://www.foldsofhonor.org/

Freedom Alliance: Scholarship resource site. http://www.freedomalliance.org

Henry H. Arnold Education Grant Program: This program provides $2000 grants to selected dependents of active duty, Title 10 AGR/Reserve, Title 32 AGR performing full-time active duty, retired reserve and deceased Air Force members; spouses (stateside) of active duty members and Title 10 AGR/Reservists; and surviving spouses of deceased personnel for their undergraduate studies. Please review website for more information, eligibility and contact information at http://www.afas.org/Education/ArnoldEdGrant.cfm

In-State Tuition Initiative Information: Find out the in-state tuition eligibility rules for your state and what is being doing to make these rules more military-family friendly.

Jason Plite Memorial Fund Scholarship: In 2010, $11,000 was awarded in scholarship funds for military children. Please visit www.jasonplitememorial.com for deadlines and rules.

The Joe Foss Institute: This site has lots to offer, but I am going to list just a couple here. Please take the time to review the website. The programs here focuses primarily on two initiatives: The veterans inspiring patriotism program, which centers on inspiring and teaching patriotism in schools; and the Joe Foss Institute Scholarship Contest Series, which awards college scholarship money to outstanding students. Go to http://www.joefoss.com/programs for further information and eligibility.

John Hopkins Scholarship: See site for information. http://www.jhsph.edu/mli/training_course/

Joseph A. McAlinden Divers Scholarship: Is offered specifically to Navy and Marine Corps Divers, whether active duty or retired, and their eligible family members. This scholarship provides financial assistance for full-time undergraduate and graduate students, who must be participating in one of the following areas of study: Oceanography, Ocean Agriculture, or Aquaculture. The McAlinden Scholarship also assists with Department of the Navy approved advanced diver training, qualifications and certifications. The scholarship is need-based and ranges from $500 up to $3,000 per academic year, for the eligible students education. There is no deadline for this program; you may apply at any time. http://www.nmcrs.org/education.html

Legacy Scholarship Fund: This Scholarship is through The American Legion and is provide to the children of **all branches** of U.S. service members who died on or after Sept. 11, 2001, and that they receive equal opportunities in their pursuit of higher learning. Please review the website for more information and rules. http://www.legion.org/scholarships

Logistics Officer Association (LOA): Is comprised of over 3,200 military officers and civilians in logistics fields around the globe. The purpose of the Logistics Officer Association is to enhance the military logistics profession. LOA provides an open forum to promote quality logistical support and logistics officer professional development.

LOA provides a great scholarship program that is intended to promote education for those who are members, children of active and corporate LOA members, and enlisted members of the armed forces. This program will allow applicants taking college classes to research and offer solutions to current logistics challenges within the Department of Defense or industry, high school students to explore and consider the implications of logistics in military operations, or other applicants to apply for scholarship awards based purely on a brief application. For more information about LOA and eligibility, rules and further guidelines go to http://www.loanational.org/.

Major James Ursano Scholarship Program: This Army scholarship program assists children of soldiers to obtain a four year undergraduate degree. Children who are eligible are dependents of soldiers on active duty, children of retired soldiers, or children of soldiers who died while on active duty or in a retired status are eligible. For more information and deadline times go to http://www.aerhq.org/education_dependentchildren_mgjames.asp.

Marine Corps Law Enforcement Foundation: This is a wonderful organization that provides various educational assistance and scholarships for military dependents. Please visit the website for further information and eligibility requirements. http://www.mclef.org/supportedorganizations.asp

Marine Corps League Foundation: Offers the Marine Corps League scholarship program and Chesty Puller Scholarship. For more information about these programs go to http://www.mclfoundation.org/scholarship_program.html for application and eligibility.

Marine Corps Scholarship Foundation: Mission is to provide financial assistance in the form of scholarships for higher education to sons and daughters of Marines and children of former Marines. http://www.mcsf.org/

Military Officers Association of America (MOAA): You can check here for educational assistance, grants, loans, or questions about deadlines, how to apply or other renewal and repayment questions. http://www.moaa.org/benefits_education/default.htm

Military Scholar: Information about the Defense Commissary Agency's Scholarships for Military Children. http://www.militaryscholar.org

Military Scholarship Finder: Will give you a list of hundreds of scholarships, grants and loans for military families to pursue their educational dreams. www.militaryscholarshipfinder.com

National High School Oratorical Contest: Offered through the Michigan American Legion and is a constitutional Speech contest designed to develop a deeper knowledge of The Constitution of The United States. The Legion awards around $15,000 to each of the three finalists. All participants receive a scholarship. www.michiganlegion.org and/or http://www.legion.org/scholarships

National Association for Unformed Services: Scholarships are available to members of all branches of services and their dependents. Visit http://www.naus.org for further information and requirements.

National Merit Scholarships: http://www.nationalmerit.org/

NMCRS Gold Star Scholarship Program: Previously called the Dependents of Deceased Service Member Scholarship Program, the Gold Star Program provides academic grants for eligible children and un-remarried spouses of deceased Sailors and Marines. Awards are based on need and the amount is determined by NMCRS Headquarters Education Division. Use the application entitled Gold Star Scholarship for Children). Children of both active duty and retired are eligible.

- The **USS STARK** Memorial Fund is a special program specifically for children of STARK crewmembers who died or were disabled as a result of the missile attack on the USS STARK in the Persian Gulf on May 17, 1987.
- The **USS COLE** Memorial Fund is a special program specifically for the children of COLE crewmembers who died as a result of the terrorist attack on the USS COLE on October 12, 2000.
- **The Pentagon Assistance Fund (PAF)** is a special program specifically for children of deceased Sailors and Marines who died as a result of the terrorist attack on the Pentagon on September 11, 2001. This program was also offered to children of active duty sailors and marines who died under hostile fire in combat operations during Operation Enduring Freedom (OEF) until 1 June 2007. Applications

for eligible children are posted on the Gold Star Program page http://www.nmcrs.org/goldstar.html in late November of each year. Application forms must be received at headquarters no later than March 1st each school year.

National Research Center on the Gifted Children: http://www.gtworld.org

Naval and Marine Corps Relief Society: Offers various educational scholarships. For further information and eligibility requirements go to http://www.nmcrs.org/education.html.

Naval Reserve Association: Offers five different scholarships for dependents of military service members. Please view http://www.ausn.org/Resources/Education/Scholarships/tabid/79/Default.aspx for further details and eligibility.

Need a Lift: "Need a Lift?" is a 152-page booklet updated annually to serve as a complete financial-aid reference guide to veterans, veterans' dependents and members of the American Legion family. The publication contains information on federal and state veteran's benefits; scholarships for veterans and their dependents, and Legionnaires and their family members; tips for applying to college and applying for financial assistance; and a comprehensive guide to colleges and universities listing tuition, room and board costs, and admission and financial aid deadlines. To search and print entries, visit: www.legion.org/needalift.

Officers Spouses' Club of San Diego, Inc. Scholarship: Provided for dependent children and spouses of active duty, retired, or deceased military officers and enlisted personal. Applicants must reside in the greater San Diego area at time of application. Send a business size SASE to: NOWC Navy Wives Clubs of American Scholarship Foundation, Scholarship Committee, P.O. Box 18-2104, Coronado, CA 92178 for an application and further information.

Oratorical Scholarship: Offered through the Michigan American Legion is a constitutional speech contest designed to develop a deeper knowledge of the constitution of the United States. www.michiganlegion.org

Order of Daedalians: The Order of Daedalians honors, as its Founding Members, all WWI aviators who were commissioned as officers and rated as military pilots no later than the Armistice on 11 November 1918. It perpetuates their names as the first to fly our country's airplanes in time of war. The Order's membership of commissioned, warrant and flight officer military pilots and WASP's, with its worldwide network of Daedalian Flights and its comprehensive awards program, supports the military services and other aerospace activities. The Awards and Scholarship Programs of the Order and Foundation encourage patriotism, integrity, and good character in our nation's youth; military careers as commissioned pilots; safety of flight, and excellence in the performance of military duties. The Daedalian Foundation's Scholarship program also promotes study in aerospace disciplines. For more information about this wonderful organization or eligibility requirements go to http://www.daedalians.org/.

The Pat Tillman Scholarship: The Tillman Military Scholarship Program supports active duty service members, veterans and their families by removing financial barriers to completing a degree or certification program of their choice. The scholarships cover not only direct study-related expenses such as tuition and fees, but also other needs, including housing and childcare. The application period opens each spring, and a new class of Tillman Military Scholars is announced in June. More information on the application process for the upcoming academic year will be available on the website, www.pattillmanfoundation.org in January.

Peterson's Undergraduate Scholarship Search (Financial Aid): http://www.petersons.com/

Presidential Freedom Scholarship: http://www.learnandserve.gov/about/programs/pfs.asp

Princeton Review Scholarships and Aid: http://www.princetonreview.com/home.asp

Reserve Officers Association of the US: This program is designed to assist deserving members of ROA, ROAL, their children, or grandchildren who wish to attend or who are now attending accredited U.S. colleges or universities. This scholarship is funded through the Henry J. Reilly Scholarship trust, which states that preference of its award will be given to those pursuing a military career. ROTC cadets, midshipmen and currently serving military graduate students are strongly encouraged to apply. The scholarship is granted to 30 applicants. For more information about ROA or this scholarship go to http://www.roa.org/.

Samsung American Legion Scholarship: To honor Korean War veterans, Samsung and The American Legion annually award $300,000 in scholarships to nearly 100 Boys and Girls State participants who are direct descendants of a veteran (**off all branches of military**) for Legion membership. The scholarship gives up to $20,000 and has a 72 year history of providing a practical; government/civics experience. They have graduated more than 40,000 Michigan Students, with many of them currently serving as law makers. See website for more information. www.michiganboystate.org and http://www.legion.org/scholarships

Sallie Mae's College Answer's Scholarship Search: http://www. collegeanswer.com/paying/scholarship_search/pay_scholarship_scholarship_ search.jsp

Scholarship.com: http://www.scholarships.com

Scholarship Resource Network Express: http://www.srnexpress.com/index. cfm

Scholarships for Military Children: Children are eligible for scholarships if either parent is active duty, Reserve, Guard, or retired military personnel, or the child is the survivor of a deceased member, and has a current military ID card. The only stipulation is that the child must be planning to attend a college or university on full-time bases. http://www.militaryscholar.org

ScholarshipHelp.org: Site provides students with information assist them in locating available scholarships as well as in skill building for future success. http://www.scholarshiphelp.org/ and http://www.mobc-online.org/

Scholarship Scams: You'll be able to avoid scholarship scams. Read the Federal Trade Commission's "Scholarship Scam's" information. http://www. ftc.gov/bcp/conline/edcams/scholarship/index.html

Scholarship for Severely Injured Service Members and Their Dependents: http://www.dantes.doded.mil/sfd/index.asp?Flag=True

Special Forces Association: The SFA Scholarship Fund was established to provide one-time scholarship grants to members, dependents and grandchildren of SFA members in good standing. For more information about this scholarship and eligibility requirements, go to http://www.specialforcesassociation.org/.

Special Operation Warrior Fund Operation: The Special Operations Warrior Foundation provides full scholarship grants and educational and family counseling to the surviving children of special operations personnel who die in operational or training missions and immediate financial assistance to severely wounded special operations personnel and their families. http:// www.specialops.org

Special Operations Warrior Foundation: Provides college scholarship grants, based on need, along with financial aid and educational counseling to the children of special operations personnel who were killed in an operational mission or training accident. http://www.specialops.org/

Student Aid on the Web: Is funded through the Department of Education. http://studentaid.ed.gov

Student.gov - Military Funding for College: Links and more links to students you get connected with educational resources. There are government and non-government links for review. http://www.students.gov/STUGOVWebApp/public

*Student Trooper Program: Priceless career option, up to $1000 scholarship and offered through the Michigan American Legion is a five day on-site career law enforcement program held at the Michigan State Police Training Academy in Lansing, Michigan. Since 1969 more than 2.000 young men and women have graduated from this program, with many choosing a law enforcement career. This program is offered in most states. *This looks like a wonderful opportunity and I would love to go and check this place out.* http://www.michiganlegion.org/trooper/index.html *I have listed Michigan's site. Check with your state's Legion site for your state program.*

Surface Navy Association: Awards scholarships to members of the Surface Navy Association, their spouses, or children working toward their first undergraduate degree. http://www.navysna.org/

Thanks USA Scholarship: Is a non-partisan, charitable effort to mobilize Americans of all ages to "thank" the men and women of the United States Armed Forces. With this scholarship they will provide college, technical and vocational school scholarships for military families. www.thanksusa.org

The American Legion Scholarship and Financial Aid Information: The cornerstone of The American Legion's Education Assistance Program is its scholarship and financial aid guide. This 152 page booklet is updated annually, and is a complete financial aid reference guide for veterans, their dependents and members of the "The American Legion Family." http://www.legion.org/scholarships.

The Council for Exceptional Children: http://www.cec.sped.org/

*The Department of Michigan Scholarships: Offers three scholarships to Michigan residents meeting the eligibility requirements. Each scholarship is for $500. The Medical Career Scholarship is available to students seeking a medical-related career. The Memorial Scholarship is for all other types of studies. The Non-Traditional Scholarship is for students over the age of 22. The $500 grant is to be applied toward the expenses of tuition, room and board fees, books and supplies necessary at any school, college, or other institution IN THE STATE OF MICHIGAN. Qualifying applicants should be in the top quarter of their class. Scholarships are restricted to high school seniors entering the first year of college.

Complete information **MUST** be given as to the applicant's family financial status. This information will be kept confidential and will be destroyed after the scholarships are awarded. Applicants **MUST** be a resident of Michigan at the time of application, and the previous year. Finally, the scholarship is to be used in the State of Michigan **only**. Please complete all questions on the application. If it does not apply, indicate with N/A. Scholarship applications and further information can be found at http://www.michalaux.org/ and to print out the rules and application form. *I have listed the state of Michigan's information because I live in Michigan. Please check with your state Auxiliary, others may/do offer grants for only residents of their states also.*

The Eight and Forty Lung and Respiratory Disease Nursing Scholarship Fund: Established to assist registered nurses with advanced preparation for positions in supervision, administration or teaching. Students must have employment prospects in specific positions in hospitals, clinics or health departments upon completion of their education and the position much have a full-time and direct relationship to pediatric lung and respiratory control. Applicants much have a current registered nurse license. Scholarship awards are $3,000 each. http://www.legion.org/scholarships

The American Legion: Scholarships: American Legion can assist with obtaining scholarships for college. http://www.legion.org/scholarships

The Survivors of Service Members SOS Fund: Provides funds to families who have lost a loved one in Iraq. http://SOSFund.us/mission.htm

The Tailhook Association: Children and grandchildren of Naval or Marine Corps Aviator, Flight Officer or Air Crewmen are eligible for scholarships through The Tailhook Association. For further information and eligibility requirements go to http://www.tailhook.org/.

United American Patriots Fund: Scholarships for military children through The Veterans of Foreign Wars Department. http://unitedpatriots.org

USS Tennessee Scholarship Fund: The scholarship provides grants of up to $2,000 for an academic year to eligible children, under the age of 23, of service members who are serving or have served aboard the USS Tennessee. Children of both active duty and retired USS Tennessee Sailors are eligible. The Tennessee application is posted on the USS Tennessee Scholarship program page in late November. Applications must be received at headquarters no later than March 1st each school year. http://www.nmcrs.org/spec-prgm.html

VFW Scholarship Programs: Besides the VFW's outstanding scholarship programs, Posts and Auxiliaries across the nation work with youth in scouting, sports, ROTC and military cadet programs. By providing leaders, funding, sponsorships and other resources, the VFW and its Auxiliaries encourage millions of American children to higher ideals and greater personal achievement. http://www.vfw.org/community/programs

Women's Army Corps Veterans Association: This wonderful scholarship has been established to recognize relatives of Army Service Women. This scholarship is based upon academic achievement and leadership as expressed through co-curricular activities and community involvement. A $1,500 scholarship will be given annually. The recipient will be notified by mail or email. The check will be forwarded to the acceptance institution. For further information and eligibility requirements go to http://www.armywomen.org/.

Women Marines Association: This great organization that offers eight scholarships a year to women marines and their dependents. For a list of these scholarships, eligibility and to download the applications go to http://www.womenmarines.org/scholarships.aspx.

SCHOLARSHIP AND FINANCIAL AID SEARCH SITES:

http://U101.com/ - *search site for all colleges by states, pretty cool site.*
www.afcea.org
www.apus.edu – *military school college*
www.campustours.com – *takes you on a tour through various colleges, pretty cool.*
www.collegeboard.org
www.collegeboard.org/clep
www.collegeIsPossible.org
www.collegenet.com
www.collegeview.com
http://www.dantes.doded.mil
www.ed.gov/directloan
http://edu.military.com/gibill
www.fafsa.ed.gov
www.feea.org
www.finaid.com
www.finaidfacts.org/scholarships.htm
www.fisherhouse.org
www.gocollege.com
www.jackkentcookedoundation.org
http://www.legion.org/scholarships
www.military.com
http://www.militaryfamily.org
www.moaa.org
www.presidentialclassroom.org

State Educational Benefits for Military Dependents: *Many states have these benefits. I apologize if I am not listing a state that is online. Please let me know if I missed one.*

> http://www.arkansasgighered.com/ -- Arkansas
> http://www.csac.ca.gov – California
> http://www.doe.state.de.us/high-ed/ -- Delaware
> http://www.in.gov/veteran/ -- Indiana
> http://www.kheaa.com/ -- Kentucky
> http://www.mdva.state.md.us/ -- Maryland
> http://www.montana.edu/ -- Montana
> http://www.hesc.com/ -- New York
> http://wwwregents.state.oh.us/ -- Ohio
> http://www.okhighered.org/ -- Oklahoma
> http://www.oregon.gov/ --- Oregon
> http://www.dmva.state.pa.us/ --- Pennsylvania
> http://www.vdva.vipnet.org/ -- Virginia
> http://dva.state.wi.us/ -- Wisconsin

OTHER MILITARY CHILD RESOURCES:

ACT Today! (Autism Care and Treatment Today) for Military Families: *ACT Today! (Autism Care and Treatment Today!)*, is a national non-profit organization whose mission is to raise awareness and provide treatment services to families that cannot afford the treatments and services their children require. Recognizing the extraordinary challenges military families experience (waging a battle on two fronts...one for their country and another for their children), *ACT Today! for Military Families* is a dedicated fund to assist military families impacted by autism. *ACT Today! for Military Families* works to improve awareness and delivery of effective autism services, and provides financial assistance to military families to help defray out-of-pocket costs associated with autism treatments and other quality of life programs. For more information please go to http://www.acttodayformilitaryfamilies.org/default.aspx.

*Air Force Sponsors Space Camp: The Air Force Services Agency is sponsoring the Air Force Space Camp at the U.S. Space and Rocket Center for eligible 12-to-18 year-olds July 25 through 30, in Huntsville, Ala. The camp is divided into two age divisions: (1) ages 12 to 14 and (2) ages 15 to 18. This program is open to family members of active duty, activated Air National Guard or Reserve, retirees, and Air Force civilian employees. Interested youth with a minimum grade point average of 2.8 can complete a nomination form at the Air Force Space Camp Program webpage at http://www.afyouthprograms.com/spacecamp.htm and submit it to their installation's youth programs. For more information, contact your local Air Force youth programs staff. *This sounds like a lot of fun; this is a camp I would have enjoyed when I was little.*

Air Force Crossroads: This site has lots of things to do: useful tools for your homework and paper-writing projects, video games, sport and art activities, and a bunch of other information and entertainment that will keep you coming back for more, come check out the site. They have other resources for families too. http://www.afcrossroads.com/?site=redirect

American Hero Hugs: This Hero Light is a perfect way for your HERO to shine as a beacon in the night for your little one. *AmericanHeroHugs* night lights are handmade and edged with coordinating red or blue ribbon and personalized with a picture you upload of your HERO.   www.americanherohugs.com

Army Child, Youth & School Service Programs: Are offered through Army Garrisons, National Guard Family State Program Offices or Reserve Regional Commands.

Army Reserve Child and Youth Services: The Army Reserve Family Program is committed to offering education, training, awareness, outreach, information, referral, and follow-up. Not only do they offer resources for military children there is also information and resources for other areas. http://www.arfp.org/skins/ARFP/home.aspx?mode=user

Believe in Tomorrow Children's Foundation: Mission is to support critically ill children of U.S. military families. http://www.believeintomorrow.org/housing_military.html

Boys & Girls Club (BGC): Has an extra program called "Military Outreach" for military children, who do not live on bases and do not receive the same care that military children would get who live on a military base. A new program called "Mission, Youth Outreach" which donates $100 to every military child to cover the annual membership fee and other expenses at the BGC. Military children are able to access all BGC services, such as Power Hour, a tutoring program, and Skill Tech, a program that nurtures technical skills. But most importantly, Guard kids can receive recognition and encouragement for their daily achievements at the BGC. The BGC is opening its doors to all military children and accepts children ages 6-18. Parents can call (800) 854-CLUB to find the nearest Boys & Girls Club. Go to www.bgca.org/military for more information.

4-H National Headquarters: Provides information to connect military youth to 4-H Programs in their hometowns. http://www.4-h.org/ Make sure you check with your state for event and programs that are offered only in your state for military families.

Dads at a Distance: This is a resource for helping fathers who spend long periods of time away from their children keep the relationship strong. http://daads.com/

*Daddy Dolls: Provides a doll with the service members' face on it; through a picture the child will be able to hug their parent. *It is really cute; my daughter had one of these. It's a very thoughtful gesture.* http://www.hugahero.com

Department of Defense, Special Needs Parent Toolkit: This kit has comprehensive information and tools that are geared towards helping military families with special needs children navigate the maze of medical and special education services, community support and benefits and entitlements. The toolkit is broken down into six colorful modules that can be easily downloaded and printed. The kit includes important facts, records, tools and sample letters. Whether you need to learn about early intervention services or want to learn how to be more effective advocate for your child, you will find the information you are searching for here. http://www.military.com/spouse/content/military-education/military-children-education/tools-for-special-needs-parents.html, and http://www.militaryhomefront.dod.mil/pls/psgprod/f?p=MHF:DETAIL1:0::::SID,CID:20.40.500.565.0.0.0.0.0,20.40.500.565.500.100.64.0.0

Department of Veterans Affairs for Kids: Provides useful tools and resources for military families. http://www.va.gov/kids/

Deployment Kids: This site offers a variety of items and resources in the form of kids to military kids to help them through deployments. http://www.deploymentkids.com

*Dog Tags for Kids: This is a wonderful group that will send an appropriate colored dog tag to the military member, inscribed for him/her to send home to their child. *Our daughter was 14 when she got this from her father. She wore it while he was deployed, stating that she felt closer to him and she was wearing it in his honor and to show support. He is not currently deployed but she still wears it. She thinks it is very cool!* www.dogtagsforkids.com

Dog Tags, Military Coins, etc: These are a couple of grassroots organizations showing support for the troops and their families. They thought of things that they could send Dad or Mom that they could easily send back to their kids. These are some of the things that they came up with that is easy to ship and something the kids can hang on to until Dad or Mom gets back home.

- www.dogtagsforkids.com has military brat dog tags and military brat coins available in each branch of service. Crest of the military wife is also available for purchase
- www.militarybrat.com sells plush uniformed teddy bears, army brat

dog tags, "My Dad Fights for our Freedom" coin

- www.miluniform.com sells *We Serve Too! (Be Strong and Courageous!)* dog tags and *We Serve Too! (We just make the best of it)* dog tags. www.weservetoo.com

*4 Military Families: Lots of military resources in all areas for military families and their dependents. *I love this website!* http://www.4militaryfamilies.com

*Geocaching: Geocaching is a high-tech treasure hunting game played throughout the world by adventure seekers equipped with GPS devices. The basic idea is to locate hidden containers, called geocaches, outdoors and then share your experiences online. Geocaching is enjoyed by people from all age groups, with a strong sense of community and support for the environment. www.geocaching.com. *My husband and daughter enjoy doing this together.*

Getting to Know Your Children Again: This resource will help the service member with the struggles of reintegration back into the home; teaching them step-by-step skills they can use to learn about their children again. Rebuilding trust and closeness takes time. Remember that children want to be close again but they don't always know exactly what to do. Hopefully these tips can help: http://www.military.com/deployment You can also take some pre-emptive steps in their program Preparing to Say Goodbye: http://www.survivingdeployment.com/preparegoodbye.html.

Hero Helpers - Lifesize Cardboard Cutout of your Military Service Member: LifeSizeCustomCutouts.com has launched a special program for military families with a loved one currently deployed on active duty. Hero Helpers are life size cardboard cutouts made from any picture you send in. www.hero-helpers.com

A Heart Apart (by Melissa Seligman, Christina Piper): Is for children 4-8 years. The thought behind this resource is that too often the focus is on the uniform; on the service member that is serving overseas. But what of the countless children who have served silently, over and over again, through sustained deployments? Where are their news stories and accounts of bravery? What about medals for their sacrifice? Their time spent, waiting?

This book is different in that it encourages children to create and share their own unique stories, upload their own photos then share it with their deployed parent overseas. Each deployment is different. And each military child is special. Taking the time to celebrate each child's uniqueness is essential in helping our war children on the road to healing and recovery. Each picture uploaded is a window into their hearts, and if a picture is worth a thousand words, these children have volumes to tell. These children serve bravely and repeatedly. They deserve the opportunity to share their story, honor their struggle, and salute their victory. Every hero should be celebrated. Seligman and Piper have written *"A Heart Apart"* to celebrate and honor the very warriors we admire most: our own children. **Free copy for service member with each purchase**. Also available; free downloadable activity sheets to complement the book http://www.herwarhervoice.com/aheartapart.

Deployment Kits and Journaling:
* http://www.militaryfamilybooks.com
* http://www.survivingdeployment.com
* http://www.survivingdeployment.com/journalingkids.html

HOOAH 4 Kids: Games, activities, information and more! http://www.hooah4kids.org

HOOAH 4 TEENS: Teens get connected with issues that are important to them, including scholarship information. http://www.hooah4kids.org

*Horses4Heroes: Based in Las Vegas and founded in 2006, mission is to make horseback riding affordable for, and accessible to, active duty service members and women, veterans, first responders, and their families as well as at risk youth, families and individuals with special needs and other whose lives would be enriched by equestrian activities, mounted and un-mounted. For all ages. Participants learn valuable leadership and team work skills, make new friends and develop a lifelong love of horses. *This sounds awesome. Wish we had one in Michigan.* http://horses4hereos.org/

Letterboxing: Letterboxing is an intriguing pastime combining navigational skills and rubber stamp artistry in a charming "treasure hunt" style outdoor quest. A wide variety of adventures can be found to suit all ages and experience levels. Click on the link to explore this fast-growing hobby. A great way to break up a road trip with a little treasure-hunt! www.letterboxing.org

Little Patriots Embraced: Mission is to help reduce the emotional and psychological stress that military family members have due to the separation, relocation or death of a loved one. They also thank military family members with a special focus on the children, for their sacrifices for our country by sending a Little Patriot Embraced family deployment package full of wonderful items for the use of military children. http://www.littlepatriotembraced.org

Military Teens: Assistance for teens on the move and MTOM for kids. http://www.defenselink.mil/mtom/

Military Teens on the Move (MTOM) and MTOM for Kids: "Life's an adventure, according to MTOM", and this site is full of tips to help military youth get the most from it. Helping kids and teens cope with relocation, the site offers practical information about installations, communities, and schools, along with ways to weather the pre- and post-move adjustment period. They have many other resources too. http://www.operationwearehere.com

Military Youth on the Move: Moving can be really exciting, but it can also be hard on military kids. The sadness and worry about losing friends, the dread of starting all over again in a new school with no knowledge of the area or friends can be in some case too much. Don't worry you are not alone, this site was created with you and many other children, just like you. This site covers topics specifically for military youth, like dealing with deployment and moving to a new location, but also everyday youth topics, like dealing with divorce, getting enough exercise and making money. Please take the time to check this site out; I think you may enjoy it. http://apps.mhf.dod.mil/pls/psgprod/f?p=MYOM:HOME:1892216818464793

My Huggy: My Huggy gives you 20 minutes of recording time to share your thoughts, feelings, wisdom, values, advice, and the love you have for your kids, in your words. My Huggy lets your personality shine through. With My Huggy nothing has to be left unspoken. Let them get to know you more, let them feel your love and support, let them hear your words of encouragement when they are sad, lonely, or discouraged. Let them hear their favorite story or that special song you sing over, and over, and over again. You can even record something fun and silly, just to bring a smile to their face. Let them know you love them, let them know no matter what you are always there for them. Whenever they want or need you, they just hug My Huggy, and feel your love and presence. www.myhuggy.com

Toys for Tots Foundation: This is a great program put in place by the United States Marines to assist low income families with toys for the holidays. But it is so much more. Please take the time to review the web site and see how they assist with literacy programs and assistance for the Native Americans and more. http://www.toysfortots.org.

ATHLETICS, CAMPS & YOUTH DEVELOPMENT

ChalleNGe Mission: To intervene in the life of an at-risk youth and produce a program graduate with the values, skills, education and self-discipline necessary to succeed as an adult. http://www.ng.mil/jointstaff/zc/ay/challenge/default.aspx

Civil Air Patrol: In 1948, Congress passed the Public Law establishing Civil Air Patrol as the auxiliary of the new U.S. Air Force. The three primary mission areas are: aerospace education, cadet programs, and emergency services. This is a great program to assist youth with growth, team work, and work ethics along with a goal for their future. Please take the time to review their website. http://www.gocivilairpatrol.com/about/

*Knights of Heroes: Mission is to provide young men and women who have lost their fathers in military service the opportunity to experience character-building events with the positive support of an adult mentor. They develop lasting friendships with similarly situated kids from across the country while participating in exciting outdoor activities in Colorado. The five elements of the "knights' code" are instilled through exposure to caring and compassionate men and women in an outdoor high adventure setting. *This organization really impresses me; I would love to visit it sometime.* http:// knightsofheroes.org/

Military Competitions: The National Guard Bureau sponsors a Military Competitions Program that allows National Guard members to compete in Department and Outside Continental United States (OCONUS) competitions representing the National Guard Bureau. The program encompasses four types of events: marathon, marksmanship, biathlon and parachuting. Nebraska, Arkansas, Vermont and Rhode Island, respectively, provide event coordinators. http://www.ng.mil/jointstaff/zc/ay/default.aspx Email:nggb-zc-ay@ng.army.mil Fax: 703-607-1744

STARBASE Mentors Kids: The STARBASE-Atlantis academy San Diego recently launched the first Navy version of the new Department of Defense (DOD) STARBASE 2.0 mentoring program for sixth-graders from a local elementary school. DOD STARBASE 2.0 is an effort to combine Science, Technology, Engineering and Math (STEM) activities in a relationship rich, school-based environment to provide enrichment for at-risk youth making the transition from elementary to middle school. There are more than 60 DOD STARBASE programs throughout the U.S. and Puerto Rico. For more information on STARBASE, visit the STARBASE website and the NETC website. For a full article on this program, visit http://www.military.com/news/article/starbase-program-mentors-at-risk-kids.html. or http://www.military.com/military-report/navy-starbase-mentors-kids?ESRC=miltrep.nl

Military Teen Adventure Camps: Thanks to a special partnership between the Department of Defense and Office of Military Community & Family Policy, the Department of Agriculture's National Institute of Food and Agriculture, and the nation's Cooperative Extension Service, military teens ages 14-18 in all service branches got to experience adventure camp opportunities the summer of 2011 throughout many different states.

The summer of 2011, Ohio State University Extension joined the partnership and offered three different camps: The Military Teen Adventure Camp, Adventure Restoration Camp and Special Needs Adventure Camp. Teens got to meet other military children from across United States while exploring camp, experience high rope courses, rappelling, cooking on a backpack stove, races and learning to wilderness navigate, backcountry cooking, basic wilderness first aid, river crossings, leave no trace and much more. Visit http://www.ohio4h.org/adventurecamp to see about 2012 camps and/or visit http://go.osu.edu/militaryteenadventurecamps to find out about all the other opportunities around the United States in 2011-2012. You can also go to http://www.operationmilitarykids.org/public/home/aspx-OMK National and http://operationmilitarykids.ohio4h.org/ - OMK & Ohio 4-H for further teen opportunities.

National Guard Family Youth Program: This site hopes to help military families with the ever-changing face and duties of the National Guard; and achieve readiness for what's ahead while remaining flexible in the present. The site offers many resources, programs and assistance that are provided to service members, spouses, parents and our youth. http://www.jointservicessupport.org/FP/Default.aspx

National Guard Youth Challenge Program: Great resource for military children to come together and make a difference. http://www.ngycp.org/site

National Military Family Association: Resources for military children. http://www.nmfa.org

National Guard Athletics & Youth Development: The Office of Military Competitions mission is to advise the Chief, National Guard Bureau, establish policy and guidance for the administration of the Marathon, Biathlon, Leapfest and Marksmanship**.**

National Guard Youth Online Community: Activities for all ages including deployment guides: Click on your state for more information at http://www.jointservicessupport.org/FP/default/aspx.

*National Guard "Patriot Academy" for Students: The Patriot Academy is a pilot program from the National Guard Bureau that offers a high school diploma opportunity for at-risk youth wanting to serve their country in the Army National Guard. The school opened its doors Aug 26th, 2009, and graduated its first class in March the following year. Students of the Patriot Academy have to join the National Guard, and they receive pay and benefits while attending the program. For more information, visit the National Guard Patriot Academy website, http://njpatriotacademy.com *I give this a thumbs up, I know a couple kids that should go to this…*☺

*Naval Sea Cadet Corps: This great programs mission is to assist military family's youth through organization and cooperation with the Department of Navy, to encourage and aid American youth to develop, train them in seagoing skills, and to teach them patriotism, courage, self-reliance and kindred virtues. *Please take the time to go to this website at* http://www.seacadets.org *and see what they have to offer.*

Operation Give a Hug Dolls: Keeping deployed loved ones close during deployment, Give a Hug Doll allows little heroes to take the service member they miss with them wherever they go. Email request to dollrequest@ operationmilitarykids.org or visit the website at www.operationgiveahug.org. www.facebook.com/operationgiveahug.

*Operation Homefront: Will provide back to school supplies and backpacks, Easter baskets and assistance with Christmas for military families. Active duty families get priority. I have listed the National website but look to your state for an Operation Homefront near you. http://www.operationhomefront.net *This is a great resource and has done a lot for military families. Our family has used this organization in the past and I also know several different military families that were blessed with their assistance too.*

*Operation Military Kids: The U.S. Army's collaborative effort with America's communities to support children and youth of **ALL BRANCHES** of military deployments. Whether families are experiencing deployment for the first time, the second or another in a series of multiple deployments, OMK's goal is to connect military children and youth with local resources in order to achieve a sense of community support and enhance their well-being. OMK will provide a variety of assistance to military children.

The American Legion Auxiliary, Boys & Girls Club and MSU Extension County offices donated time, money and material to this organization to help valuable information and resources get to military families, these are called "hero packs". OMK provides summer camps and a variety of fun days put together so military children can get out and meet other kids who have family members deployed. In Michigan, OMK works daily with an Army National Guard Youth Programmer to provide save and useful information for military families. Check with your local department. *They also work with your local 4H Clubs and some things are free of charge. This is a great resource.* http://www. operationmilitarykids.org

Operation MOM: A support group and a site full of resources for families of all branches of service. http://www.operationmom.org/

*Operation Purple Camp: Funding through National Military Family Association provides a safe and fun environment for military children. The National Military Family Association's Operation Purple camps are a time for having fun, making friends, and reminding military kids that they are the Nation's youngest heroes. The mission of the Operation Purple program is to empower military children and their families to develop and maintain healthy and connected relationships, in spite of the current military environment. They do this through a variety of means, including the healing and holistic aspect of the natural world. The program is joint or "purple" and open to children and families of active duty, National Guard or Reserve service members from the

Army, Navy, Air Force, Marine Corps, Coast Guard, or the Commissioned Corps of the US Public Health Service and NOAA.The Operation Purple program also includes camps for teens, family retreats at the national parks, and camps geared to address the needs of children and families of our nations wounded service members. Please direct questions regarding the Operation Purple program to OPC@militaryfamily.org. *This is a wonderful organization. Hopefully someday my daughter can attend one of these camps; I have heard awesome comments about these camps.* http://www.militaryfamily.org/our-programs/operation-purple/

*Our Military Kids:** Provides tangible support to the children of all branches of active duty deployed including and severely injured wounded warriors' and National Guard soldiers and Reserves in the form of grant money for fine arts, sports, and tutoring that nurture and sustain the children during the time their parent is away. Grant is in the form of $500 and is paid to the company. You may use this grant twice during the deployment and EACH child in your household is entitled to a grant. *I LOVE this grant! They are so considerate and the turnaround is very fast. I would not have been able to get the tutoring needed for our daughter without this organization. I cannot speak enough on how wonderful they are.* http://www.ourmilitarykids.org/

Operation Outreach Christmas: Is through Soldier's Angels and their mission is to adopt military families for the holiday season. Nothing personal will ever be asked or solicited. If you would like to nominate a military family or nominate your selves for Operation Outreach Christmas please complete the questionnaire, and return it to cvink@soldiersangels.org.

*Operation We Are Here:** This is a wonderful website that offers 24 different organizations that dedicate their time to training service dogs, home companion dogs and residential companion dogs to assist individuals who have a wide range of physical and cognitive disabilities for children and wounded warriors and veterans. Please take the time to review each organization as they differ in locations and abilities. All are wonderful organizations. The website has other information about military families that will be of interest to you also. http://www.operationwearehere.com/MilitaryServiceDogs.html and http://www.operationwearehere.com

Over There Activity Book (Daddy version, Mommy version): Here is an opportunity to create your own "Over There" children's book! Download the PDF (either the mommy version or the daddy version, depending on which parent is deployed), print it out, and attach photos that represent the spirit of the text. If you and your child are feeling extra creative, you can even draw your own illustrations. Do whatever feels right to capture your family's unique deployment story. After completing the book, keep it on hand and read it to your child as often as each of you would like. www.zerotothree.org

Purple Heart Ranch (Sterling City, TX) - Military Warriors Hero Support Foundation: Purple Heart Ranch is open exclusively to combat wounded heroes and to Gold Star families. The ranch is also open to children of combat wounded heroes and those who have a parent currently deployed to a combat zone. Both the families of the wounded heroes and the parents of the children are encouraged to come and enjoy the experience with the hunters. There is fishing available at both properties and many other activities for the families. Both ranches are rich in history and are littered with Native American artifacts, especially arrow heads. http://militarywarriors.org/skills4life

Real Time Activities with Deployed Parent: Allows you to read interactive books, play games and do activities with your child in real time from anywhere in the world. The site allows users to see and hear one another while they read books, play games and do art activities together—all in real time. Free for military families. www.mychildmymilitary.com

Sesame Street Family Connections: The Defense Centers of Excellence for Psychological Health and Traumatic Brain Injury (DCoE) in collaboration with Sesame Street Workshop recently unveiled the "Sesame Street Family Connections" website. This interactive website, similar to Facebook, allows Soldiers, Sailors, Airmen, Marines and their families to stay connected in a safe and nurturing environment surrounded by their favorite Sesame Street friends. It's a private place where only the family and friends you invite can post messages, create and share artwork, upload photos and record videos. www.sesamestreetfamilyconnections.org

*SesameWorkshop: Provides resources for military children in the form of books, tapes and deployment kits. *I have seen the material from this organization and it is very useful for military children. I thought the video tapes were very cute.* http://www.sesameworkshop.org/initiatives/emotion/tic

Sittercity: This site provides free access to hundreds of local quality babysitters and nannies in your neighborhood. You can review detailed sitter profiles featuring their experience, background checks, references, reviews and photos. Membership is available at no cost to all Army, Marines, Navy and Air Force families (active and Reserve Guard). In addition to quality local babysitters and nannies, you can also find elder care providers, dog walkers, housekeepers and tutors. Go to www.sittercity.com/dod for more information.

*Talkatoo: This is a really cool recordable key chain, designed for kids (yet hip for parents), it comes as a necklace or as a clip-on charm for backpacks, lunchboxes, purses or even belt loops. Just press the little button to record a message, then the big one to hear it back (repeat as desired). From silly to sentimental, it's perfect for whenever you're apart. 30 seconds of recording time. Lockout switch protects messages. *This looks so cool, I plan on ordering one.* www.talkatoo.com

*Thousand Thanks for Military Kids: This project is a partnership with Warner Brothers and their Looney Tunes characters. Children of deployed service members receive a letter from the parent's choice of cartoon characters (Bugs Bunny, Daffy Duck, Scooby Doo, etc.). The letter thanks the child for sharing their deployed parent to make the world a better place. There is no charge for this service and letters can be requested from a simple form on the Salute Our Services web site at http://saluteourservices.org/main/page_thousand_thanks. html. For more information or questions you can email sos@saluteservices.org or call (703) 234-1773. *Very cute! Too bad our daughter is a teenager; she would have enjoyed this when she was little.*

Tikatok: Creating a book with Tikatok is a simple and fun way for you and your child to express imagination and creativity. www.tikatok.com
1.   Write your story.
2.   Add pictures.
3.   Order your book (hard cover, soft cover, or e-book download)

The Patriot Academy: Patriot Academy is a five-day leadership and political training camp for students ages 16-25 and is held each summer in Austin, TX. Students experience the political process from the inside out as they file legislation, debate bills, campaign for office and pass laws. In addition, students are trained in media skills, public speaking, leadership, today's issues and America's heritage, all from a Biblical worldview. Conservative leaders from all areas of the political field mentor students through the process, sharing their experience and wisdom.

Students are housed at the DoubleTree Guest Suites, within walking distance of the Texas State Capitol. All training is held at the Capitol. Students use the Capitol committee rooms and meeting rooms and present their bills on the Floor of the Texas House of Representatives. For more information about scholarships, costs and the foundations and skills that they learn, go to http://www.patriotacademy.com/about-2/.

Upward Sports: This is a great organization that will assist military kids of deployed parents with sports. For more information go to www.upward.org/military.

*United Through Reading: They issue kits to soldiers so they can tape their voices reading books. These books and tapes are mailed to the children of the soldier's family. *My husband mailed one to our daughter and all his nieces and nephews. They absolutely loved these. Great organization!!* http://www.unitedthroughreading.org/military/

*USS KIDD: *I am adding the program to the book because it is a wonderful opportunity offered through the collaboration of Louisiana Army National Guard Reintegration Office's Child and Youth Program, Louisiana Operation*

Military Kids, and the 4-H Program once a year to host an overnight event and several camps for military children throughout the year. Go to http://www. arng.army.mil/News/Pages/LouisianaGuardsmen,FamiliesSpendNightonUSS Kidd.aspx *for more information on the wonderful opportunities in the great state of Louisiana. This is a perfect example of what hard work and great team work can provide. What a great opportunity for children to be a part of.*

*VA Kids – Helping Kids Learn About Being a Vet: The Department of Veterans has designed this site to help kids understand what it means to be a vet. *This is a wonderful site.* http://www.va.gov/kids

VFW National Home for Children: Helps military families in a variety of ways. For example, they have safe and clean homes for families to stay in during their time of need and they assist with food, clothing and education for military children along with other programs. *This is a wonderful organization. I hope other states have one. The state of Michigan does and it has been helpful to many families.* http://www.vfwnationalhome.org

You're Never Far Away (by Jan Krystkowiak): *Where in the World Books*, created by children's author Jan Krystkowiak, are personalized children's books that incorporate the child's name into the story and photos with state of the art print technology. This is a personalized photo book for a child who knows someone in the military. The child's name is in the story and cleverly implemented into the photos. Children feel the story is written only about them. See the look on their faces as they see their name in a cereal bowl, in fireworks, and much more. 26 pages with your child's name in the story over 24 times, plus your child's name on the cover! https://www.webstore.teuteberg.com/wepersonalizeitall/choose. cgi?x=76&y=31

Youth Military Employment Training: http://www.doleta.gov/jobseekers/ youth.cfm

*Young Marines: This mission of the Young Marines is to positively impact America's future by providing quality youth development programs for boys and girls (age eight through 18) that nurtures and develops its members into responsible citizens who enjoy and promote a healthy, drug-free lifestyle. The Young Marines promotes the mental, moral, and physical development of its members. The program focuses on character building, leadership, and promotes a healthy, drug-free lifestyle. The Young Marines is the focal point for the U.S. Marine Corps' Youth Drug Demand Reduction efforts. Please view the website for further information on Training, National Programs and more. http://www. youngmarines.com/ *This looks like a great organization. I would love to go and review one of these summer programs. I think a lot of kids would enjoy going and would learn a lot about themselves and life in general.*

MILITARY FAMILY SUPPORT

The one thing military families need to remember is that it is okay to need assistance and that you are NOT failing when you ask for help. Many little and big issues will come up during every deployment, whether you planned for them or not. These organizations are here to help you and most are CONFIDENTIAL! It does not affect any security clearances to get assistance.

FINANCIAL AND OTHER ASSISTANCE

Army and Air Force Mutual Aid Association (AAFMAA): Provides emergency assistance to Army and Air Force members and families. http://www.aafmaa.com

Army Career and Alumni Program: The Army Career and Alumni Program (ACAP) provides Soldiers and their eligible family members transition and job assistance services at most Army installations. ACAP services include pre-separation counseling and employment assistance.

For more information go to: http://myarmybenefits.us.army.mil/Home/
Benefit_Library/Federal_Benefits_Page/Army_Career_and_Alumni_
Program_(ACAP).html.

Army Community Covenant: This program is designed to foster and sustain
effective state and community partnerships with the Army to improve the
quality of life for soldiers and their families, both at their current duty stations
and as they transfer to other states. It is a formal commitment of support by state
and local communities to Soldiers and Families of the Army (Active, Guard
and Reserve). While Community Covenant is an Army program, it extends to
the other military services as well, recognizing that many community efforts
support all service members and their families regardless of the uniform they
wear. http://www.army.mil/community/

Army Community Services: The Army Community Service Center is a
resource haven for soldiers and family members. The many programs offered
within are designed to enhance and directly deal with quality of life issues and
needs. http://www.drummwr.com/ArmyCommunityService.htm

***Army Family Health Care:** This site offers information about TRICARE,
dental, life insurance, family members with special needs and more. This is a
pretty informative website. *You will be surprised at all they discuss. Please
review this site at* http://www.goarmy.com/soldier-life/army-family-strong/
health-care/family-health-care.html.

Air Force Aid Society: Provides emergency assistance to Air Force members
and families. http://www.afas.org

Air Force Services: The Air Force Services team provides mission sustaining
combat support and community service to Airmen and their families every day
at deployed and home station locations. Their contribution to the Air Force
mission is evident in their involvement in worldwide deployments. They are
there feeding troops, managing tent cities, operating field exchanges, attending
to fallen comrades, and providing fitness activities and off-duty sports
programs. Air Force Services delivers a unique capability anywhere in support
of Global Reach and Global Power. http://www.afsv.af.mil/

Air Force Reserve, U.S. – USAFR – DoD: Provides emergency assistance to
soldiers, airmen, Reserves and their families. http://www.afreserve.com

Air National Guard, U.S. – ANG: Provides emergency assistance to soldiers
and their families. http://www.ang.af.mil

***America Supports You**: A 501(c)3 non-profit organization out of Texas that
supports military service members and their families by promoting public
awareness across the United States. They provide support by assisting currently
deployed military service members and their families with financial assistance
to meet the emergency needs that arise from deployments. They host various
family support activities, Welcome Home Rallies, and Return to Duty Rallies

for military members. They support and host patriotic events, parades on all military holidays, host and sponsor the annual America Supports You Texas Cookout honoring our military, veterans and their families. They also host and sponsor the annual Armed Forces Day "Celebrating Freedom & Honoring Service" Banquet and the annual Washington, DC Veterans Tour, honoring Texas Veterans. For emergency assistance go to: http://americasupportsyou. mil *I hear a lot about this organization in the news, wonderful group.*

*Army Emergency Relief Fund: Provides emergency financial assistance in the form of grants and no interest loans to Army soldiers and their families. You can go to any American Red Cross for assistance with this organization. *I have used this organization to assist military families and they are a great organization. You will need certain documentation and a current ID card to be given assistance. Wonderful organization!* http://aerhg.org

Armed Force Relief Trust: Provides contact information and useful information to Army Emergency Relief, Coast Guard Mutual Assistance, Air Force Aid Society and Navy – Marine Corps Relief Society. http://www. afrtrust.org/contact.asp

Coast Guard Reserve: Provides emergency financial assistance for Coast Guard Reservists and their families. http://uscg.mil/reserve/

Coast Guard Mutual Assistance: Within the limits of CGMA policies as described in the Coast Guard Mutual Assistance Manual, when verified, documented and justified, assistance is provided for families. Assistance can be provided for emergency, medical and dental, survivor, general, education, housing and more. Please go to the website for further information and applications. http://www.cgmahq.org/Assistance/programs.html

Federal Employee Educational Assistance Fund: This is the only non-profit organization dedicated solely to helping civilian federal and postal employees. FEEA provides assistance through three signature programs and partnered with over a dozen membership organizations, unions and federal agencies to administer special programs that are available only to members. The three areas programs are: Scholarship Competition, Emergency Financial Assistance and Child Care Subsidy. For further information about these programs and eligibility requirements go to http://www.feea.org/.

Military.Com Base Guides: Is sponsored by NFCU, and is your one-stop source for what you need to know about life on base or in the city around your area. Get the scoop on your area now. http://military.com/baseguide

Military Family Support Centers, Inc: Provides support and information to families of deployed service members including military and civilian programs and benefits, telecommunication services such as video conferencing, broadband Internet access, support groups, home and car repair assistance, transportation, child care, food and clothing, counseling and more. www. milfamily.org/

Military 4 Life: Is a website dedicated to military families and work daily to bring the latest information about military pay, MWR, military lifestyle, discounts, education and more. http://military4life.com/

National Veterans Foundation: Mission is to serve the crisis management, information and referral needs of all U.S. veterans and their families through the management and operation of the nation's only toll-free helpline for all veterans and their families. Assist with public awareness programs and assist with outreach programs that provide veterans and families with food, clothing, transportation, employment and other essential resources. http://www.nvf.org/about-us

Navy Community Services: The Navy Community Service Center is a resource haven for seamen and family members. The many programs offered within are designed to enhance and directly deal with quality of life issues and needs. http://www.cnic.navy.mil/NDW/About/CommunityServices/index.htm

Navy-Marine Corps Relief Society: Provides, in partnership with the Navy and Marine Corps, financial, educational, and other assistance to members of the Naval Services of the United States, eligible family members, and survivors when in need; and to receive and manage funds to administer these programs. http://www.nmcrs.org

Navy Fleet and Family Support Center: Provides emergency assistance to sailors and their families. http://www.nffsp.org

Navy Reserve, U.S.: Provides emergency assistance for naval reservists and their families. http://navyreserve.navy.mil

*Operation Homefront: Provides emergency financial assistance and other assistance to service members, wounded warriors and their families. This organization also provides uplifting services in other areas, especially around the holidays. *I worked for this organization and we offered Easter baskets, Christmas and Thanksgiving Baskets, Back to School Supplies and other programs to help military families get through some rough times while lifting their spirits. I can't say enough good things about this organization. They are great!* http://www.operationhomefront.net

Pentagon's Homeowners Assistance Program: Program to assist military families with their homes if they are going through foreclosure. http://www.military.com/news/article/housing-assistance-program-expansion.html.

Reserve Aid: Provides assistance to Reserve and National Guard Members **ONLY.** Soldiers must have been activated and deployed between 1 Jan 2008 to present. Assistance is provided for rent, mortgage, utility bills, car payments and insurance in the form of a onetime payment to companies owed. Maximum grant is $2500. www.reserveaid.org

Supportive Services for Veteran Families: Under this program, the certain agencies in the state of Michigan will be able to provide a range of services to eligible low income veterans and their families. This will include services for rent, utilities, deposits and moving costs. http://www.va.gov/HOMELESS/SSVF.asp

*The American Legion: The American Legion's Family Support Network stands ready to assist you and your family, as you serve our country. They assist with grocery shopping, childcare, lawn care, car care, emergency financial assistance, assistance with scholarships, and countless other challenges to the military spouse. *Great organization, I have worked with them in the past.* http://www.legion.org

The Armed Forces Foundation: Provides comfort and assistance through financial support, career counseling, housing assistance and recreational therapy. Assistance is provided to active duty, retired, National Guard, reserve components and their families. http://www.armedforcesfoundation.org

The G.I.Go Fund: Provides transition assistance to all military veterans, with a focus on veterans from the Iraq and Afghanistan conflicts, by preparing veterans for the twenty first century economy, securing education and health benefits, and providing aid assistance to low income and homeless veterans. http://www.gigofund.org

The Murray Grey Foundation: Provides assistance to serving soldiers and veterans from **ALL** branches in need. The support is in the form of financial assistance to families facing home foreclosure, support for food, clothing, utility payments, transportation, home repairs and other critical resources to military families. The Murray Grey Foundation makes unrestricted need based grants. http://themurraygreyfoundation.org/

*United Service Automobile Association (USAA): Provides financial, banking and insurance services. *Our family uses this service and they are very professional and work to make your life easier. Our family has never had a problem with this organization.* http://www.usaa.com

*Unmet Needs (Veterans of Foreign Wars): This was created to provide emergency financial support to families of military personnel. Funds from donations are available to the five branches of service (Army, Navy, Air Force, Marines and Coast Guard), as well as members of the Reserves and National Guard. Funds awarded by the program are offered in the form of grants, not loans, so recipients don't need to repay them. *Wonderful organization, they assisted my family in 2006 with an issue with our roof. I have also used this organization to assist military families in the past. Great organization!!!* http://www.vfw.org/Assistance/National-Military-Services/

*USA Cares: USA Cares exists to help bear the burdens of service by providing post-9/11 military families with financial and advocacy support in their time of need. Assistance is provided to all branches of service, all components,

Military Family

all ranks while protecting the privacy and dignity of those military families and veterans who request our help. *Wonderful organization, I have used this company to assist many military families. They are a great organization!!* http://usacares.org/

VA Home Loans Foreclosure: Provides you information to assist you and your families to avoid foreclosure. http://www.benefits.va.gov/homeloans

Vet Success: This site provides assistance with a variety of military family needs from job resources, benefits and more. http://www.vetsuccess.gov/

*Veterans of Foreign Wars (VFW): Offers a vast amount of resources to military families. From burial, help with retirement or disability paperwork, emergency financial grants, scholarships, food drives, spousal assistance around home when soldier deployed, care packages. The list goes on. *I highly recommend this organization, they have always been a huge support for military families and I cannot see that ending anytime soon.* http://www. vfw.org

OTHER RESOURCES

Army Housing OneStop: It's time to move and we all know how stressful that can be. Thanks to the One Stop Army website, you can get a sneak preview of what your new post and housing will be like. The Army OneStop site offers information on each post as well as floor plans that are available through on post housing. In addition, you will find maps of the local area and information on temporary lodging that is available both on post and off post. This website is jam packed with information and all you need to know about your new home. http://marriedtothearmy.com/army-housing-onestop-website/

Army and Air Force Mutual Aid Association (AAFMAA): Provides military families with various resources; for example, low cost life insurance, assisting survivors with Survivor Assistance Services, loans and more. Go to http://www.aafmaa.com/AboutUs/Overview.aspx.

Army One Source: Provides family and program services for military families. www.armyonesource.com

Army Reserve Family Program: Provides information on family programs and support, mobilization and readiness, tools, handbooks, news and much more. http://www.arfp.org/skins/ARFP/home.aspx

Coaching into Care: A program launched by Department of Veterans Affairs to provide assistance to family members and friends trying to encourage their veteran to seek VA care in their community. The program offers unlimited, free coaching with family members or friends over a series of telephone calls. Callers can reach VA's Coaching into Care program at the toll-free number 888-823-7458, 8 am-8 pm, Mondays through Fridays and online. As always, veterans can reach immediate help at the Veterans Crisis Line at 800-273-8255, press 1 for veterans. http://www.mirecc.va.gov/coaching/

Coast Guard Work-Life Programs: Coast Guard's Work-Life Program is managed by the Office of Work-Life, a Headquarters program manager staff within the Health, Safety and Work-Life Directorate, reporting to the Assistant Commandant for Human Resources. This staff is responsible for establishing, developing and promulgating Work-Life policy and interpreting program standards for Coast Guard-wide implementation. The overall objective is to support the well-being of active duty, reserve and civilian employees and family members. Please review the site as it offers other helpful information for Coast Guard military families and the service members. http://www.uscj.mil/worklife/

Family Support Network: Military families in need of help can turn to The American Legions Family Support Network. In countless ways, Legionnaires can provide support and services to families affected by the obligations of military service. Families needing help are encouraged to call the toll-free number to get connected with a nearby American Legion Post. Toll free: (800) 504-4098 and forms to seek assistance are available online at www.legion.org.

*Guardian Angels for Soldier's Pets: This organization's mission is supporting our military, veterans, and their beloved pets to ensure the pets are reunited with their owners following a deployment (combat or peace-keeping mission) in harm's way to fight the global war on terrorism or unforeseen emergency hardship impacting their ability to retain their pet's ownership rights. Please go to the website to get further information on eligibility. *I am a huge fan of organizations that assist pets. Love this organization.* http://guardianangelsforsoldierspet.org

Home Alarms: Provides free home alarms systems for military families. Eligibility is for family members of currently deployed service members or service members who will be deploying soon and have been issued his orders. Protect our Troops will provide free alarm system for home, free upgrades for your current alarm system or a home alarm fee reimbursement. For more information, rules and eligibility www.protectourtroops.org.

Iraqi and Afghanistan Veterans of American (IAVA): Connect with other veterans, get access to critical resources, and play a role in tackling issues that impact our community. http://iava.org/membership

Military Community and Family Policy: This newsletter will come to your email each month and offer various information and resources for military families. For further an example of what to expect, this is a sample of an October 2011 newsletter at: http://apps.mhf.dod.mil/pls/psgprod/f?p=EMAG2:COVER:0::::MONTH,YEAR:October,2011. To subscribe for the monthly newsletters go to http://apps.mhf.dod.mil/pls/psgprod/f?p=AMS:SUBSCRIBE:0.

Military Family Books: Offers a variety of books and deployment kits for military children. http://www.militaryfamilybooks.com

*Military Family Network: Is a great resource that lists TONS of resource, some you will see listed in this book. *Check out the website, I give this a star because I liked the website so much.* www.themilitaryfamilynetwork.org

National Guard Family Program: With this website, senior leadership is trying to achieve readiness for what's ahead while remaining flexible in the present. Through the brand new website, family program offices, you can find out about the services, programs and assistance that are provided for service members, spouses, parents and military children. http://www.jointservicessupport.org/FP/

National Military Family Association: *LOVED, LOVED this website. It is loaded with resources for all branches of military and veterans. Check it out.* http://www.military.org

Operation Military Family - Support Network, Action Plan, Resources, and Book: As a veteran who traveled many parts of the world, Mike Schindler knew the complexities and adventures surrounding deployments. When his best friend was deployed to Afghanistan, Mike captured his experiences by compiling his friend's notes, emails, pictures and instant messages in order to put them in a keepsake for his best friend's son (Mike's godson).

Like many ideas, it grew into more than a keepsake. Mike went on to interview numerous military couples, marriage experts, chaplains, and support organizations in an effort to uncover what keeps military couples together. Thus was born the book "Operation Military Family" that later became endorsed by leading marriage experts and former Commander in Chief, US Central Command General Tommy Franks.

The book was only the beginning. Couples wanted not only a road map but a peer to peer, mentoring type program. So Mike, along with his wife, Keri, founded the organization Operation Military Family, and set out to develop a mentoring program that would move beyond the classroom and into the community.

Teamwork often makes a dream work with collaboration being the key. Mike teamed up with Jeff Kemp, who is the eldest son of the Honorable Jack Kemp and the president of Stronger Families to ensure this dream became a reality. Stronger Families, formerly Families NW, has been a leader in the marriage movement for over 15 years, having been recognized for dropping divorce rates, helping establish community marriage initiatives, and rallying communities around strengthening relationships.

Now a division of Stronger Families, Operation Military Family delivers "Oxygen for Your Relationship" workshops and seminars to military service members and family members with the help and expertise of the staff at Stronger Families. www.operationmilitaryfamily.org

*Operation Once in a Lifetime: This organization is comparable to "Make a Wish Foundation" but helps only military soldiers and their families participate in a "once in a lifetime events and activities." *This is a wonderful organization and I hope to hear more about it in the future.* http://operationonceinalifetime.com

Operation We Are Here: This is a wonderful website that offers information and links to resources for military families and veterans about retreats, books, youth links, links for parents of service members, emotional support, marriage, and much more. Please review the site at http://www.operationwearehere.com.

Operation Touch: A website designed exclusively for the commissary & exchange shopper. Sign up today for FREE access to coupons, sale prices, recipes, health & lifestyle tips, and contest! www.operationtouch.com

*Project Sanctuary: Is a wonderful non-profit organization whose mission is to provide therapeutic, curative, supportive and recreational activities to veterans, active military personnel, their spouses and children in a leisure environment. Please view the website for further information and eligibility requirements. http://www.projectsanctuary.us/retreats.html. *This retreat looks amazing, I hope to be able to check it out sometime. Looks like a great place to reconnect with your service member and family.*

Save and Invest: Free, unbiased financial information for military families and older investors. Save and Invest is your source for objective answers and unbiased investing resources. They offer a multifaceted program that includes online and on-the ground training to make sure you are supported at every financial milestone. Whether you're saving for a down payment on a home, preparing for deployment or PCS, or putting money away for retirement, Save and Invest wants to help you make smart financial decisions and avoid financial fraud. http://www.saveandinvest.org/Military/index.htm

Sitter City Corporate Program: Military families now have free access to an online network of quality caregivers who can assist with everything from babysitting to dog walking. Sittercity is the nation's largest online source for local babysitters, nannies, elder care providers, dog walkers, housekeepers and tutors, and contains more than a million caregiver profiles. The Sittercity Corporate Program, funded by the Defense Department, offers military families, including active duty, Guard and Reserve, with a paid membership to the site. To get more information and to activate your free membership goes to http://www.sittercity.com/dod.

*Strong Bonds: Strong Bonds Family includes singles, couples, spouses and children, and helps them work together to face the challenges of military life. Children ages eight and up are invited to participate. Strong Bonds Pre- and Re-deployment is designed to help keep families close throughout deployment and reintegrate them after long term separation. These events are scheduled in conjunction with the Yellow Ribbon program to coincide with the Army Force Generation Cycle so that skills can be practiced prior to separation. Events are also scheduled 30, 60 and 90 days after return from deployment. To learn more about Strong Bonds or to find an upcoming event in your area, contact your unit chaplain or visit www.StrongBonds.org. *I have been able to attend this a couple of times here in Michigan and I really enjoyed it and learn great skills. This is money by the military spent well.*

*A Warrior's Wish Foundation: The Warrior Wish Foundation enhances the lives of United States military veterans and their families who are battling a life-limiting illness. Through the fantastic financial support of generous donors, the financial contributions of Veterans' Service Organizations, their volunteer network and corporate partnerships, they are able to grant the wishes of those who have served. A wish may be as simple as a new hearing aid or scooter chair, or as involved as one last family vacation or reunion. http:// awarriorwish.org/. *This is a great organization doing wonderful things.*

Wish 4 Our Heroes: Grants wishes for active duty soldiers, sailors, marines, airmen and their families. The foundation strives to relieve the burdens of family separation, re-integration for deployed soldiers, hardship circumstances, and other means of assistance not covered by existing charities. They do not assist in bill payments or other financial obligations. See website for more information and examples of what this wonderful organization does. http:// wish4heroes.org

CAREER/JOBS

Department of Labor Veterans' Employment & Training Service: To foster, promote, and develop the welfare of the wage earners, job seekers, and retirees of the United States; improve working conditions; advance opportunities for profitable employment; and assure work-related benefits and rights. http:// www.dol.gov/opa/aboutdol/mission.htm

*Employer Support of Guard and Reserve (ESGR): www.esgr.mil. *Great group of people, they work hard to maintain service member's rights.*

RETREATS FOR MILITARY FAMILIES

Coming Home Project–California: Offers free, confidential and professional service providers along with group support and stress management retreats for OIF and OEF veterans, service members and their families. A multidisciplinary team of veterans, family members, psychotherapists and interfaith leaders, are devoted to providing innovative, compassionate care to address the mental, emotional, and spiritual and relationship problems veterans and service member's face. For more information and eligibility requirements, go to http://www.cominghomeproject.net/retreats.

Compass Retreat Center (Loveland, Ohio): Provides a supportive setting for National Guard Members, Reservists and their families following deployment with emphasis on renewing relationships and strengthening family bonds. www.compassretreatcenter.org

DET3 FOUNDATION: Mission is to make life a bit brighter for the troops, and also for the children around them. They will try to help in any way they can. See site for examples of their generosity. http://www.det3.us/whatwedo.html

Disabled Veterans Rest Camp (Washington County, Minnesota): This camp provides and facilities opportunities for recreation, rest, and wellbeing for all women and men who have served or are serving in the Armed Forces of the United States, along with their families. The campground is open to all military personnel in good standing: Active duty, Reservists/Guard, veterans, disabled, retirees, families and friends. www.vetscampmn.org

House in the Woods, Inc. (Maine): A free, outdoor self-help program, which remains flexible to the needs of those who serve. The only expense to participants is their transportation to Lee, Maine. Using the recreational, therapeutic, and educational properties of Maine's great wilderness and outdoor heritage, we form short-term retreats for participants to meet others with common military-related challenges and experiences. Activities are led by licensed Maine guides and staffed with caring volunteers and assistance from the local VA Center and health professionals from the community upon request. Maine is a four-season climate, so activities will be dependent on weather and availability. http://houseinthewoods.org/Home.html

Hunters Helping Soldiers: The mission of *Hunters Helping Soldiers* is to provide a means to enhance physical and emotional healing through comradely during hunting and fishing trips as well as mentorship to help ease the transition from military life to civilian life and help families of returning, wounded, and mortally wounded soldiers cope with the challenges they face. www.huntershelpingsoldiers.org

Operation Oasis at Sandy Cove (Maryland): Sandy Cove Ministries has created Operation Oasis as a way to say thank you for the sacrifices made by our military with the goal of making Sandy Cove an "oasis" for moms and dads and boys and girls–a place to rest and reconnect with one another after deployment.

Any service man or woman, including those in the Reserve and National Guard, returning home from deployment in support of OIF or OEF can come to Sandy Cove with their immediate family for FREE! This includes comfortable accommodations in the Chesapeake Lodge or Pioneer Campground cabins, all meals, recreation and program if scheduled. Five-nights for a family of four would normally cost up to $2100, but through generous donations, Sandy Cove is able to offer this as a FREE gift to military families to help you bond together and relax in a Christian atmosphere. www.sandycove.org

Operation Open Arms (SW Florida, Eastern Maryland): Is a nationally acclaimed military outreach program. Founded in 2005, *OOA* has a very simple mission statement: "To provide US servicemen/women visiting SW FL or the Eastern Shore of Maryland every conceivable benefit during their two week combat leave or return from any foreign duty station." *Operation Open Arms* provides extraordinary benefits such as free limo service, lodging, restaurants, fishing charters, golf, tennis, bowling, kayaking, biking, emergency dental care, and a cutting edge approach for the treatment of PTSD. *Operation Open Arms* is self-administrating. There is no paid staff or volunteers to assist you. Making a reservation or appointment within OOA is no different than making arrangements within the military. All *Operation Open Arms* sponsors will require a DA-31 and valid military ID prior to hotel stays, golf, fishing charters, or any other benefits. All *OOA* participants will be as punctual and cooperative as your days in basic training. http://www.operationopenarms.com/

Operation Purple Family Retreats - National Military Family Assoc. Family Retreats: Operation Purple Family Retreats are designed to allow families to reconnect after experiencing the stresses surrounding a deployment. They are a great opportunity to spend time outdoors, try new things, make friends, and enjoy quality time together as a family. These four-day retreats take place in beautiful National Parks and are led by experienced outdoor educators. www.militaryfamily.org/our-programs/operation-purple/family-retreats/

Operation R&R - (South Carolina): Reconnect after deployment on Hilton Head Island at little or no cost. Operation R&R is a non-profit organization designed to provide our service men and women an opportunity to reconnect with their spouses and children upon their return from Iraq or Afghanistan. Property owners, represented by many property management companies, are donating their homes and villas on Hilton Head Island, SC for this purpose. All of this is to ensure that our military families have a chance to spend some time away from their everyday lives to strengthen relationships that have been strained due to long separations and extreme circumstances. www.operationrestandrelax.org

Purple Heart Ranch (Sterling City, TX): Military Warriors Hero Support Foundation: Purple Heart Ranch is open exclusively to combat wounded heroes and to Gold Star families. The ranch is also open to children of combat wounded heroes and those who have a parent currently deployed to a combat zone. Both the families of the wounded heroes and the parents of the children are encouraged to come and enjoy the experience with the hunters. There is fishing available at both properties and many other activities for the families. Both ranches are rich in history and are littered with Native American artifacts, especially arrowheads. http://militarywarriors.org/skills4life

HEALTH

Caregiver Access: Military families have FREE access to an online network of quality caregivers who can assist with everything from babysitting to dog walking through SitterCity. The Sittercity Corporate Program, funded by the Defense Department, offers military families, including active duty, Guard and Reserve, with a paid membership to the site. The paid membership enables military families entry to a custom-built Defense Department website portal where they can match up caregivers to their situation; gain instant access to caregiver profiles that include background checks, references and reviews; and find military-certified care providers as well as caregivers who are military-subsidized and authorized access to a military installation. Military members and their families can activate their membership by going to http://www.sittercity.com/dod.

Coast Guard Community Services: The Army Community Service Center is a resource haven for soldiers and family members. The many programs offered within are designed to enhance and directly deal with quality of life issues and needs.   http://www.military.com/Community/Home/1,14700,COASTG,00.html

Exceptional Family Member Program: The Military Services use the term Exceptional Family Member Program (EFMP) to refer to two different functions: a personnel function and a family support function; it was put in place to ensure that military members and their families with health or special needs get the medical care and assistance that they require. http://www.public.navy.mil and http://www.navymil

Family Support During Deployment: Today's military family faces a lifestyle that is comprised of frequent deployments, which results in increased family separations. This often proves to be a stressful challenge for military families. To assist the military's efforts to keep both troops and their families prepared, there are several programs supporting the readiness of families. The information in this section will assist ALL service members and their families in preparing for and coping with deployments. This site contains family support links for each of the services, as well as information for children, locating service members and deployment entitlements. http://fhp.osd.mil/deploymentTips.jsp

HOOAH 4 Parents: Is geared towards parents of children of all ages. Many of these pages will concentrate on the needs of parents from pregnancy to talking with your teenager. There is also information for veterans and health information for family members who are over 50. http://www.hooah4health.com/4life/hooah4parents/default.htm

In Our Hearts: Blue Star Banners for deployed families to display. www.inourhearts.org

Marine Corps Community Services: The Army Community Service Center is a resource haven for soldiers and family members. The many programs offered within are designed to enhance and directly deal with quality of life issues and needs. http://usmc-mccs.org/

Military HomeFront: Is the official Department of Defense website for reliable Quality of Life information designed to help troops and their families, leaders and service providers. Whether you live the military lifestyle or support those who do, you'll find what you need. This site will provide information about pre-deployment, deployment and reintegration. Go to http://www.militaryhomefront.dod.mil/.

Military OneSource: Education, health, relocation, parenting, stress—you name it—Military OneSource can help with just about any need. Available by phone or online, this free service is provided by the Department of Defense for active-duty, Guard, and Reserve service members and their families. The service is completely private and confidential, with few exceptions. http://www.militaryonesource.com/MOS.aspx

7-Day Love Challenge: This is a program set up as a challenge for your married relationship. Each day a simple challenge will be given to you in hopes that you will take it on and see a new spark start within your marriage, or will continue to fan the flame that is already burning. The daily challenges are simple and the benefits undeniable. The *7-Day Love Challenge* is renewing romance and bringing marriages into deeper intimacy than they have ever experienced before. Site includes free downloads *50 Ways to Love Your Spouse* and *50 Valentine's Day Ideas*.   http://www.strongerfamilies.org/7-day-love-challenge-2/

VET CENTER: Vet Centers provide readjustment counseling and outreach services to all veterans who served in any combat zone. Services are also available for their family members for military related issues. All benefits are provided at no cost. http://www.vetcenter.va.gov

LINKS FOR MILITARY PARENTS

Military Moms: http://militarymomsmm.com/

Michigan Military Moms: www.michiganmilitarymoms.com

Network Dearborn: www.networkdearborn.com/michiganmilitarymoms

Operation Love: http://operation-love.com/michiganm...rymoms.htm

Marine Parents: http://www.marineparents.com/connec...search.asp

Blue Star Moms: http://www.bluestarmothers.org/mc/p...orgld=bsma

MILITARY MOVE RESOURCES

Active duty military families are required to pick up their homes and families and move all over the world many times throughout the service member's career. Sometimes even Reserve and National Guard service members are required to move for jobs and/or promotions. Moving when you are single can be stressful, but moving a family away from everything they are familiar with and even their own families can be even harder. I hope some of these resources can make that move easier.

BR Anchor Publishing: For nearly 20 years, *BR Anchor Publishing's* books have been providing the most current relocation advice. The company's books differ from other relocation publications in that they focus on the employee's entire family, providing cost-effective and practical relocation advice, checklists and valuable resources. www.branchor.com.

Military OneSource: Getting ready to relocate as a military family can be stressful. When you receive Permanent Change of Station (PCS) orders, you're bound to have mixed feelings. You're likely to be excited about the upcoming change and the chance to meet new people and see new places. But you're also likely to feel stressed about the logistics of the move and about helping family members—especially children and teenagers—with the transition. Fortunately, there are steps you can take and resources available to help you make plans, stay organized, help your children and keep a step ahead while you move. www.militaryonesource.com

Move.mil - Official DPS Portal: In an effort to make moving a little bit easier for you, the US Department of Defense (DoD) United States Transportation Command (USTRANSCOM) and the Military Surface Deployment and Distribution Command (SDDC) developed the Defense Personal Property Program, or DP3. As part of the DP3 mission, an internet-based system to manage DoD household goods moves was created. It's called the Defense Personal Property System (DPS). Find out more at www.move.mil.

Moving with the Army (Married to the Army): Topics include: Moving Time Basics, After the PCS Move Checklist, Shipping your POV, Full Replacement Value Coverage, How to Make a House a Home, On Post Housing Information, Tips for Moving Day, Resources if You're House or Apartment Hunting, One Clause Your Lease Must Have!, Army Posts, Plan My Move, Automated Housing Referral Network, Can You Move to Korea?, and information on PCS Weight Allowance. www.marriedtothearmy.com

DITY Movers: Do-It-Yourself Moving has never been so popular! They can help you make the most of your move. You may not have a choice of when or where to move, but you can make your move work for you! www.ditymovers.com

Household Goods Portal - Move.mil: DoD household goods portal. www.move.mil

Base of Preference: Will list the most commonly researched base information and also give the numbers and website for housing, childcare, central appointments, military lodging, and the base public affairs office. In addition, they will offer you the opportunity to review the bases you have been to and read others' reviews. This site wants you to tell them and other military families about the area. Give your opinion. Love it? Hate it? This is your forum to express your opinions. www.baseofpreference.com

Military Avenue: Created by a team of military and Internet veterans, *MilitaryAvenue.com* offers community information about more than 240 Military Installations. They have listings of more than 5,000 businesses that offer some kind of military "reward" or discount! Their company acts as an advocate for the military family and community, searching for and finding businesses that work hard to serve the military. Don't forget to sign up for their monthly Military Family Newsletter! www.militaryavenue.com

Military Concierge Company: The *Military Concierge Company™* is the only concierge company worldwide that exclusively serves members of the U.S. military and government personnel overseas. To date, they have successfully assisted thousands of American military families, soldiers and contractors living across Europe with recommendations, concierge services and direct referrals to quality home and lifestyle service providers, restaurants, events and other businesses.

The *Concierge Quickfinder™* section of their website features easy-to-access referrals, covering military installations in Bavaria and beyond, with new installations being added in the future. Members can also find help with booking airport shuttles, planning travel itineraries, looking up emergency plumbers, making hotel and restaurant reservations, arranging for flowers, cakes and gifts to be delivered, coordinating appointments with service providers and generally helping military clientele enjoy as seamless and as stress-free a home life as possible. www.mymilitaryconcierge.com

Military Duty Stations: Moving to a new area? Read what other military families have to say. Looking for particular information? Search the categories on the installation pages to find the information you are looking for. Make your experiences count! Review, write about and rate your current military duty station! The site also includes these tools:

- Free PCS Guide: Sign up for our free PCS guide. Whether you are new to the military or a seasoned PCS veteran, you will find it packed with valuable moving tips and suggestions to make you PCS with less stress!
- Cost of Living: Find out how much your income can buy at your new location.
- Great Schools: Public and private school ratings, reviews and parent community.
- Crime Reports: Crime statistics from 700 law enforcement partners across North America and Sex Offender Data for all 50 States.
- City Compare: Statistics that help paint a picture about where you move.
- Military Installations - Your official DoD source for installation and state resources available to active duty, Guard and Reserve service and family members.
- View articles, photos, major unit listings and contacts for programs and services worldwide. If you can't find an international location, try visiting the Department of State country information.
- View articles and local, state and national resource directories.
- A customizable calendar tool to create a unique personal moving

plan. The calendar contains to do lists, checklists, phone lists, and links to critical moving information from budget planners to choosing a school. www.militarydutystations.com

Military Portico: MilitaryPortico.com is a new free website targeted specifically for service members and their dependents, devoted to providing military families' invaluable relocation information and useful links to over 400 military installations throughout the world, as well as 40 categories of links to local businesses and services all in one site. Whether it's a kennel near Ramstein AFB, Germany or the best steak around Ft. Gordon, Georgia...no more spending hours surfing the Internet researching duty locations when it's time to PCS. www.militaryportico.com

My Base Guide: Their mission is to provide essential information to all military personnel and families relocating to a different part of the country. As a newcomer, you can find out about registration, rules, maps, and the history of the base's commands, installations, and units. You will also find a wealth of information regarding housing, employment, education and schools, health care and dental services, as well as community activities and recreation. www.mybaseguide.com

PCS America: PCS America is a very targeted relocation network for the United States military community including active members, Guard and Reserve, the DoD civilian workforce, retirees, veterans, and their families. Over 200 US military installations and their local communities linked into one Network, plus nearly 100 overseas installations! www.pcsamerica.net

Military Move It: Organize your military move with this website's tools that include itinerary, calendar, lists & notes, research on neighborhoods, homes & schools. www.militarymoveit.com

Where Is My POV: To reduce the amount of time spent in the turn-in and pick-up of your vehicle, they will provide a quick and easy means for you to schedule an appointment at *Vehicle Processing Centers* should you so desire. Just click on the "Make an Appointment" button on the left of the website. Once you have turned in your vehicle, you can track its shipment progress, or view the maintenance history of your car if in storage. www.whereismypov.com

Just Moved with Susan Miller: A website and study program designed to bring hope, comfort and encouragement to all military women in their transition and adjustment of moving. It is written by and for military spouses, moms, those who are single and those who serve on active duty. As you read about women, like yourself, who are going through the same feelings and emotions, may it encourage you to know that you are not alone. As you hear other testimonies of God's faithfulness, may it bring you hope. As you embrace God's word from others, may it bring you comfort. www.justmoved. org

TRICARE: Your TRICARE eligibility does not change when you move. But, certain things about your benefits may change once you move, such as your TRICARE plan. This site will allow you to enter your profile so they can give you the most accurate information about what to do when you move. When selecting where you live, tell them where you live now (where you're moving from). Click here http://tricare.mil/mybenefit/ProfileFilter.do;jsessio nid=Nb2QNvRn32jRktL1105LWv1yymhvQSp2bwJJL2RGlQYRfcGhTyvP !1109199768?puri=%2Fhome%2FLifeEvents%2FMovingAndPCS for more information.

The AHRN: The Automated Housing Referral Network (AHRN.com) is sponsored by the Department of Defense and is designed to improve the process of securing available housing for relocating military members and their families. www.ahrn.com

Homeowners Assistance Program (Department of Defense): The Department of Defense (DOD) is proud to offer the *Homeowners Assistance Program* (HAP) to eligible service members and federal civilian, including non-appropriated fund, employees. The program is authorized by law, and administered by the US Army Corps of Engineers (USACE) to assist eligible homeowners who face financial loss when selling their primary residence homes in areas where real estate values have declined because of a base closure or realignment announcement. The American Recovery and Reinvestment Act of 2009 (ARRA) temporarily expands the HAP to assist service members and DOD employees who are wounded, injured or become ill when deployed, surviving spouses of service members or DOD employees killed or died of wounds while deployed, service member and civilian employees assigned to BRAC 05 organizations, and service members required to permanently relocate during the home mortgage crisis. http://hap.usace.army.mil/

Homes for Heroes Real Estate Savings Program: Learn more about the *Homes for Heroes* real estate savings program. Substantial home buying and selling savings are available including reduced commissions and/or discounted lender fees. The program offers full service at a discounted rate and is able to offer more savings than anyone else because of their strong business relationships with Home for Heroes Affiliates. Here is the Homes for Heroes promise: No forms, no red tape, no fine print, no hidden fees, no catch…for more information go to www.homesforheroes.com.

Military by Owner: Provides a comprehensive, low-cost means for military members and their families to advertise their home for sale or rent to military members across the nation. They will link up buyers and sellers of homes along with landlords and prospective tenants. www.militarybyowner.com

Military Moves: MilitaryMoves.com offers a unique web resource that allows service members to search for homes near their new installation before they've even arrived. The company works with realtors, landlords, and homeowners in military locations to show you the best that each location has to offer. www.militarymoves.com

REMilitary: REMilitary.com is designed to help families find military housing, sell their homes by owner, and assist agents and brokers in reaching a unique and powerful market. REMilitary.com is the most comprehensive listing of houses for sale and rent near military installations. www.remilitary.com

DEPLOYMENT RESOURCES

With most families there are a great number of issues that come up before, during and after a service member is deployed. These issues range from school, social, financial, physical, spiritual and much more. I hope I have listed resources that you will find helpful.

Adopt a Platoon: Register to send service members care packages, letters, etc. http://adoptasoldierplatoon.org

After Deployment: After Deployment is a website designed to assist all branches of service members and their families in all areas of self-care solutions targeting post-traumatic stress, depression, and other behavioral health challenges commonly faced after a deployment. Please review site for more information and questions you may have http://www.afterdeployment. org.

American Patriot Heroes Fund: Provides emergency assistance to ALL veterans from past, present and future armed forces. http:// americanpatriotheroesfund.org/

MyArmyLifeToo: The following site includes information about benefits and support for military families. www.myarmylifetoo.com

Air Force Cross Roads: The following sites include information about benefits and support for military families. www.afcrossroads.com, www.afcommunity. af.mil, and http://www.afcrossroads.com

*Air Force Aid Society: Provides great resources worldwide. For example, emergency assistance, sponsoring education programs, base community enhancement programs and more. Please visit the website for further information. http://www.afas.org *Great resource!*

*America's Adopt-A-Soldier: Was founded in 2009 in an effort to formalize a program to better serve and respond to the support demands of veterans, soldiers and their families. The mission is to make a difference in the lives of veterans, soldiers and their families. This is accomplished through strategic community/corporate partnerships, outreach to generous donors and the assistance of thousands of nationwide "grassroots" volunteers giving back. The volunteers establish local America's Adopt-A-Soldier chapters, which will raise public awareness by hosting packing events, raising funds for postage and event support, collecting-packing-shipping packages. They will also give back through sponsoring of local and national events that focus on soldiers, veterans and their families. www.americasadoptasoldier.org *Great resource that shows how generous Americans are!*

American Military Family: Provides financial support and services to members of the United States military and their families, in appreciation to all those who serve to protect the United States of America. www.amf100.org

Any Soldier Inc.: Started as a way for parents to send care packages to their soldiers in Iraq. Support for the effort grew rapidly, and Any Soldier Inc. became a nonprofit organization in 2003 and assists deployed service members all over the world. www.anysoldier.com

*Army Family Health Care: This site offers information about TRICARE, dental, life insurance, family members with special needs and more. This is a pretty informative website. http://www.goarmy.com/soldier-life/army-family-strong/health-care/family-health-care.html *You will be surprised at what all they discuss. Please review this site!*

*Armed Forces Foundation: Is dedicated to providing comfort and solace to members of the military community through financial support, career counseling, housing assistance and recreational therapy programs. They provide assistance to active duty and retired personnel, National Guard, Reserve Components, and their loved ones. http://www.armedforcesfoundation.org/about.php. *Great resource!*

Armed Forces Tax Guide: IRS Publication 3, at www.irs.gov explains special tax rules for deployed military personnel.

Army One Source: Provides family and program services for military families. www.armyonesource.com

Army MWR-Child & Youth Services (CYS): The following site includes great information and deployment resources for military families. http://www. armymwr.com/family/childandyouth/default.aspx

Army Wounded Warrior Program: The Army Wounded Warrior Program (AW2) is the official U.S. Army program that assists and advocates for severely wounded, ill, and injured soldiers, veterans and their families, wherever they are located, regardless of military status. Warriors in Transition (WTs) who qualify for AW2 are assigned to the program as soon as possible after arriving at the WTU. AW2 supports these soldiers and their families throughout their recovery and transition, even into veteran status. This program, through the local support of AW2 Advocates, strives to foster the WT's independence.

For more information on the support AW2 provides, please watch the AW2 video, For As Long As It Takes. And for more information and eligibility requirements go to http://wtc.army.mil/aw2/index.html.

*BuildASign: Is a wonderful company that will provide to military families a one time free customized welcome home banners, or jumbo cards to send to loved ones who are deployed. Check out the cool options at www.buildasign. com/troops. *Lots of really cools signs from this company, I wish I would have ordered one for my husband.*

*Buddy to Buddy Program: Links trained vets to veterans struggling with reintegration. http://buddytobuddy.org *I have heard great things about this program.*

Coaching Into Care: Is a new national call center service developed by the Department of Veterans Affairs to support, inform and aid friends and family of veterans and to help their veteran gain appropriate care. Many service men and women who return from combat each year and resume their family lives suffer from problems with readjustment, post-traumatic stress, anger, alcohol abuse, or depression. Family members and others close to these veterans are often the first to notice these difficulties and need help in how to approach the veteran about seeking services. Veterans often do not recognize the signs of Post-Traumatic Stress Disorder, or they may allow medial issues to expand. They are proud of the strengths they showed under the tremendous stress of military life and may not understand the sudden discomfort of feeling lost, sad and disconnected from loved ones.

In many cases, these veterans do not seek out and accept the various services offered by the Department of Veterans Affairs.

Coaching Into Care also provides a "coaching" service for family and friends who recognize that their veterans need help. Coaching aids the caller in discovering how to be effective in motivating their veteran to seek services. The service is free and provided by licensed clinical social workers and psychologists. Coaching Into Care is available from 8am– pm Eastern Standard Time Monday through Friday to receive calls from family and friends of veterans at, **888-823-7458**. They can be reached by email at coachingintocare@va.gov. If a veteran is currently in an acute crisis, immediate help can be reached by calling 1-800-273-8255, pressing 1 for veterans.

Coast Guard Child Care Program: The Coast Guard Child Care Subsidy Benefit program was created to assist Coast Guard Members who use any federal child care center, or any state licensed child care facility in the Continental US (CONUS) and outside the Continental US (OCONUS) which includes child development centers as well as in home child care providers to provide childcare for their children—especially during deployment. Go to the following website for further information and regulation and rules for the program and other resources. http://gsa.gov/portal/content/102063

Coast Guard Mutual Assistance: Within the limits of CGMA policies as described in the Coast Guard Mutual Assistance Manual, when verified, documented and justified, assistance is provided for families. Assistance can be provided for emergency, medical and dental, survivor, general, education, housing and more. Please go to the website for further information and applications. http://www.cgmahq.org/Assistance/programs.html

Coming Home Project–California: Offers free, confidential and professional service providers along with group support and stress management retreats for OIF and OEF veterans, service members and their families. A multidisciplinary team of veterans, family members, psychotherapists and interfaith leaders, are devoted to providing innovative, compassionate care to address the mental, emotional, and spiritual and relationship problems veterans and service member's face. For more information and eligibility requirements, go to http://www.cominghomeproject.net/retreats.

Compass Retreat Center (Loveland, Ohio): Provides a supportive setting for National Guard Members, Reservists and their families following deployment with emphasis on renewing relationships and strengthening family bonds. www.compassretreatcenter.org

Department of Defense Education Activity (DODEA): DODEA's mission is to plan, direct, coordinate, and manage the education programs for eligible dependents of U.S. military personnel and civilian personnel of the DoD. DoDEA provides an exemplary education that inspires and prepares all students for success in a dynamic, global environment. Dependents of military personnel face unique challenges to their educational attainment. They move more frequently than typical students and are also subject to the stress that accompanies the potential deployment of parents to combat. DoDEA schools provide students with a uniform curriculum and standards that mitigate the stress of frequent moves. DoD challenges faced by military dependents— especially during deployments. http://www.dodea.edu/home/about.cfm

Deployment Parent Checklist Pre-Deployment: Use these checklists to help you prepare yourself and your family for your deployment. http://www.carlisle.army.mil

Deployment Health and Family Readiness Library: Provides service members, families, veterans and healthcare providers an easy way to quickly find deployment health and family readiness information. Within this library you will find access to fact sheets, guides, and other products on a wide variety of topics published by the services and organizations that serve you. You will also find additional website links to other organizations and resources devoted to the health and welfare of the service member and their family. http://deploymenthealthlibrary.fhp.osd.mil

Deployment Tips: A Collection of Official Military Websites. The information listed in this section will assist service members and their families in preparing for and coping with deployments. This site contains family support links for each of the services, as well as information for children, locating service members and deployment entitlements. http://fhp.osd.mil/deploymenttips.jsp

Faith Deployed: Offering hope, community and spiritual encouragement for spouses of deployed troops through two books, *Faith Deployed* and *Faith Deployed: Again*, and also through their website at http://faithdeployed.com.

*Family and Medical Leave Act: The Labor Department has written new rules the expand Family and Medical Leave Act benefits that represent a dramatic change in how National Guard and Reserve members and caregivers responsible for seriously combat injured troops will be treated by employers. Please review this information carefully so you and your families are aware of your rights before, during and after deployments. http://www.blr.com/hrtips/FMLA *Make sure you are familiar with the Family and Medical Leave Act. This is important to your rights!*

*Family Program Office: Establishes and facilitates ongoing communications, involvement, support and recognition between National Guard families and the National Guard. Become familiar with yours in your area. There are a lot of programs and resources that they will be able to share with you and your family. Each military installation has a Family Program or Family Support office be sure to ask your commander if you can't find it.

*Family Support During Deployment: Today's military family faces a lifestyle that is comprised of frequent deployments, which results in increased family separations. This often proves to be a stressful challenge for military families. To assist the military's efforts to keep both troops and their families prepared, there are several programs which support the readiness of families. The information in this section will assist ALL service members and their families in preparing for and coping with deployments. This site contains family support links for each of the services, as well as information for children, locating service members and deployment entitlements. http://fhp.osd.mil/deploymentTips.jsp

*F.I.S.H. Fishermen in Support of Heroes: This organization was organized as a way to show appreciation to military service members for the job they do protecting our country. They have combined a passion for fishing and admiration for military families. This group primary focus on the Wounded Warriors who come back from Iraq and Afghanistan to Camp LeJeune and Fort Bragg to recover from their injuries and they organize trips to take them fishing. Donations of private boats, charter boats, ocean piers and other venues are used take military families fishing. All the gear, licenses, food, drinks and bait are provided. Plenty of volunteers are also there to help bait hooks, demonstrate techniques, clean fish, and other chores as needed. *This group is way cool; I would love to go fishing sometime.* www.fishheroes. org

Freedom Calls Foundation: Provides a way for families and troops overseas to communicate for free with each other. www.freedomcalls.org

Freedom Hunters: Saluting the noble work of our courageous men and women of the Armed Forces is their mission. They by take select active duty and combat veterans on outdoor adventures. Long deployments away from the fields and streams can be hard on those who love the tradition of hunting and fishing. Some servicemen can miss several seasons between training before the deployment and the actual deployment. In an effort to boost morale, they select a few individuals who are currently deployed to go on dream adventures when they return home. www.freedomhunters.org

Free Phones for Soldiers: Provides a communication link between military families and the deployed service members through cell phone and calling cards. http://cellphonesforsoldiers.com/

Department of Veterans Affairs: VA Loan site includes detailed information about VA loans. www.homeloans.va.gov

DeploymentLink: Mission is to enhance communication regarding the health of our service members and their family. The site provides information to: safeguard the health and well-being of service members and their families, promote and sustain a healthy and fit force, prevent injuries and illness and protect the force from health hazards, and sustain world class medical and rehabilitative care to the sick and injured anywhere in the world. http://www.arfp.org/skins/arfp/display.aspx?ModuleID=75d46deb-74a1-4d47-abef-9acf907199bf&Action=display_user_category_objects&CategoryID=57aaf078-bfb3-4cbb-b6ab-f966dc587f5d

Guardian Angels for Soldier's Pets: This organizations mission is supporting military, veterans, and their beloved pets to ensure the pets are reunited with their owners following a deployment (combat or peace-keeping mission) in harm's way to fight the global war on terrorism or unforeseen emergency hardship impacting their ability to retain their pet's ownership rights. Please go to the website to get further information on eligibility. http://guardianangelsforsoldierspet.org

Home Alarms: Provides free home alarms systems for military families. Eligibility is for family members of currently deployed service members or service members who will be deploying soon and have been issued orders. Protect our Troops will provide, free alarm system for home, free upgrades for your current alarm system or a home alarm fee reimbursement. For more information, rules and eligibility www.protectourtroops.org

House in the Woods, Inc. (Maine): A free, outdoor self-help program. The only expense to participants is their transportation to Lee, Maine. Using the recreational, therapeutic, and educational properties of Maine's great wilderness and outdoor heritage, they form short-term retreats for participants to meet others with common military-related challenges and experiences. Activities are led by licensed Maine guides and staffed with caring volunteers and assistance from the local VA Center and health professionals from the community upon request. Maine is a four-season climate, so activities will be dependent on weather and availability. http://houseinthewoods.org/Home.html

Hunters Helping Soldiers: The mission of Hunters Helping Soldiers is to provide a means to enhance physical and emotional healing through comradely during hunting and fishing trips as well as mentorship to help ease the transition from military life to civilian life and help families of returning, wounded, and mortally wounded soldiers cope with the challenges they face. www.huntershelpingsoldiers.org

Iraqi and Afghanistan Veterans of American (IAVA): Connect with other veterans, get access to critical resources, and play a role in tackling issues that impact our community. http://iava.org/membership

Marine Corps: The following site includes information about benefits and deployment support for military families. www.usmc-mccs.org

Marine Corps Association: Following site offers deployment resources and other information for military families. http://www.mcafdn.org/

Marine Corps Aviation Association (MCAA): The MCAA mission is to promote and recognize professional excellence in Marine aviation, support the fraternal bond of its membership, preserve Marine aviation heritage and safeguard the future of Marine aviation through awards programs, events and publications. This site also offers links to other programs and events. http://www.flymcaa.org/

Military.com: Helps active duty service members, reservists and family members of the National Guard with everything from how to send care packages to counseling and scholarship information, Military.com maintains a long list of organizations and agencies where you can lend financial or material support. www.military.com/deployment and/or www.military.com/benefits/resources/support-our-troops

MilitaryHomefront–Deployment Connections: This site provides information for service members, families, parents, spouses, and children about pre-deployment, deployment, and return/reintegration. http://www.militaryhomefront.dod.mil

Military One Source: Education, health, relocation, parenting, stress - you name it - Military OneSource is here to help with just about any need. Available by phone or online, this free service is provided by the Department of Defense for active-duty, Guard, and Reserve service members and their families. The service is completely private and confidential, with few exceptions. http://www.militaryonesource.com/MOS.aspx

Military Pets Foster Project: Nationwide network of foster homes cares for the pets of deployed personnel. http://www.netpets.org/militarypet/foster.php

Military Sentinel (Federal Trade Commission): Recommends putting your identity (credit report information) on military deployment status. Your credit report will be placed on hold. This will in effect make it impossible for anyone to open any credit without written permission from you. And if anything does accidently get on your report you will be able to get it off fairly easy. This DOES NOT put a hold on your obligations you currently have. Make sure you pay everything on time. https://www.ftccomplaintassistant.gov/faq.html https://www.ftccomplaintassistant.gov/index.htm

National Guard Family Program: With this website senior leadership is trying to achieve readiness for what's ahead while remaining flexible in the present. Through the brand new website and family program offices, you can find out about the services, programs and assistance that are provided for service members, spouses, parents and military children. http://www.jointservicessupport.org/FP/

National Military Family Association: Features resources to help military families prepare for deployment and deal with other financial issues. www.nmfa.org

National Guard Psychological Health Program: National Guard members and families should never weather emotional and behavioral challenges alone. That is why this site has Directors of Psychological help in every state, Territory, and the District of Colombia. Find information and contacts to help you and your family build resiliency, including education to support overall wellness, support for family members and friends, and immediate access to help if you are experiencing troubling symptoms. Their library is home to numerous online resources on topics ranging from Post-Traumatic Stress Disorder to Traumatic Brain Injury and more. http://www.jointservicessupport.org/PHP/Default.aspx

National Veterans Foundation: Mission is to serve the crisis management, information and referral needs of all U.S. veterans and their families through management and operation of the nation's only toll-free helpline for all veterans and their families. They also assist with public awareness programs and assist with outreach programs that provide veterans and families with food, clothing, transportation, employment and other essential resources. http://www.nvf.org/about-us

Deployment Resources

Navy: The following site includes information about benefits and support for military families. www.nffsp.org

Naval and Marine Corps Relief Society: Offers various emergency assistance from loans, grants, survivor benefits, visiting nurse, educational and more. Please visit their website and see the great resources they have to offer. http://www.nmcrs.org

Operation: Care and Comfort: Offers support in three ways: sending care packages, tickets to special events, parks, and concerts and adopting a soldier. http://www.occ-use.org

Operation Gratitude: Sends care packages to U.S. military members serving overseas. http://www.operationgratitude.com

Operation Homelink: Provides refurbished computers to the spouses or parents of junior enlisted (E1-E5) U.S. deployed service members, enabling email communication with their loved ones deployed overseas. Operation Homelink does not accept individual requests for computers; instead they are sent to units slated for deployment. For more information, visit the Operation Homelink website at http://myarmyonesource.com/News/2010/02/OperationHomelink.

Operation Hero Mile: This program is comprised of individual airlines whose passengers donate their frequent flyer miles to assist service members and their families. Specifically, Fisher House Foundation provides free airline tickets to military men and women who are undergoing treatment at a military or VA medical center incident to their service in Iraq or Afghanistan, and their families. Visit their website for further information regarding eligibility and rules. http://www.fisherhouse.org/programs/hero-miles/

Operation Love Reunited: Everyone needs to check this site out. These are some beautiful photos. They provide one free photo and you must have a VALID military ID card. Other restrictions apply, see site for details. http://oplove.org

Operation Military Pride: Ideas to assist with putting together a care package for your service member. http://www.operationmilitarypride.org/

Operation Oasis at Sandy Cove (Maryland): Sandy Cove Ministries has created Operation Oasis as a way to say thank you for the sacrifices made by our military. Any service man or woman, including those in the Reserve and National Guard, returning home from deployment in support of OIF or OEF can come to Sandy Cove with their immediate family for FREE! For more information please visit www.sandycove.org.

Operation Open Arms (SW Florida, Eastern Maryland): Is a nationally acclaimed military outreach program. Founded in 2005, OOA has a very simple mission statement. "To provide US Servicemen/women visiting SW FL or the

Eastern Shore of Maryland every conceivable benefit during their two-week combat leave or return from any foreign duty station." Operation Open Arms provides extraordinary benefits such as free limo service, lodging, restaurants, fishing charters, golf, tennis, bowling, kayaking, biking, emergency dental care, and a cutting edge approach for the treatment of PTSD. http://www. operationopenarms.com/

Operation Purple Family Retreats - National Military Family Assoc. Family Retreats: Operation Purple Family Retreats are designed to allow families to reconnect after experiencing the stresses surrounding a deployment. They are a great opportunity to spend time outdoors, try new things, make friends, and enjoy quality time together as a family. These four-day retreats take place in beautiful national parks and are led by experienced outdoor educators. www.militaryfamily.org/our-programs/operation-purple/family-retreats

Operation R&R - (South Carolina): Reconnect after deployment on Hilton Head Island at little or no cost. Operation R&R is a non-profit organization designed to provide our service men and women an opportunity to reconnect with their spouses and children upon their return from Iraq or Afghanistan. Property owners, represented by many property management companies, are donating their homes and villas on Hilton Head Island, SC for this purpose. All of this is to ensure that our military families have a chance to spend some time away from their everyday lives to strengthen relationships that have been strained due to long separations and extreme circumstances. www. operationrestandrelax.org

Operation Military Family: Support network, action plan, resources and book to support families during deployments. A division of Stronger Families, Operation Military Family delivers "Oxygen for Your Relationship" workshops and seminars to military service members and family members with the help and expertise of the staff at Stronger Families. www.operationmilitaryfamily. org

*Operation Once in a Lifetime: This organization's mission is to make the dreams of service members and their families come true by providing free financial and moral support. Operation Once in a Lifetime was created on the bases that "a service member knows what a service member needs," and a service member does not need to worry about providing beds for his kids, worrying if his electricity will still be on when he goes home or if his house will be foreclosed on when serving his/her country. A service member needs a program that will provide free financial assistance regardless of his rank, race, branch of service, physical condition or his deployment status. A service member needs a program that can help make a life altering contribution when he/she is in their greatest need. Operation Once in a Lifetime hopes to be that organization for you. *This is a wonderful organization; I wish I would have heard about them earlier in my past positions. Michigan soldiers could use this organization. I will be passing this information on to the Family Assistance Coordinators*. Please go to www.operationonceinalifetime.com.

Operation Paperback: Provides gently used books and ships overseas to our service members. http://www.operationpaperback.org/

Operation UpLink: With the advancement of technology in combat zones, they are no longer sending phone cards overseas but provide bi-monthly FREE call days through SPAWAR cafes. If you or your loved one is stationed in Iraq, Afghanistan or Kuwait there are locations near them. There are restrictions and rules for using this program. Please read instructions at http://www.operationuplink.org.

Outward Bound: Adventure and challenge, solitude, reflection, and renewal, the wilderness has always symbolized a new beginning - a place for discovery and fulfilling adventure. The Outward Bound Program for veterans provides an opportunity for camaraderie and has proven to be a powerful tool helping veterans readjust after leaving the combat zone. Their newest programs offer numerous wilderness adventures exclusively for combat veterans, and are fully funded for all participants to include their round-trip stateside travel costs between home and the excursion site. There goals include helping participating veterans build a supportive community with other war veterans; facilitating discussions on readjustment and transition challenges; and re-energizing and reinvigorating our veterans' spirits with adventures and challenges in the beautiful outdoors. www.outwardbound.org

*Operation We Are Here: This is a wonderful website that offers information and links to resources for military families and veterans about retreats, books, Youth links, links for parents of service members, emotional support, marriage, and much more. Please review the site at http://www.operationwearehere.com.

*Picture a Hero: Offers individual and family portraits to members of the U.S. military who are preparing to deploy. *This looks like a great opportunity, the web site is awesome. Check out the site to get more information.* http://www.pictureahero.org

*Project Evergreen: This is another organization that I truly LOVE. They assist military spouses with lawn care and snow removal free of charge while your spouse is deployed. *I cannot say enough how helpful it was for me this past year to have them come over and plow my driveway! There is NO way I would have been able to do it myself. They were early and very efficient.* http://www.projectevergreen.com/gcft

Project Sanctuary: Is a wonderful non-profit organization whose mission is to provide therapeutic, curative, supportive and recreational activities to veterans, active military personnel, their spouses and children in a leisure environment. Please view the website for further information and eligibility requirements. http://www.projectsanctuary.us/retreats.html

Purple Heart Ranch (Sterling City, TX) - Military Warriors Hero Support Foundation: Purple Heart Ranch is open exclusively to combat wounded heroes and to Gold Star families. The ranch is also open to children of combat wounded heroes and those who have a parent currently deployed to a combat zone. Both the families of the wounded heroes and the parents of the children are encouraged to come and enjoy the experience with the hunters. There is fishing available at both properties and many other activities for the families. Both ranches are rich in history and are littered with Native American artifacts, especially arrow heads. http://militarywarriors.org/skills4life

ReserveAid: Is a nonprofit organization committed to providing financial support to the families of Reserve service members from all services who have been called to active duty and are experiencing financial difficulty. The goal is to alleviate the emotional and financial burdens placed on the men and women called to serve by supporting their families at home. www.reserveaid.org

Returning from the War Zone - Guides for Military and Families: The days and weeks after a homecoming from war can be filled with excitement, relief, and many other feelings. This guide is to help military family members with reintegration. While going through your transition period, this guide should help answer questions and provide guidance. http://www.ptsd.va.gov/PTSD/public/reintegration/guide-pdf/familyguide.pdf and http://www.ptsd.va.gov/public/reintegration/returning_from_the_war_zone_guides.asp

Return the Favor: Provides assistance to military personal and their families providing services that include financial assistance grants for housing, medical or basic needs, prepaid phone cards, assistance filing disability and benefit claims, and "Welcome Home" and "Send-off" events for troops. Visit http://www.vfwonthehill.org/2011/03/usaa-provides-250000-sponsorship-for.html for more information.

7 Day Love Challenge - Find Oxygen for Your Relationship: Is a program set up to challenge yourself in your marriage. Each day a simple challenge will be given to you in hopes that you will take it on and see a new spark start within your marriage, or will continue to fan the flame that is already burning. The daily challenges are simple and the benefits undeniable. Site includes free downloads 50 Ways to Love Your Spouse and 50 Valentine's Day Ideas. http://www.strongerfamilies.org/7-day-love-challenge-2/

Sarge's List – (Sell or Donate Your Stuff): Is a brand new website that helps military members lighten their load during PCS, or every day, by selling or donating their stuff to other military families locally or globally. With over 500 installations worldwide, this FREE and made just-for-military community's website offers local PCS information as well as local classifieds for household goods, cars, real estate, pets, yard sales, military savings and more! www.sargeslist.com

Sitter City Corporate Program: Military families now have free access to an online network of quality caregivers who can assist with everything from babysitting to dog walking. Sittercity is the nation's largest online source for local babysitters, nannies, elder care providers, dog walkers, housekeepers and tutors, and contains more than a million caregiver profiles. The Sittercity

Corporate Program, funded by the Defense Department, offers all military families a free membership to the site. To get more information and to activate your free membership go to http://www.sittercity.com/dod.

Soldiers Angels: Assistance for service members, "Adopt a Soldier Program." http://www.soldiersangels.org

*Strong Bonds: This unit based, chaplain-led program helps service members and families build and maintain strong relationships. The program is available to singles, couples, and family members both during and after a deployment. Strong Bonds helps provide skills the service member can use to strengthen his or her marriage or other relationships. To maximize the benefits, training is done in a retreat format, where service members and family members can get away and focus on building key relationship skills. To see more about this program and if one is near to you, go to www.StrongBonds.org. *I have been a part of this program with my husband and it was wonderful and full of useful information. Hope to go to another one someday.*

Supportive Services for Veteran Families: Under this program, the certain agencies in the state of Michigan will be able to provide a range of services to eligible low income veterans and their families. This will include services for rent, utilities, deposits and moving costs. http://www.va.gov/HOMELESS/SSVF.asp

Thanks-a-Bunch: This organization helps the community say "thank you" to a military service member or family through the purchase of gift cards. Check on line how you can donate. http://www.thanksabunch.org

*The American Legion's Family Support Network: Provides immediate assistance to service personnel and families whose lives have been directly affected by Operation Iraqi Freedom and America's war on terror which include family assistance like grocery shopping, childcare, mowing the grass, fixing the family car and other routine household jobs.

   To address these issues, The American Legion has a nationwide toll-free telephone number, (800) 504-4098, for service members and their family members to call for assistance. Applicants can apply online by clicking the assistance form at the top of the page. Calls are referred to The American Legion department, or state in which the call originated. Departments relay the collected information to a local American Legion post. The local post then contacts the service member or family to see how assistance can be provided locally. Since the creation of the Family Support Network during the first Persian Gulf War, thousands of posts have responded to meet these families' needs. *Is a wonderful organization, they are there when you need them. I have used their services in the past to help military families.* http://www.legion.org/familysupport

The Deployment Dilemma - Pets of Military Personnel: Whether deployments extended, or the service member is redeployed or newly deployed, they face a number of difficult decisions regarding home and family. And one of the biggest worries is pets. Hopefully you will find contentment and security with these options.   http://www.americanhumane.org/animals/adoption-pet-care/issues-information/fostering-military-pets.htm

The Mission Continues: Mission is to build on America where EVERY returning veteran, wounded or otherwise can serve again as a citizen leader, and where together they honor the fallen by living their values through service. http://www.missioncontinues.org

Trees for Troops Program: Organization is out of Missouri and they are helping military families keep Christmas spirit alive for deployed families. http://www.christmasspirtfoundation.org

*Tutoring: The Defense Department launched a free, online tutoring service for service members and their families. The site http://www.tutor.com/military offers round the clock professional tutors who can assist with homework, studying, test preparation, resume writing and more. *This site looks really interesting and cool. I wish I would have used it for my daughter last year.*

*Unmet Needs (Veterans of Foreign Wars): Was created to provide emergency financial support to families of military personnel. Funds from donations are available to the five branches of service (Army, Navy, Air Force, Marines and Coast Guard), as well as members of the Reserves and National Guard. Funds awarded by the program are offered in the form of grants, not loans, so recipients don't need to repay them. *Wonderful organization, they assisted my family in 2006 with an issue with our roof. I have also used this organization to assist military families in the past. Great organization!!!* http://www.vfw.org/Assistance/National-Military-Services/

*USA Cares: USA Cares exists to help bear the burdens of service by providing post-9/11 military families with financial and advocacy support in their time of need. Assistance is provided to all branches of service, all components, all ranks while protecting the privacy and dignity of those military families and veterans who request our help. *Wonderful organization, I have used this company to assist many military families. They are a great organization!!* http://usacares.org/

USMiles: Is a leading auto loan provider designed exclusively for active duty military. Recognized for their integrity, they will only finance quality vehicles that are affordable for service members and their families. Their loans are financed by US Bank, the fifth largest bank in the United States. Through consistent payments made through an allotment, and by having a major national lender on their credit report, customers are building the foundation for good credit. To learn more about how MILES protects and works with service members to be able to get a new vehicle go to http://www.usmiles.com.

U.S. Department of Justice: This is a service members and veterans' rights page and provides information about special legal rights of members of the military and veterans. www.servicemembers.gov

USO: Not a government agency, as many believe, the USO is a congressionally chartered nonprofit organization. Since 1941, the mission of the USO has been to provide morale, welfare and recreation-type services to service members and their families. USO is located all over the world on bases and at some airports for the use of military families and service members. They provided all sorts of assistance to snacks, electronic usage, communication and more. www.uso.org

*VFW Military Assistance (MAP): A quality of life initiative that focuses on easing the financial emergencies of deploying service members and supporting them and their family through the hardships of deployments. They offer grants for emergency situation and at different locations assistance with job search and scholarships for children. *Wonderful organization, I have worked with them in the past.* http://www.vfw.org/Assistance/Family-Assistance/

Veteran Affairs of Government: http://www.va.gov and http://www.seamlesstransition.va.gov/res_guard.asp

*Veterans of Foreign Wars of the United States: http://www.vfw.org

Veterans License Plates: Provides information about the different military license plates that are offered. http://www.dmv.state.pa.us/militaryCenter/licensePlates.shtml

Veteran Resource: A VA newsletter offers resource for Iraq and Afghanistan veterans interested in learning more about benefits, health risks and current news. The Operation Enduring Freedom/Operation Iraqi Freedom Review can be accessed online at www.publichealth.va.gov/exposures/oefoif. Click on "Resources and Materials" in the upper right box to link to an electronic edition. Veterans also can order free hard-copy subscriptions at the site as well.

Warrior Gateway: Provides steps for easier reintegration into home communities. Please read site for further information. http://www.warrorgateway.org

Welcome Home – A Guide To A Healthy Family Reunion: This guide will give you tips and tools to help you and your family with re-integration. http://www.redcross.org/www-files/documents/pdf/corppubs/welcome.pdf

Wild Rivers on the Fly (New Mexico): Fly fishing trips in New Mexico; returning veteran's fish free! www.wildriversonthefly.com

Warrior Support Program: Provides a transition assistance advisor in each state and territory to help Guard members and their families with accessing Veterans Affairs benefits and filing claims, TRICARE, state benefits, and access to community resources. https://www.hnfs.com/content/hnfs/home/tn/common/care/warrior_care_support_program.html/pp/content/hnfs/home/tn/bene

A Warrior's Wish Foundation: The Warrior Wish Foundation enhances the lives of US military veterans and their families who are battling a life-limiting illness. Through the fantastic financial support of generous donors, the financial contributions of Veterans' Service Organizations, their volunteer network and our wonderful corporate partnerships, they are able to grant the wishes of those who have served this great nation of ours. A wish may be as simple as a new hearing aid or scooter chair, or as involved as one last family vacation or reunion. http://awarriorwish.org/

Wish For Our Heroes: Is a Phoenix group that launched a non-profit foundation in November of 2009 that grants wishes for active duty soldiers, sailors, marines, airmen, and their families. The Foundation strives to relieve the burdens of family separation, re-integration for deployed service members, hardship circumstances, and other means of assistance not covered by existing military charities. The Foundation is driven by an interactive website allowing anyone to request a wish for active duty members of our Armed Forces. The website allows 'wish granters' to view wishes and contribute donations. www.wish4ourheroes.org

Yellow Ribbon Program: The Yellow Ribbon program provides information, services, referrals and proactive outreach programs to Guard soldiers and Reserves and their families. Yellow Ribbon offers pre-deployment events to update Guard members and their families on programs such as TRICARE, Military OneSource, VA Benefits and Employer Support benefits. After deployment, Yellow Ribbon holds events for Guard Families at 30, 60, and 90 day intervals. Post-deployment events, including marriage and counseling services, address the physical and mental health of the service member and remind families about their resources. http://www.yellowribbon.mil/

Yellow Ribbon Reintegration Program (National Guard and Reserve): All service members and their families may face challenges throughout the deployment cycle, from pre-deployment to reintegration. But National Guard and Reserve members can face additional challenges, as they may not live near military facilities or have community supports in place. To help National Guard and Reserve members and their families overcome these challenges, the Yellow Ribbon Reintegration Program proactively provides information about benefits, referrals, programs and services for health and well-being. The Yellow Ribbon Reintegration Program consists of a series of events at key stages in the deployment cycle such as: pre-deployment, during deployment (just for families), 30 days after deployment, 60 days after deployment and 90 days after deployment. http://www.realwarriors.net/guardreserve/reintegration/yellowribbon.php

LINKS TO STATE SPECIFIC
ARMY NATIONAL GUARD WEBSITES

Arizona: www.guardfamily.org

Colorado: www.guardfamily.org, (720) 250-1190

Florida: www.floridaguard.army.mil, click on "programs" then "family programs" (904) 823-0360

Georgia: www.gahro.com/familyprogram, (678) 569-5065

Hawaii: www.guardfamily.org, (808) 672-1442

Illinois: www.guardfamily.org

Iowa: www.iowanationalguard.com/family, (515) 252-4416

Kansas: www.guardfamily.org

Massachusetts: http://states.ng.mil/sites/ma/pages/default.aspx, (508) 233-7222

Michigan: www.michigan.gov/dmva, click on "Michigan National Guard" (517) 481-8361

Mississippi: www.guardfamily.org, (601) 313-6379

Missouri: www.moguard.com/familyreadiness, (573) 638-9827

Nevada: http://www.nv.ngb.army.mil/family.cfm, (775) 887-7346

New Hampshire: www.guardfamily.org, (603) 225-1340

North Carolina: www.guardfamily.org, (919) 664-6054

North Dakota: www.guardfamily.org, (701) 333-2058

Oklahoma: http://www.ok.ngb.army.mil/famprog, (405) 228-5843

Pennsylvania: www.pngfamilyprogram.state.pa.us, (717)861-9676

South Dakota: www.guardfamily.org, (605) 737-6728

Tennessee: www.guardfamily.org

Vermont: www.vtguard.com/famread, (802) 338-3391

Wisconsin: www.wingfam.org, (608) 242-3424

Wyoming: www.guardfamily.org

WOUNDED OR DECEASED

This is a subject that is never easy to think about let alone talk about. But these are resources that you need to be aware of and familiar with in the event the unthinkable happens. And to those that are in this situation, I hope some of these resources can bring you some peace and hope.

DECEASED WARRIOR

HEALTH

A Survivors Guide to Benefits - Taking Care of Our Own: This guide in intended to aid you as you work through the difficulty and pain of losing a loved one who was serving in the military. http://www.militaryhomefront.dod. mil

*American Fallen Soldiers Project: The American Fallen Soldiers Project was formed to help provide comfort and healing to the mourning families of our fallen military men and women. With the mission to honor, respect and forever memorialize those who have sacrificed their lives while protecting our freedom. This 501c3 non-profit organization makes available to the families, at no cost, an original portrait of their fallen loved one that fully captures their appearance and personality. http://www.americanfallensoldiers.com/ *Please visit this website, these portraits are beautiful and touch my heart. What a thoughtful gesture and a wonderful organization!*

*American Gold Star Mothers: Resource for parents who have lost their child in time of war. *This is a great organization and website.* http://www.goldstarmoms.com

American Widow Project: This non-profit was launched in 2008 by Taryn Davis who became a widow at the age of 21 years. It is dedicated to the newest generation of war widows, including some who lost their spouses to non-combat causes with an emphasis on healing through sharing stories, tears and laughter. The organization has a camaraderie that their spouses had and their hotline is staffed with fellow widows, not by grief counselors. Official events include surfing and skydiving, rather than speakers and seminars. This is an organization that strives and encourages each other with hope for the future. http://www.americanwidowproject.org

Bereavement Counseling for Surviving Family Members: Support to people with emotional and psychological stress after the death of a loved one. It includes a broad range of transition services, including outreach, counseling, and referral services to family members. http://www.vetcenter.va.gov/bereavement_counseling.asp

CACO's Survivor Benefits Guide: This is a guide that has been provided by Headquarters Marine Corps. The information is useful to all military service members and their families. Individuals should contact their specific service casualty representative–especially to make sure the guide is up-to-date. http://www.emilitary.org/links.php

Survivor Outreach Services: To build a unified support program which embraces and reassures survivors that they are continually linked to the Army Family for as long as they desire. Their website has resources available for your needs. http://www.myarmyonesource.com/FamilyProgramsandServices/SurvivingFamilies/default.aspx

Tragedy Assistance Program for Survivors (TAPS): Is an organization for families who are grieving the loss of a fallen service member. It offers support groups, seminars, grief camps and other resources. Since families of suicide victims are often affected differently from families of service members fallen in combat, TAPS developed programs and events geared directly for this group. http://www.taps.org or the toll free crisis line at 800-959-TAPS

TRICARE, Transitional Survivor and Survivor Benefits for Active Duty Family Members: Family Members are entitled to TRICARE benefits as transitional survivors or survivors if their active duty service sponsor died while serving on active duty for a period of more than 30 days. TRICARE pays transitional survivor claims at the active duty family member payment rate and pays survivor claims at the retiree payment rate. Transitional survivors pay no enrollment fees or copayments to use TRICARE Prime. They will, however, pay cost shares and deductibles at the active duty family member rate to use TRICARE Standard or TRICARE Extra. http://www.military.com/benefits/tricare/tricare-survivor-benefits

*VFW: Great emergency assistance and resource during this time of need. http://www.vfw.org/. *They have resources for many different needs during this time and for the future of your children and grandchildren.*

Educational Scholarships

American Legion Legacy Scholarship: Was created to assist children whose parents have been killed while serving our country with obtaining a higher education. Scholarships are for undergraduate study at an accredited institution of higher education within the United States. The amount of aid and number of awards depend upon the income derived from the trust. Scholarship recipients may reapply for the award. Applications must be post marked no later than April 15th. For more information about additional American Legion scholarships and college financial aid, review the scholarships page or direct inquires to Mr. Charles Graybie, Program Coordinator at (317) 630-1212. http://www.legion.org/scholarships/legacy

Army Nurse Corps Association (ANCA): ANCA awards scholarships to U.S. citizen students attending accredited baccalaureate or graduate nursing or anesthesia nursing programs. This scholarship is in honor of Cpt. Joshua M. McClimans, AN, USAR, who was killed in a mortar attack in April 2011 while assigned to the Combat Support Hospital at Forward Operating Base Salerno in Afghanistan. For more information about this scholarship and eligibility requirements go to http://e-anca.org/ANCAEduc.htm.

Army Ranger Association: This scholarship program is memorial to selfless service and contributions made to our country by USARA members. These awards are given in their honor. This program provides an opportunity to provide financial assistance to qualified dependents of USARA members in furthering their education. The scholarship committee seeks to award scholarships to applicants displaying the potential for a degree in higher education, whether it is technical, university or professional. Each year the scholarship committee evaluates the scholarship applicants and selects the most outstanding submissions to be awarded to USARA Legacy Scholarship. For further information about this scholarship and eligibility requirements go to http://www.ranger.org/.

Army Reserve Association: Offers scholarships for dependents of service members. Please review the website at http://www.armyreserve.org for further information and eligibility.

Children of Fallen Soldiers Relief Fund: Was founded as a means to provide college grants and financial assistance to surviving children and spouses of our U.S. military service members who have lost their lives in the Iraq and Afghanistan wars. The program will assist disabled service member families too. For further information or to apply for assistance, go to http://www.cfsrf. org/.

*Educational Benefits for Children of Disabled or Deceased Veterans: This tuition grant program is administered by the Michigan (or your state) Higher Education Assistance Authority in the Michigan Department of Treasury provides payment for the education of the children of a veteran who is totally disabled from service-incurred causes, was killed in the line of duty, has died subsequently from a service-related disability, was totally disabled before death from a service-connected illness or injury, or who is listed by the federal government as missing in action in a foreign country. A student may be eligible for a tuition waiver of up to $2,800 annually for undergraduate study. Recipients must meet certain eligibility requirements. Information on eligibility and application forms are available at www.michigan.gov/ studentaid or by calling toll-free 888-447-2687. *Check with you state for this same support.*

Folds of Honor: This organization was created to provide scholarships to families of men and women killed or wounded while serving, no matter how young or old they are. For more information or application go to www. foldsofhonor.org.

National Guard Association of the United States: Provides scholarships for the children of fallen National Guardsmen who have lost their lives protect this great nation. For more information and eligibility requirements, go to http:// www.ngaus.org/.

Association of Naval Aviation: This scholarship is provided by The Philip H. Jones Family and the Association of Naval Aviation to honor the service and sacrifice of LCDR Philip H. Jones, USN (RET), who started his Naval Aviation career as an Aviation Pilot during WWII. This scholarship is provided for the sons and daughters of Naval Aviators and Navy, Marine Corps and Coast Guard Air crewmen who died while on active duty serving in the United States Navy, Marine Corps or Coast Guard. Please review the website for further information and eligibility requirements and contact information at http://www.anahq.org/ scholarship2011.htm.

Special Operation Warrior Fund Operation: The Special Operations Warrior Foundation provides full scholarship grants and educational and family counseling to the surviving children of special operations personnel who die in operational or training missions and immediate financial assistance to severely wounded special operations personnel and their families. http://www.specialops.org

State Provided Educational Benefits: Educational benefits for families, particularly children of deceased, MIA, POW, and disabled veterans, may be available in some states. Military.com has developed an on-line general summary of educational benefits for veterans, surviving spouses and their dependents. www.military.com and/or http://www.military.com/benefits/content/survivor-benefits/surviving-spouse-and-family-education-benefits.html, or http://www.military.com/benefits/content/survivor-benefits/survivors-resource-list.html

Stateside Spouse Education Assistance Program (SSEAP): This scholarship program assists Army spouses obtain a four year undergraduate degree. Spouses of active duty soldiers, spouses of retired soldiers, and widows/widowers of soldiers who died either on active duty or in a retired status are eligible. http://www.aerhq.org/education_spouseeducation_StateSide.asp

OTHER RESOURCES

*Air Force Enlisted Village: The Air Force Enlisted Village was founded in 1967 to provide a safe, secure and dignified place for indigent surviving spouses of retired Air Force personnel. The Village's primary goal and focus is to provide a home and financial assistance to these women. The surviving spouse with the greatest need is cared for first and none are refused assistance due to financial status. Low pay and frequent military moves leave some spouses without careers, home equities, retirement plans or any significant assets. Surviving spouses requiring financial assistance live here among peers sharing memories of Air Force life without the stigma normally associated with subsidized housing facilities. Explore our site for more details! http://afenlistedwidows.org/ *What a great place! This looks amazing!*

*American Legion: Great resource during this time of need for wounded soldiers and spouses of deceased soldiers. http://www.legion.org. *I have worked with the two local ones in my area and they are amazing, hardworking, generous people!*

AmVets: Has a proud history of assisting veterans and sponsoring numerous programs that serve our country and its citizens. AmVets assists in many different ways. http://www.amvets.org

Armed Forces Service Corporation (AFSC): Begun in 1879 as a non-profit established to care for the surviving spouses from "The Battle of Little Big Horn". The Military Service Relief Societies have partnered with the Armed Forces Services Corporation (AFSC) to provide lifetime AFSC membership for the surviving spouse and/or surviving children of service members who die while on active duty. http://www.afsc-usa.com

Department of Veterans Affairs: Burial & Memorials: The National Cemetery Administration honors veterans with final resting places in national shrines and with lasting tributes that commemorate their service to our nation. http://www.cem.va.gov/ and http://www.va.gov/

eVetRecs Request Copies of Military Personnel Records: Military veterans and the next of kin of deceased former service members may now use a new online military personnel records system to request documents. The NPRC has established a website for veterans and next of kin to access the Department of Defense Form 214. http://www.lafbraomilitaryretireenews.org/militaryrecords.html

Fallen Patriot Fund/The Mark Cuban Foundation: Was established to help families of U.S. Military personnel who were killed or seriously injured during Operation Iraqi Freedom. Go to http://fallenpatriotfund.org/ for eligibility and further information.

Family Support Network: Military families in need of help can turn to The American Legions Family Support Network. In countless ways, Legionnaires can provide support and services to families affected by the obligations of military service. Families needing help are encouraged to call the toll-free number to get connected with a nearby American Legion Post. Toll-free: (800) 504-4098 and forms to seek assistance are available online at www.legion.org.

Fannie Mae Military Forbearance Option: If you're facing a financial hardship due to a death or injury of a service member on active duty, you may be eligible for a special military forbearance option. Forbearance is an agreement between you and your mortgage company to temporarily suspend or reduce your monthly mortgage payments for a specific period (usually between 90-180 days) of time. This option lets you deal with your short-term financial problems by giving you time to get back on your feet and bring your mortgage current.

With a military forbearance, you may qualify for additional benefits such as a longer forbearance period—up to six months—and no adverse impact to your credit score (all credit reporting related to your mortgage loan will be suspended during the forbearance period). Additionally, a special hotline has been set up for additional guidance about this option and other mortgage assistance programs—877-MIL-4566. www.knowyouroptions.com/Military

Forgotten Eagles of Michigan: This wonderful organization works to heighten awareness and to publicize the POW/MIA issues, to educate the public on the plight of POW/MIA's, to advocate for the fullest possible accounting of all of America's POW/MIAs, to heighten awareness and education of the public on the effects of Agent Orange/Dioxin and of the chemical, biological and radiological weapons testing on the U.S. Military Personnel. To promote physical and cultural improvement, growth and development, self-respect, self-confidence and usefulness of America's Veterans and Families, to assist America's disabled in-need veterans, their dependents and the widows and orphans of deceased veterans, and to help not-for-profit organizations that have

similar interests at heart. Please view the website for other useful informat.
and resources. http://forgotteneagles.org/

*Gold Star Wives of America: Is an organization of military widows/
widowers whose spouse died while on active duty or from service-connected
disabilities. This military survivor's organization has been serving war widows
from all conflicts and service-connected disabilities since it was founded in
1945. *This is another great organization and website.* http://goldstarwives.
org/

Headstones and Markers Information: www.military.com/benefits/content/
headstones-and-markers.html

The Joint Munitions Command (JMC): If your VFW Post uses weapons
issued through the ceremonial rifle pro-am at the U.S. Army TACOM Life
Cycle Management Command in Warren, Michigan; you are eligible to
request one or two boxes of blank ammo and clips per event. The request must
be made by the Post Commander. The Joint Munitions Command provides the
blank ammo to VFW Posts free of charge to perform military funeral honors
and parades. This function has been performed by JMC since the end of WWII.
For information about the ceremonial ammo program, contact JMC at 1-877-
233-2515 or email ROCK-JMCceremonialammorequests@conus.army.mil.
The ceremonial rifle program can be contacted at DAMI_Donations@conus.
army.mil or visit www.tacom.army.mil/ceremonial_rifle. Please check with
your state for your rights regarding this program.

MAPCentral Casualty and Mortuary Affairs: (Military Assistance Program
Central) Guidance of military funeral support is available in one location to
help ensure proper honors are paid to our nations fallen. Information includes
mortuary policy and other casualty policies and procedures. This site will
help the grieving families of deceased military personnel and the ceremonial
paying of respect at their memorials; provide the final demonstration of our
nation's gratitude to those who faithfully defended our nation. http://osd.dtic.
mil/mapcenteral/casualty.html

The Marine Corps Causality Assistance Program: Has signed a
Memorandum of Agreement with TAPS, which allows closer coordination
between the groups. Together they will provide comfort and care to anyone
who has suffered the loss of a military loved one, regardless of the relationship
to the deceased or the circumstances of the death. For more information go to
www.manpower.usmc.mil and click on the link for causality assistance.

Military Assistance Program Central: Assistance with Casualty and
Mortuary Affairs. http://osd.dtic.mil/mapcentral/casualty.html

Office of Survivors Assistance (OSA): Was created in 2008 to serve as a
resource regarding all benefits and services furnished by the Department
to survivors and dependents of deceased veterans and members of
the Armed Forces. If you have any questions you can contact OSA at

officeofsurvivors@va.gov for further information about your benefits, go to http://www.va.gov/survivors/, click on right side of page to "view available benefits for survivors" you will be given a option for "death in service" or "death after service." Other options offered on this website are OSA Outreach, VA benefit Administration, National Cemetery Administration, Support for Caregivers, Bereavement Counseling, CHAMPVA benefits, and other useful links. Link to view chapter by chapter booklet of Federal Benefits for Veterans, Dependents and Survivors is http://www1.va.gov/OPA/publications/benefits_book.asp.

Office of Personnel Management (OPM)–Federal Jobs for Veterans: Certain veterans, principally those who are disabled or who served on active duty during specified times, are entitled to preference for federal civil service jobs filled by open, competitive exams. Preference is also provided for widows/widowers not remarried mothers of personnel who died in service, and spouses of service-connected disabled. This preference includes five or ten points added to passing scores on examinations. Individuals interested in federal information should contact the personnel officers of the federal agencies in which they wish to be employed. Or, contact any Office of Personnel Management (OPM) Service Center. The centers are listed in telephone books under U.S. Government, or you can visit the web site at http://www.opm.gov. Federal job opportunities can be found at http://www.usa.jobs.opm.gov. Also check out http://www.fedshirevets.gov.

Operation Family Fund: Provide emotional and emergency assistance to the families of fallen soldiers. http://www.operationfamilyfund.org/

Our Survivors: After the death of your loved one, there are so many questions, required forms, and changes that it is easy to overlook some of the necessary paperwork and procedures that need to be completed. It is easy to feel overwhelmed. The military will assign a casualty representative (who will be a military service member) to assist you with this transition you will need to take. The following is a list where you can find the paperwork you will need; *Not all of the items will pertain to you or your circumstances; I just wanted to make sure they are brought to attention. Remember these are guides and reference points to assist with the challenge at hand. They will be available to print in PDF format for your convenience.*

- http://www.army.mil/standto/archive/2009/03/06/
- http://www.vba.va.gov/survivors/index.htm
- http://www.military.com/benefits/survivor-benefits/survivor-benefit-plan-explained

*Patriot Guard: The Patriot Guard Riders are honored to assist with service members military funerals. They work to protect you and your family's privacy. http://www.patriotguard.org. *I love this group, they drive all over the country and work diligently to ensure you and your family have the honor and respect that should be given in your time of need. They touch my heart every time I see them.*

Project Compassion: This wonderful organization provides an 18 x 24 oil portrait of fallen soldiers to family members. Family members can mail a few photographs to Project Compassion and within a month they will receive their oil portrait free of charge. For more information go to www.heropaintings.com.

The Survivors of Service Members SOS Fund: Provides funds to families who have lost a loved one in Iraq. http://SOSFund.us/mission.htm

WOUNDED WARRIORS

**At the time of publication, all OIF/OEF personnel who have sustained a TBI (concussion) while serving in Iraq or Afghanistan and sustained symptoms from the encounter may now qualify for Purple Heart Medals under new Army guidelines. The change, which was reported in March 2011 means thousands of soldiers may qualify for the medal, which is awarded for wounds or injuries resulting from combat.*

Sentiment has been slowly changing the 10 years of the global war on terrorism. Unfortunately earlier attempts at adding concussions to the list of qualifying wounds was derided by those who thought conventional wounds only should be on the list. But as traumatic brain injury has become more of a signature wound from road-side bombs and mental health issues thinking has begun to change.

Soldiers who suffer from concussions and were denied the medal are being encouraged to seek review of their cases. They can do so by calling 888-276-9472 or sending an email to hrc.tagd.awards@concus.army.mil.

***The VA has broadened its list of undiagnosed illnesses afflicting 1991 Persian Gulf War veterans. As of Aug 15th 2011, functional gastrointestinal disorders, such as irritable bowel syndrome or chronic constipation and diarrhea when lasting months or longer, are now considered eligible for presumptive service-connected disability care and compensation. Service members should make every effort to review their records for claims for these disorders if they were in the Gulf War and previously denied.*

***As of September 2011 service members who are catastrophically wounded, ill or injured are now eligible for compensation designed to offset the economic burden primary caregivers incur when assisting them. The Special Compensation for Assistance with Activities of Daily Living (SCAADL) is designed to mitigate this financial hardship. Monthly payment amounts are based upon the U.S. Department of Labor's bureau of Labor Statistics wage rate for home health aides and are adjusted by several factors. Applications for SCAADL require DD Form 2948 which must be completed by a licensed DoD or VA physician. For more information, go to http://www.military.com/military-report/special-compensation-for-wounded-warriors?ESRC=miltrep.nl.*

*****An important update service members need to know is you can access, apply and learn about your military benefits easier online with the Health Benefits Renewal Form (10-10EZR) at www.va.gov/healtheligibility or call VA at toll free 1-877-222-VETS. The online form is available at http://www.1010ez. med.va.gov/sec/vha/1010ez/Form/1010ezr/pdf.*

HEALTH

*Aid and Attendance Pension Program: This program is not widely known or used. But this is a great program that can help low income; disabled veterans receive needed medical, nursing, and home health care without depleting their savings. It can be used to pay for adult day care, skilled nursing care and home care. It also can be used to pay for a family member other than a spouse to care for the veteran at home. The Aid and Attendance Program began in 1953, but most veterans do not know about it. The program differs from the disability pension provided by the U.S. Department of Veterans Affairs. For more information, visit the Military.com website. Applications can be submitted online through the VA's VONAPP portal. For more information, visit the Department of Veterans Affairs website at www.va.gov or contact your local veteran's service organization. *Great program, more veterans need to be aware of it.*

Air Force Wounded Warrior: The AFW2 program works hand-in-hand with the Air Force Survivor Assistance Program and Airman & Family Readiness Centers to ensure Airmen receive professional support and care from the point of injury, through separation or retirement, for life.

- Advocate for services on Airman's behalf
- Coordinate with closest A&FRC to ensure wounded warriors receive face-to-face, personalized services
- Provide professional services such as transition assistance, employment assistance, moving assistance, financial counseling, information and referral, and emergency financial assistance
- Assist in integrating Airmen and their families back into their local communities
- Connect Airmen and their families with the Joint Family Support Program in each state
- Coordinate benefits counseling and services provided by the DoD, Department of Veterans Affairs, Department of Labor, Social Security Administration, TRICARE, and other helping agencies. Please view the website for further useful information. www.woundedwarrior. af.mil/

*American Legion: Great resource during this time for wounded soldiers and spouses of deceased soldiers. http://www.legion.org. *Have great resource for service members and their families in all areas.*

Army Wounded Warrior Program: The Army Wounded Warrior Program (AW2) is the official U.S. Army program that assists and advocates for severely wounded, ill, and injured soldiers, veterans, and their families, wherever they are located, regardless of military status. Warriors in Transition (WTs) who qualify for AW2 are assigned to the program as soon as possible after arriving at the WTU. AW2 supports these soldiers and their families throughout their recovery and transition, even into Veteran status. This program, through the local support of AW2 Advocates, strives to foster the WT's independence. Please go to the website to see guidelines, requirements and further information. www.aw2.army.mil

Army Medical Action Plan (AMAP): The purpose of AMAP is to develop a holistic approach to develop a sustainable system that supports, treats, and vocationally rehabilitates service members to prepare them for successful return to duty or transition to active citizenship. AMAP will ensure that the needs of the Army, the Soldier and their families are jointly met. Visit http://www.armymedicine.army.mil/news/amap/amap.html.

Brain Injury Association of Michigan: The Brain Injury Association of America (BIAA) is the country's oldest and largest nationwide brain injury advocacy organization. Their mission is to be the voice of brain injury. Through advocacy, education and research, they bring help, hope and healing to millions of individuals living with brain injury, their families and the professionals who serve them. Please go to the website listed to see all areas of this wonderful organization. http://www.biausa.org/About-Us/about-brain-injury-association.htm

Compensation and Benefits Handbook: For seriously ill and injured members of the Armed Forces.

- http://turbotap.org
- http://www.nko.navy.mil
- http://www.npc.navy.mil
- http://www.aw2.army.mil
- http://www.my.af.mil/gcss-af/USAF/AFP40/d/1073755231/Files/C&BHandbook

Computer/Electronic Accommodations Program (CAP): The CAP program realized years ago that some of our service members return every day from deployment in OIF/OEF to Military Treatment Facilities (MTFs) because of injuries they sustained in the Global War on Terror. CAP works closely with wounded service members across the nation to ensure they receive appropriate accommodations and support services for their needs by introducing assistive technology during recovery and rehabilitation at MTFs.

Accommodations are available for service members with injuries that have caused: Dexterity Impairments, including upper extremity amputees, Vision loss, Hearing loss, Cognitive Injuries, including Traumatic Brain Injuries (TBI). The CAP staff is dedicated to ensuring all resources and assistive devices are available to assist our nation's service members in their rehabilitation process and employment search. For more information, please contact the wounded service member team at wsm@tma.osd.mil and visit their website at http://cap.mil/Programs/WSM.aspx.

DCoE Outreach Center for Psychological Health and Traumatic Brain Injury Information and Resources: (866) 966-1020 www.dcoe.health.mil

Defense and Veterans Brain Injury Center: The mission of the Defense and Veterans Brain Injury Center (DVBIC) is to serve active duty military, their beneficiaries, and veterans with traumatic brain injuries (TBIs) through state-of-the-art clinical care, innovative clinical research initiatives and educational programs. DVBIC fulfills this mission through ongoing collaboration with military, VA and civilian health partners, local communities, families and individuals with TBI. In 2008, DVBIC's mission expanded to include Force Health Protection and Management.

This encompasses the following Department of Defense (DoD) programs: TBI Surveillance, TBI Registry, Pre-deployment neurocognitive testing, Family Caregiver Curriculum, 15 year longitudinal study of TBI, and Independent study of automated neurocognitive tests and more. DVBIC has been named the Office of Responsibility or Executive Agency for these programs. DVBIC's multi-center network design and collaborations with forward medical commands allows for clinical innovation along the entire continuum of care: from initial injury in the war zone through to medical evacuation, acute care, rehabilitation and ultimately a return to community, family, and work or continued duty when possible. Please review the website for more information and resources at http://www.dvbic.org/About-DVBIC.aspx.

Department of Defense Wounded Warrior Resource Center: The Department of Defense announced on September 8th that the Military OneSource service has established a Wounded Warrior Resource Center telephone number and e-mail address for service members and their families, if they have concerns or other difficulties during their recovery process. Service members and their family members can now call (800) 342-9647 or e-mail wwrc@militaryonesource.com 24/7 to request support. Assistance provided by the resource center will not replace the specialized wounded warrior programs established by each of the military services, but it will offer another avenue of assistance for military facilities, health care services, and/or benefits information. Specially trained consultants will ensure consistent, quality customer-centric support. The consultants will identify the appropriate "warm hand-off" to either a military service or federal agency with authority to resolve the matter. The resource center consultant will maintain communication with the caller until the issue or concern is resolved. Please review site for more information at http://info.helmetstohardhats.org/content/career/wounded-warrior-resource-center-opens.

Disabled American Veterans: Is an organization of disabled veterans who are focused on building better lives for disabled veterans and their families. The organization accomplishes this goal by providing free assistance to veterans in obtaining benefits and service earned through their military service. It is fully funded through its membership dues and public contributions. It is **NOT** a government agency and receives no government funds. http://www.dav.org

Disability Benefits for Wounded Warriors: Military service members can receive expedited processing of disability claims from Social Security. Benefits available through Social Security are different than those from the Department of Veterans Affairs and require a separate application. The expedited process is used for military service members who become disabled while on active military service on or after October 1, 2001, regardless of where the disability occurs. This website will allow you an answer to the most common questions that are asked and will hopefully speed up your process and give you a better understanding of your benefits and what you need to do. http://www.ssa.gov/woundedwarriors/

DOL ReaLifelines: This site will guide wounded and injured service members and veterans access valuable online resources and contact information for one-on-one employment assistance to assist with the transition into the civilian workforce. You can contact 888-774-1361 for a ReaLifelines advisor or go to http://www.dol.gov/vets/programs/Real-life/main.htm.

DoD's T2 Virtual PSTD Experience: Accessed through the Second Life virtual-reality program, T2 allows service members to anonymously learn about symptoms of PTS, and where to get help. A service member can create an avatar to navigate through realistic scenarios in Second Life. These include a simulation demonstrating how PTS may be acquired during a combat-related traumatic event, an explanation of the connections between danger cues and triggers, the role of avoidance in the development of PTS, and how PTS is a normal human response to traumatic events. www.t2health.org/vwproj

Dryhootch of America: A nonprofit formed by combat veterans to help others returning home, officially opened its first veteran's center in Milwaukee on August 27, 2010. Rebuilding Together, a nonprofit group led the effort by partnering with The American Legion, Sears and local plumbers union 75 to help make the veterans center a reality. Dryhootch of American mission is to give returning soldiers a peace of mind and any further assistance they may need to transition back to civilian life. For further information go to Dryhootch of America facebook page.

Fisher House Foundation: Provides a safe home for military families to be close to loved one during hospitalization from an illness, disease or injury. http://www.fisherhouse.org

Gift from Within-PTSD Resource: A non-profit organization dedicated to those who suffer post-traumatic stress disorder (PTSD), and those who care for traumatized individuals. It provides information for survivors and caregivers. http://www.giftfromwithin.org

A couple of other sites of interest regarding PTSD Issues are:
- http://www.ptsdinfo.org
- http://www.giveanhour.org
- http://www.notalone.com

Healers and Heroes: Created by the Medical Society of New Jersey and the state's Department of Military and Veterans Affairs, the program gives returning service members opportunities to meet with consultations and referrals. www.njhealersandheroes.com

Marine Corps Wounded Warrior Regiment: Family Care is a very important part of the Wounded Warrior Regiment. The Regiment strives to identify and solve the unique family support needs of staff and wounded, ill, and injured (WII) Marine, their families, and caregivers. The Regiment provides information to families of the Wounded Warrior Regiment staff through Family Readiness Officers (FRO) and to the families of warriors on their recovery path through Family Support Coordinators (FSC). They offer a 24hour/7 day a week, 365 days a year contact at 1-877-487-6299 and their website is http://www.woundedwarriorregiment.org/FRO/FRO.cfm.

Military Assistance Program Central: Assistance with Casualty and Mortuary Affairs. http://osd.dtic.mil/mapcentral/casualty.html

National Center for PTSD: The Center aims to help U.S. veterans and others through research, education and training on trauma and PTSD. www.ptsd. va.gov

National Guard Psychological Health Program: National Guard members and families should never weather emotional and behavioral challenges alone. That is why the National Guard Psychological Health Program is here for you, with Directors of Psychological help in every state, territory and the District of Columbia to ensure you receive the care you deserve. You will find information and contacts to help you and your family build resiliency, including education to support overall wellness, support for family members and friends, and immediate access to help if you are experiencing troubling symptoms. Their library is home to numerous online resources on topics ranging from Post-Traumatic Stress Disorder to Traumatic Brain Injury and more. http://www. jointservicessupport.org/PHP/Default.aspx

National Veterans Services Fund, Inc: (Located in Darien, Connecticut) This organization provides case-managed social services and limited medical assistance to Vietnam-Persian Gulf War Veterans and their families, with focus on families with disabled children. http://www.angelfire.com/ct2/natvetsvc/

National Association of American Veterans: Assisting all veterans and families, from WWII, Korean War, Vietnam, Desert Storm, Enduring Freedom and Operation Iraqi Freedom who are severely wounded by helping to access health benefits, improving communication and coordination and collaborating among health agencies, medical professional organizations, educational organizations and the public. http://www.naavets.org

National Intrepid Center of Excellence (NICoE): NICoE is a treatment center in Bethesda, MD that blends cognitive and holistic therapies in a plan that also includes family education and reintegration support. Family members stay at a

Fisher House during treatment. You can call (866) 966-1020 for more information or email resources@dcoeoutreach.org. www.dcoe.health.mil/componentcenters/nicoe.aspx.

Navy Bureau of Medicine and Surgery: The Navy Bureau of Medicine and Surgery (BUMED) is the headquarters command for Navy Medicine. Under the leadership of the Navy Surgeon General, Navy Medicine provides high quality health care to beneficiaries in wartime and in peacetime. Highly trained Navy Medicine personnel deploy with sailors and marines worldwide - providing critical mission support aboard ship, in the air, under the sea and on the battlefield. At the same time, Navy Medicine's military and civilian health care professionals are providing care for uniformed services' family members and retirees at military treatment facilities around the globe. Every day, no matter what the environment, Navy Medicine is ready to care for those in need, providing world-class care, anytime, anywhere. Today, BUMED is the site where the policies and direction for Navy Medicine are developed to ensure our Patient and Family Center Care vision carried out. http://www.med.navy.mil/BUMED/Pages/default.aspx

Navy Safe Harbor: Navy Safe Harbor is the Navy's lead organization for coordinating the non-medical care of wounded, ill and injured sailors, coast guardsmen and their families. Through proactive leadership, they will provide a lifetime of individually tailored assistance designed to help the service member succeed in recovery, rehabilitation, and reintegration activities. Please go to the website for further information regarding this organization. www.persnit.many.mil/commandsupport/safeharbor/

National Suicide Prevention Lifeline: If you or someone you know feels like they just can't handle life anymore, please immediately call this toll free number: (800) 273-8255 or go to www.suicidepreventionlifeline.org.

***Not Alone:** Is an online confidential personal, virtual or group counseling site for military families, wounded warriors, and much more. *This site comes highly recommended to me by a friend.* www.notalone.com

Paralyzed Veterans of America: This wonderful organization's mission is to change the lives and build brighter futures for the seriously injured heroes and empower them with what they need to achieve the things they fought for: freedom and independence. This organization was founded by a band of service members who came home from World War II with a spinal cord injury. They returned to a grateful nation, but also to a world with few solutions to the challenges they faced. They are a group of fine service members who made the decision not just to live, but to live with dignity as contributors to society. They created Paralyzed Veterans of America, an organization dedicated to veterans' service, medical research and civil rights for people with disabilities. For further information about this group and contact information, go to http://www.pva.org/.

Real Warriors Campaign: (866) 966-1020, www.realwarriors.net

Real Warriors (Combating Psychological Health Care Stigma): SAMHSA is partnering with the Department of Defense's Centers of Excellence for Psychological Health and Traumatic Brain Injury (DCoE) on its Real Warriors Campaign. Real Warriors focuses on combating the stigma associated with seeking care and treatment for psychological health concerns. With the campaign theme, "Real Warriors, Real Battles, Real Strength," the web site features resources on psychological health issues. They also feature video interviews with service members, their families, and others dealing with psychological health or traumatic brain injury issues. Every page of the site lists the Veterans Suicide Prevention Hotline (1-800-273-TALK, press 1 for veterans), which is a partnership between SAMHSA and the Department of Veterans Affairs. Please review the site for more important information about this subject. http://www.samhsa.gov/SAMHSAnewsLetter/Volume_17_Number_3/RealWarriors.aspx

Ride 2 Recovery: Is produced by the Fitness Challenge Foundation, (a 501c3) in partnership with the military and VA Volunteer Service Office to benefit mental and physical rehabilitation programs for our country's wounded veterans that feature cycling as the core activity. For more information about this program or how to participate you can go to the website at www.ride2recovery.com.

*Soldiers Best Friend: Is a program that pairs shelter dogs with veterans who have Post Traumatic Stress Disorder. After training, the former shelter dogs are actual service dogs that veterans can take anywhere they go. For more information, visit the Soldiers Best Friend website at http://soldiersbestfriend.org/. *Great organization, love the work they are doing!*

Women Veterans of America (WVA): Female veterans face their own array of issues after they have finished active duty. WVA was created to be a resource for female veterans and for the families and friends who support them. On this site you can learn about women veteran's health issues, information on military sexual trauma and the balancing of motherhood with service. The site will provide assistance with understanding military benefits and direct you towards organizations and resources advocating for women veterans. These resources are for current and past members of the military service. http://www.womenveteransofamerica.com/about

Wounded Warrior Regiment: Will provide daily support for the non-medical and medical care of wounded, ill and injured reserve marines. The majority of the Wounded Warrior Regiments staff consists of reserve marines, which allows a heightened awareness with regard to reserve specific issues. For more information, visit the Wounded Warrior Regiment website at www.woundedwarriorregiment.org or call 877-487-6299.

The Wounded Warriors Traumatic Brain Injury Project: Is a collaborative effort between Grand Valley State University and Mary Free Bed Rehabilitation Hospital, with funding from the Department of Defense. The program is designed to provide a comprehensive, individualized outpatient rehabilitation services to wounded warriors with traumatic brain injury addressing their physical, cognitive and psychosocial needs. Service members will also be able to access online information and training about traumatic brain injury that is geared towards recovery. Services may include but are not limited to: Occupational, physical, and speech therapies, psychological counseling, on-the-job coaching, social work, driver's rehabilitation and family and group support. Eligibility includes: experience a traumatic brain injury on active duty or training status within the last nine years and no pre-existing neurological or psychiatric condition before injury. For more information you can call 888-736-0208 or visit www.maryfreebed.com/woundedwarriors, or email woundedwarrior@maryfreebed.com.

Veterans Airlift Command: Provides FREE air transportation to wounded veterans and their families for medical and other compassionate purposes, through a national network of volunteer aircraft owners and pilots. Their priority is for the veterans of OIF and OEF. http://www.veteransairlift.org/

Veterans & Families United: Assists with physical and mental issues with soldiers. http://www.veteransfamiliesunited.org/how_to_get_help.html

Veteran Homestead: (Based out of Fitchburg, MA) Provides medical, psychological, and spiritual care to veterans who are diagnosed with a terminal illness, the elderly, and/or the disabled or otherwise needed. http://www.veteranhomestead.org

Voice of Warriors: The goal of Voice of Warriors is to help veterans connect with resources available to them at a local and national level. They address topics such as military suicide, traumatic brain injury, PTSD, multiple deployments to war zones. They provide online forums, information, a radio show and community awareness projects. http://voiceofwarriors.com

***Warrior Care:** This site hopes to set an example for military well being, and serves as a portal to various resources ranging from specific programs to sources of information. Whether you are currently active-duty military, veteran, a family member or a concerned neighbor, the links on this site will provide answers to your questions or ideas for where to turn next. www.warriorcare.mil *This is a really nice website that offers assistance for not only the wounded but also has links to resources for other services for military families.*

Wounded Soldier and Family Hotline: (800) 984-8523

***Wounded Warrior Project:** Mission is to honor and empower wounded warriors and to foster the most successful, well-adjusted generation of wounded warriors in this nation's history. Their purpose is to raise awareness and enlist the public's aid for the needs of injured service members, to help injured service members with aid and assist each other, and to provide unique, direct programs and services to meet the needs of injured service members. *This is a wonderful organization; please check out their website to see* *what all they have to offer.* http://www.woundedwarriorproject.org/mission.aspx. *This is a great group of volunteers and employees. I have met several of them throughout the years. Great organization!!*

A Warrior's Wish Foundation: The Warrior Wish Foundation enhances the lives of United States military veterans and their families who are battling a life-limiting illness. Through the fantastic financial support of generous donors, the financial contributions of veterans' service organizations, a volunteer network and wonderful partnerships, they are able to grant the wishes of those who have served. A wish may be as simple as a new hearing aid or scooter chair, or as involved as one last family vacation or reunion. http://awarriorwish.org/

EMERGENCY ASSISTANCE

*American Patriot Hero's Fund: Is a non-profit organization that is committed to supporting veterans by making wishes come true for disabled veterans through charitable donations, by providing emergency funding for active and reserve military veterans, by providing care packages to veteran facilities and troops overseas and by offering direct services at a discounted price for all veterans. Some of these services include: job placement, estate planning, mortgage and tax consultations, insurance advice and health care services. For more information and application assistance go to http://americanpatriotheroesfund.org/. *Great organization with great ideas!*

American Military Families: Provides emergency financial assistance and assistance with remodeling wounded warriors homes. They offer assistance and resources in other areas too. Please go to website for more information. http://www.amf100.org/AMFWoundedWarriorProgram.html

American Red Cross Armed Forces Casualty Travel Assistance Program: The service to the Armed Forces Casualty Travel Assistance Program (CTAP) is a one-time grant available to up to two immediate family members who are not on Invitational Travel Orders (ITOs) or government funded. The program provides assistance for travel, lodging and food expenses for: A) Travel to the bedside of a service member injured in a combat zone in the CENTCOM Area of Responsibility (AOR), who is hospitalized in a medical facility in the continental United States/U.S. Territories. Assistance will be provided upon the recommendation of the attending medical authorities. B) Travel to the funeral or memorial service for a service member killed in action in the CENTCOM AOR. For more information about this program you can go to, http://www.redcross.org/portal/site/en/menuitem.d8aaec f214c576bf971e4cfe43181aa0/?vgnextoid=a6181b655eb3b110VgnVCM100000 89f0870aRCRD&vgnextfmt=default. To locate your local Red Cross chapter you can go to: http://myarmyonesource.com/News/2010/02/RedCross.

AmVets: Has a proud history of assisting veterans and sponsoring numerous programs that serve our country and its citizens. AmVets assists in many different ways. http://www.amvets.org

Heroes to Hometowns: The American Legion works closely with VA and DoD in local communities to provide support for severely wounded military personnel trying to restart their lives at home. Family support, entertainment, claims assistance and vehicle adaptation are among the ways the Legion can help. www.legion.org/heroes or email heroestohometowns@legion.org

Injured Marine Semper Fi Fund: Provides financial grants and other assistance to the marines, sailors and families of those injured serving our nation. http://semperfifunding.org/

National Resource Directory: Online resource for wounded, ill, or injured service members, veterans and their families and those who support them. The directory provides information and contacts for those in the armed forces community to find support in a multitude of areas. www.nationalresourcedirectory.gov

Operation Family Fund: Provides emotional and emergency assistance to the families of fallen soldiers. http://www.operationfamilyfund.org/

The Patriot Fund: This fund is for all disabled service members and their families with needed funds, jobs, information, equipment and medical care as our resources permit. For more information go to http://www.patriotfund.us/.

Patriot Fund Endowment: Sponsored by The American Legion Department of Michigan and offered to Michigan Veterans of all eras and their families in times of financial hardship, especially those who may not qualify for assistance under the existing Legion, county, and VA programs. Funds get distributed after approval of the State Adjutant in concert with the State Reconnect Chairman. For more information go to http://www.michiganlegion.org/pdfs/endow_fund.pdf or your local American Legion office for assistance.

OTHER RESOURCES

Armed Forces Foundation: Is dedicated to providing comfort and solace to members of the military community through financial support, career counseling, housing assistance and recreational therapy programs. They provide assistance to active duty and retired personnel, National Guard, Reserve Components, and their loved ones. http://www.armedforcesfoundation.org/about.php

Bold Brave Courageous: This organization provides comfort items for injured military personnel returning from Afghanistan and Iraq. http://www.boldbravecourageous.com/frameset.htm

Fannie Mae Military Forbearance Option: If you're facing a financial hardship due to a death or injury of a service member on active duty, you may be eligible for a special military forbearance option. Forbearance is an agreement between you and your mortgage company to temporarily suspend or reduce your monthly mortgage payments for a specific period (usually between 90-180 days) of time. This option lets you deal with your short-term financial problems by giving you time to get back on your feet and bring your mortgage current.

With a military forbearance, you may qualify for additional benefits such as a longer forbearance period—up to six months—and no adverse impact to your credit score (all credit reporting related to your mortgage loan will be suspended during the forbearance period). Additionally, a special hotline has been set up for additional guidance about this option and other mortgage assistance programs 877-MIL-4566. www.knowyouroptions.com/Military

Forgotten Eagles of Michigan: This wonderful organization works to heighten awareness and to publicize the POW/MIA issues, to educate the public on the plight of POW/MIA's, to advocate for the fullest possible accounting of all of America's POW/MIAs, to heighten awareness and education of the public on the effects of Agent Orange/Dioxin and of the chemical, biological and radiological weapons testing on the U.S. Military Personnel. To promote physical and cultural improvement, growth and development, self-respect, self-confidence and usefulness of America's veterans and families, to assist America's disabled in-need veterans, their dependents and the widows and orphans of deceased veterans, and to help not-for-profit organizations that have similar interests at heart. Please view the website for other useful information and resources. http://forgotteneagles.org/

Guardian Angels for Soldier's Pets: This organizations mission is supporting our military, veterans, and their beloved pets to ensure the pets are reunited with their owners following a deployment (combat or peace-keeping mission) in harm's way to fight the global war on terrorism or unforeseen emergency hardship impacting their ability to retain their pet's ownership rights. Please go to the website to get further information on eligibility. http://guardianangelsforsoldierspet.org

Homes for Our Troops: Provides homes for the severely wounded and disabled since Sep 1, 2004 at no cost to the veterans or their families. An eligible Veteran or service members may receive a Veterans Administration Specially Adapted Housing Grant up to a maximum amount of $63,780. Homes for Our Troops assistance covers all costs over and above this grant to ensure that the home is provided at no cost to the recipient. View the website for more information and assistance requirements/application. *This is a wonderful organization, I got an opportunity to work with a couple people who were fixing a veterans house in Michigan. Great group!!* http://www.homesforourtroops.org

Honor Flight Network: Is a non-profit organization created solely to honor America's veterans for all their sacrifices. They will transport our heroes to Washington, D.C. to visit and reflect at their memorials. Top priority is given to the senior veterans—World War II survivors, along with those other veterans who may be terminally ill. For more information, go to http://www.honorflight.org/.

Iraqi and Afghanistan Veterans of American (IAVA) Connect with other veterans, get access to critical resources and play a role in tackling issues that impact our community. http://iava.org/membership

Luke's Wings: Provides travel planning services and airplane tickets for the families of wounded warriors currently hospitalized at medical and rehabilitation centers all over the country. www.lukeswings.org

Military One Source: Education, health, relocation, parenting, stress—you name it—Military OneSource helps with just about any need. Available by phone or online, the free service is provided by the Department of Defense for active-duty, Guard and Reserve service members and their families. The service is completely private and confidential, with few exceptions. http://www.militaryonesource.com/MOS.aspx

Military Order of the Purple Heart: Mission is to foster an environment of goodwill and camaraderie among Combat Wounded Veterans, promote patriotism, support necessary legislative initiatives, and most importantly, provide service to all veterans and their families. http://www.purpleheart.org

Military Pathways: An online self-screening program for mental and emotional health. (877) 877-3647 www.militarymentalhealth.org

National Resource Directory: A revitalized Department of Labor online directory promises access to services and resources for wounded troops, veterans and their families. The National Resource Directory provides links to national, state and local sources that support recovery, rehabilitation and community reintegration. The site offers information for vets seeking education, training and employment. It also provides help for employers who want to hire veterans, understand employment laws and make workplace accommodations for disabled vets. For more information go to http://www.nationalresourcedirectory.gov.

Operation Comfort Warriors: Helps to purchase comfort items for U.S. troops recovering from combat wounds and illnesses. The fund has provided items ranging from sweat suits to video-game players at various military hospitals since 2008, when it was launched. For more information or assistance go to http://www.legion.org/troops/operationcomfort.

Operation Hero Mile: This program is comprised of individual airlines whose passengers donate their frequent flyer miles to assist service members and their families. Specifically, Fisher House Foundation provides free airline tickets to military men and women who are undergoing treatment at a military or VA medical center incident to their service in Iraq or Afghanistan, and their families. Visit their website for further information regarding eligibility and rules. http://www.fisherhouse.org/programs/hero-miles/

***Operation Heroes & Hounds:** A wonderful program that offers injured members of the United States Armed Forces an opportunity to live with and coach (play/train) shelter dogs. Participants include the "walking wounded" of the U.S. military suffering from non-visible ailments such as post-traumatic stress disorder and traumatic brain injury. Shelter dogs that are chosen for the program need to be coached (play/trained) to be well-mannered dogs, which the wounded warriors accomplish through the kind, nonaggressive teaching of "the loved dog method." Together the soldiers and dogs can heal their emotional wounds while gaining new life skills. For more information and contact information go to http://www.petconnect.us/article/helping/operationheroes.htm. *Wonderful organization, I love what they are doing!*

Operation Second Chance: Committed to serving wounded, injured and all combat veterans. The organization will give support while the service member is recovering in hospitals. Please see site for more details. http://www.operationsecondchance.org/

*Operation We Are Here (Service Dogs): This is a wonderful website that offers 24 different organizations that dedicate their time to training service dogs, home companion dogs and residential companion dogs to assist individuals who have a wide range of physical and cognitive disabilities for wounded warriors and veterans. Please take the time to review each organization as they differ in locations and abilities. *All are wonderful organizations. The website has other information about military families that will be of interest to you also.* http://www.operationwearehere.com/MilitaryServiceDogs.html

*Operation We Are Here: This is a wonderful website that offers information and links to resources for military families and veterans about retreats, books, Youth links, links for parents of service members, emotional support, marriage, and much more. Please review the site at http://www.operationwearehere.com.

P2V: Founded by Air Force Veteran and PTS sufferer David Sharpe, P2V pairs up specially trained dogs with active-duty personnel, veterans and emergency first responders, as well as spouses and survivors. Other organizations, such as Patriot PAWS and Hounds4Heroes, offer similar services. DoD and VA are studying the effects of such programs. You can email any questions to info@pets2vets.org or call (877) 311-4728. www.P2V.org.

Paint a Miracle Art Studio: Is for injured veterans and individuals with disabilities and is uniquely designed for people with traumatic brain injuries and other disabilities. Dr. Dale Propson, a TBI survivor and a former captain in the Air Force, created the organization. For more information about this wonderful organization, go to www.paintamiracle.org or you can contact Rachelle Propson Tyshka, Executive Director at shelly@paintamiracle.org or 248-652-2702.

*Pets2Vets: Pairs homeless pets with combat veterans, law enforcement/emergency personnel, and those affected by PTSD. An Air Force Senior Airman who, after returning home from Iraq, struggled with his own experience started Pets2Vets. He went to a pit-bull rescue facility and adopted a puppy. Through his own success, he started the group. This group has made two or three matches a week since its creation. The group's objective is to assist our nation's heroes and their families with rehabilitation through pet therapy, save sheltered pets from being euthanized by providing them with homes, and to raise public awareness of PTSD. To learn more about this wonderful group, go to http://myarmyonesource.com/News/2010/02/VetsDogs or http://www.awla. org/pets2vets.shtml. *Great organization with wonderful people!*

Rebuilding Together Quad Cities: Rehabilitates the home of low-income homeowners, particularly the elderly, disabled and families with dependent children. www.rebuildingtogetherquadcities.org/

Rebuilding Together-Veterans Housing Initiative: Fills the gaps in housing modification and repair services for retired and active duty service members and strives to provide safe and accessible housing for all low-income veterans. Partners with Project H.E.R.O. (Homes Eliminated of Restrictions and Obstacles), an innovative program to make homes accessible to disabled veterans across the United States. www.rebuildingtogether.org/section/ initiatives/vet

Sentinels of Freedom: Provides life-changing opportunities for men and women of the U.S. Armed Forces who have suffered severe injuries and need the support of grateful communities to realize their goals and dreams. http:// www.sentinelsoffreedom.org

Stars and Stripes: Their mission is to fly WWII veterans and terminally ill veterans from other wars to see their memorials in Washington, D.C. They also work closely with schools throughout Wisconsin to ensure that the heroic stories of veterans are built into the curriculum so that future generations will fully appreciate the sacrifices made on their behalf. http://starsandstripeshonorflight.org/

The Mission Continues: To build an America where EVERY returning veteran, wounded or otherwise can serve again as a citizen leader, and where together who honor the fallen by living their lives through service. http://www. missioncontinues.org

Transition Warrior Care: Will ensure equitable, consistent, high-quality support and service for all branches of wounded warriors and their families, as well as transitioning members of the Armed Forces, through effective outreach, interagency collaboration, policy and program oversight. http://warriorcare. dodlive.mil/about/

United We Serve: Provides a safe haven for all military branches, veterans and family members during times of difficulty and crisis. http://www. unitedweservemil.org/about-us

VA Benefit - VA Automobile & Special Adaptive Equipment Grants: You may qualify for the VA benefit of automobile assistance if you have: A) a service connected loss or permanent loss of use of one or both hands or feet or B) A permanent impairment of vision of both eyes to a certain degree; or C) Entitlement to compensation for alkalosis (immobility) of one or both knees or one of both hips. VA provides a one-time payment of not more than $11,000 toward the purchase of an automobile or other vehicle. The VA also pays for adaptive equipment and for repair, replacement or reinstallation required because of disability. To apply for this benefit or request further information, contact the nearest VA Regional Office or call 800-827-1000. www.vba.va.gov/VBA/benefits/factsheets/serviceconn

VFW: Great emergency assistance and resource during this time of need. http://www.vfw.org/

Voice of Warriors: Voice of Warriors is an organization made up of military veterans, their family members and concerned American Citizens. Their mission is to bring awareness to the American population on obstacles our military families face daily and hope to connect them to resources that are available to them at local and national levels. At VOW, they endeavor to help veterans connect with resources available to them at local and national level. http://voiceofwarriors.com/about/

Warrior Transition Program: This website is a primary means for the Warrior Transition Office (WTO) to communicate with WT Cadre, Supported Commands, senior military leaders and others with an interest in keeping abreast of the various aspects of the Army's Warrior Transition Program. http://www.army.mil/info/organization/offices/eoh/wtc/

CAREER/JOB TRANSITION

Center for Veteran Enterprise (Veteran Business Opportunities): Vetbiz.gov is a veteran resource information web site designed to assist veteran entrepreneurs who want to start and expand their businesses in the Federal and private marketplace. This site provides up to the minute information from the Federal Government as it pertains to service disabled and veteran owned small businesses. http://www.vetbiz.gov/

Civilians Working for National Defense: The Department of Defense (DoD) provides employment opportunities for disabled men and women who honorably served on behalf of our nation. As the largest federal employer of veterans, they state they are committed to providing every disabled veteran who wants to serve our country as a Department of Defense civil servant the opportunity to do so. http://www.godefense.com/, http://www.godefense.com/entry-level.html, and http://www.military.com/vetcareers?ESRC=ggl_mem_car_civilian.kw&np=1&nipkw=civilian%20jobs&ppcseid=6110&ppcsekeyword=civilian+jobs&mmtctg=212002230&mmtcmp=5072820&mmtmt=5&mmtgglcnt=0&mmtadid=4980302640&niadgrp=Civilian+Careers&nicmp=Hiring+and+jobs&nichan=Google

Coalition to Salute America's Heroes: Mission is helping disabled wounded veterans find their way to a "New Beginning" and a better life. http://saluteheroes.org/

Entrepreneurship Boot Camp for Veterans with Disabilities (EBV): Offers cutting-edge, experiential training in entrepreneurship and small business management to post-9/11 veterans with disabilities resulting from their service to our country. The EBV is designed to open the door to business ownership for our veterans by 1) developing your skills in the many steps and activities associated with launching and growing a small business, and by 2) helping you leverage programs and services for veterans and people with disabilities in a way that furthers your entrepreneurial dreams.

Six universities offer the all-expenses paid program that teaches disabled veterans how to run their own business. Besides Syracuse, the program also is offered at the University of California-Los Angeles, Florida State University, Texas A&M University, Purdue University and the University of Connecticut. The nine-day "residency" exposes vets to the nuts and bolts of business ownership through workshops and lessons from faculty. Participants will also receive yearlong mentorships. Visit http://www.whitman.syr.edu/ebv/ for more information and eligibility requirements. You can contact Ellie Komanecky, EBV's National Program Administrator at: (315)-443-6007, (315) 443-6899 or email ebvinfor@syr.edu.

Military Franchising (JOBS): If you are looking to earn extra income on the side and operate a business out of your home, a home-based franchise may interest you. This website is a list of home-based franchise opportunities for military spouses and veterans. Find "military-spouse/veteran friendly" home-based franchise opportunities. http://www.militaryfranchising.com/spouse/default.aspx

Network of Champions: Is a project formed in 2008 by defense contractor Northrop Grumman to help wounded service members return to civilian life. More than 60 employers are dedicated to hiring vets suffering from injuries or illnesses incurred while deployed in Operation Iraqi Freedom or Operation Enduring Freedom. Essentially, if you apply for a job with any company in this network, if the company does not have a job that fits your skills, they will circulate your resume (with your permission) to other companies within the network.

Some of the companies that are a part of this program are: Able Forces, Aerotek, Inc., Bank of America, Best Buy, Boeing, Capital One Bank, Colonial Circuits, Cubic, Deloitte & Touche, Federal Staffing Resources, General Electric, General Motors, Helmets to Hardhats, Homeland Security Careers, Homeland Security Management Institute, Long Island University, HR Works, Kelly Connect, Lockheed Martin Corporation, National Glass Association, NAVAIR, NAVSEA, Nielsen Associates, Pinkerton Government Services, Pinnacle Solutions, Quantum Executive Group, Raytheon, Silverstar Consulting Inc., Smart Solutions, SunTrust Bank, TASC, Team River Runners, TELEDYNE, The Sierra Group, Travelers Insurance Company, US Naval Sailing Association (USNSA), US Naval Sailing Foundation (USNSF). http://careers.northropgrumman.com/network_of_champions.html. If your company (and/or if you know of a company) has an interest in supporting career opportunities for wounded warriors, you can contact them at operationimpact@ngc.com.

SBA Patriot Express: The SBA "Patriot Express" loan program helps the military community open their own small business. SBA loans up to $500,000

and may be used for business startup, expansion, equipment purchase, working capital, inventory or business-occupied real estate purchase. Interest rates generally are 2.25% to 2.75% above the prime rate, based upon the amount and maturity of the loan. Veterans' business development officers man SBA district offices in every state. They can provide lists of area Patriot Express lenders as well as additional small business advice and resources.

In addition, the Veterans Business Outreach Program provides entrepreneurial development services such as business training, counseling and mentoring to eligible veterans owning or considering starting a small business. Check into your local SBA and see what all they have to provide for you and your family. Patriot Express Loans are available to veterans, service-disabled veterans, active-duty military eligible for the military's Transition Assistance Program, Reservists and National Guard members, current spouses of any of these groups, and surviving spouses of members or veterans who died during service or from a service-connected disability. http://www.sba.gov/content/patriot-express

U.S. House Wounded Warrior Program: Was established to create fellowships that provide employment opportunities within the House of Representatives. The fellowship will provide veterans with experience and exposure to ultimately broaden their scope of transition opportunities. Positions are available in Congressional member district offices nationwide. Wherever possible, those selected for the program will be given the opportunity to transition into full-time employment. However, full-time employment is not guaranteed at the conclusion of the two-year fellowship.

Applicants must have served on active duty since September 22, 1001, have a 30% or greater service-connected disability rating and less than 20 years of service. If a fellowship is located within a members' district, the appointment is contingent on the Representative's continuous representation of that district. In addition to a current resume, applicants must submit a copy of their DD214 and a VA letter confirming that they have at least a 30% service-connected disability rating. For more information and contact information, go to http://www.cao.house.gov/wwp-about.shtml.

EDUCATION/SCHOLARSHIPS

Army Nurse Corps Association (ANCA): ANCA awards scholarships to U.S. citizen students attending accredited baccalaureate or graduate nursing or anesthesia nursing programs. This scholarship is in honor of Cpt. Joshua M. McClimans, AN, USAR, who was killed in a mortar attack in April 2011 while assigned to the Combat Support Hospital at Forward Operating Base Salerno in Afghanistan. For more information about this scholarship and eligibility requirements go to http://e-anca.org/ANCAEduc.htm.

Army Ranger Association: This scholarship program is a memorial to selfless service and contributions made to our country by USARA members. These awards are given in their honor. This program provides an opportunity to provide financial assistance to qualified dependents of USARA members in furthering their education. The scholarship committee seeks to award scholarships to applicants displaying the potential for a degree in higher education, whether it is technical, university or professional. Each year the scholarship committee evaluates the scholarship applicants and selects the most outstanding submissions to be awarded to USARA Legacy Scholarship. For further information about this scholarship and eligibility requirements go to http://www.ranger.org/.

Army Reserve Association: Offers scholarships for dependents of service members. Please review the website at http://www.armyreserve.org for further information and eligibility.

Children of Fallen Soldiers Relief Fund: Was founded as a means of providing college grants and financial assistance to surviving children and spouses of our U.S. military service members who have lost their lives in the Iraq and Afghanistan wars. The program will assists disabled service member families too. For further information or to apply for assistance, go to http://www.cfsrf.org/.

Sgt. Dakota Meyer Scholarship: This scholarship is in partnership with the Marine Corps Scholarship Foundation to help education the children of wounded Marines and Navy Corpsmen. http://www.dakotameyer.com/

Disabled Patriot Fund: Is an all-volunteer group of area business people and local officials who have come together to help disabled American veterans who have fought in the war on terror. An Illinois not-for-profit corporation, their mission statement is "To provide financial relief for local U.S. Military families who have been adversely affected by the War on Terror." To review eligibility and contact information go to http://disabledpatriotfund.com.

*Educational Benefits for Children of Disabled or Deceased Veterans: This tuition grant program is administered by the Michigan (or your state) Higher Education Assistance Authority in the Michigan Department of Treasury provides payment for the education of the children of a veteran who is totally disabled from service incurred causes, was killed in the line of duty, has died subsequently from a service-related disability, was totally disabled before death from a service-connected illness or injury, or who is listed by the federal government as missing in action in a foreign country. A student may be eligible for a tuition waiver of up to $2,800 annually for undergraduate study. Recipients must meet certain eligibility requirements. Information on eligibility and application forms are available at www.michigan.gov/studentaid or by calling toll-free 888-447-2687. *Check with your state for this same support.*

Fallen Patriot Fund/The Mark Cuban Foundation: Was established to help families of U.S. Military personnel who were killed or seriously injured during

Operation Iraqi Freedom. Go to http://fallenpatriotfund.org/ for eligibility and further information.

Fold of Honor Foundation Scholarship: Provides scholarships for dependents and spouses of service members that have been killed or disabled as a result of their military service. http://www.foldsofhonor.org/

*Military to Medicine: Offers an easy way for service members and military families to gain a career in health care that can move with you. Whether you have experience and/or education currently or just starting out this program can help you. Military to Medicine's online training is in partnership with The Claude Moore Health Education Program and provides students with real-life job standards and role expectations. Both students and healthcare employers can feel confident that Military to Medicine course work demonstrates realistic, healthcare workplace skills. Military to Medicine is committed to participants' long-term career success. Before specific career courses begin, Military to Medicine assesses each student's interests and abilities, this information helps students set career goals and select career courses.

At the writing of this book, tuition for the initial assessment was $599, for the career-specific courses (front office medical assistant or medical records and health information assistant), the tuition was $1,850. The tuition includes the eBooks, eLearning materials and completion certificates, Scholarships are available. This program is available for military spouses, wounded warriors and their caregivers, veterans, National Guard, Reserve and their Spouses and service members transitioning to civilian employment. For more information go to www.militarytomedicine.org.

Scholarships for Severely Injured Service Members and Their Dependents: http://www.dantes.doded.mil/sfd/index.asp?Flag=True

Society of Sponsors of the United States Navy Centennial Scholarship Program: Offered to Iraq-Afghanistan combat wounded veterans who are pursuing a degree that leads to license and certification as a teacher. The Society of Sponsors of the United States Navy, is an organization of women who serve as ship sponsors, and dedicated to promoting educational opportunities for the men and women who serve in the United States Navy and Marine Corps. In support of this goal, the Society has established scholarships for Navy-Marine Corps veterans who were injured in combat. The Society will support individuals who pursue a career in education, by making available five $3,000 annual scholarships for "education related" expenses. There is no deadline for this program; you may apply at any time. For an application and more information go to http://www.nmcrs.org/education.html.

Special Operation Warrior Fund Operation: The Special Operations Warrior Foundation provides full scholarship grants and educational and family counseling to the surviving children of special operations personnel who die in operational or training missions and immediate financial assistance to severely wounded special operations personnel and their families. http://www.specialops.org

State Provided Educational Benefits: Educational benefits for families, particularly children of deceased, MIA, POW, and disabled veterans, may be available in some states. Military.com has developed an on-line general summary of educational benefits for veterans, surviving spouses and their dependents.

- www.military.com
- http://www.military.com/benefits/content/survivor-benefits/surviving-spouse-and-family-education-benefits.html
- http://www.military.com/benefits/content/survivor-benefits/survivors-resource-list.html.

Stateside Spouse Education Assistance Program (SSEAP): This scholarship program assists Army spouses obtain a four year undergraduate degree. Spouses of active duty soldiers, spouses of retired soldiers, and widows and widowers of soldiers who died either on active duty or in a retired status are eligible. http://www.aerhq.org/education_spouseeducation_StateSide.asp

VETS Scholarship Program: Provides hope and opportunities for wounded veterans in the Baltimore and Washington, DC Metro Region. For more information please go to http://www.usamarylandjobs.com/2011/02/08/project-vets-scholarship-program-provides-hope-and-opportunities-for-wounded-veterans-in-the-baltimore-and-washington-dc-metro-region/.

Veteran's Scholarship Fund, VFW Post 5855: This VFW Post out of Portage, Michigan offers a $500 grant to be awarded twice a year. This grant is open to **all Michigan veterans only** that are attending higher educational institutions. This is a onetime per person and grants will be sent to schools financial aid departments. For more information, eligibility requirements and to download the applications go to www.vfw5855.org. Or you can contact Mr. Al Mar at (269) 324-2371.

RETREATS/CAMPS

Disabled Veterans Rest Camp (Washington County, Minnesota): This camp provides and facilities opportunities for recreation, rest, and wellbeing for all women and men who have served or are serving in the Armed Forces of the United States, along with their families. The campground is open to all military personnel in good standing: Active duty, Reservists/Guard, veterans, disabled, retirees, families and friends. www.vetscampmn.org

*F.I.S.H. Fishermen in Support of Heroes: This organization was organized as a way to show appreciation to military service members for the job they do protecting our country. They have combined a passion for fishing and admiration for military families.

This group primary focus on the Wounded Warriors who come back from Iraq and Afghanistan to Camp LeJeune and Fort Bragg to recover from their injuries and they organize trips to take them fishing. Donations of private boats, charter boats, ocean piers and other venues are used take military families fishing. All all the gear, licenses, food, drinks and bait are provided. Plenty of volunteers are also there to help bait hooks, demonstrate techniques, clean fish, and other chores as needed. *This group is way cool; I would love to participate in this some time!* www.fishheroes.org

Fishing for Freedom - (Quincy, Illinois): By their very nature, outdoor recreational activities are extremely therapeutic and have been shown through recent examples to make a difference in our returning warrior's lives. Although angling is only one of those outdoor activities, it is one that can help our returning heroes escape the hardships of combat deployments and begin the process of assimilation back into to everyday life.

Inspired by the Army Bass Anglers, and fishing guides to take wounded warriors and GWOT veterans out for a day of tournament bass fishing. With assistance from a network of bass anglers throughout the region and caring local and corporate sponsors, the Bi-State Basser's Bass Club will be hosting their annual Fishing for Freedom event in June at the Quincy IL fishing on the mighty Mississippi River. www.fishingforfreedomquincy.org

Fly-Fishing Therapy Resources: These organizations are here to help wounded soldiers get back their life and rebuild skills and goals for the future.

- **Project Healing Waters:** www.projecthealingwaters.org
- **Trout Unlimited:** www.tu.org (800) 834-2419
- **Federation of Fly Fishers:** www.fedflyfishers.org (406) 222-9369
- **Warriors & Quiet Waters Foundation:** www.warriorsandquietwaters.org
- **River of Recovery:** www.riversofrecovery.org (303) 801-8022
- **Sun Valley Adaptive Sports** www.svasp.org (208) 726-9298

Freedom Hunt: Is provided by many community sponsors in partnership with the Fort Custer Training Center in Augusta, Michigan. The Freedom Hunt is an early firearm deer hunt (occurring in Mid-October) for disabled individuals, free of charge. In order to participate in the early hunt, applicants must have a disability that satisfies one of the following categories: 100% disabled or deemed individually unemployable as determined by the U.S. Veterans Administration; legally blind; possess a permit to hunt from a standing vehicle from the Michigan Department of Natural Resources and Environment. Lodging, meals and assistance are provided. Anyone interested in volunteering or getting more information about opportunities for disabled hunters can contact Jonathan Edgerly at 269-731-6570 or jonathan.edgerly@us.army.mil.

Hunters Helping Soldiers: The mission of *Hunters Helping Soldiers* is to provide a means to enhance physical and emotional healing through comradely during hunting and fishing trips as well as mentorship to help ease the transition from military life to civilian life and help families of returning, wounded, and mortally wounded soldiers cope with the challenges they face. www.huntershelpingsoldiers.org

Operation Open Arms (SW Florida, Eastern Maryland): Is a nationally acclaimed military outreach program. Founded in 2005, *OOA* has a very simple mission statement: "To provide US Servicemen/women visiting SW FL or the Eastern Shore of Maryland every conceivable benefit during their two week combat leave or return from any foreign duty station." *Operation Open Arms* provides extraordinary benefits such as free limo service, lodging, restaurants, fishing charters, golf, tennis, bowling, kayaking, biking, emergency dental care, and a cutting edge approach for the treatment of PTSD.

 Operation Open Arms is self-administrating. There is no paid staff or volunteers to assist you. Making a reservation or appointment within OOA is no different than making arrangements within the military. All *Operation Open Arms* sponsors will require a DA-31 and valid military ID prior to hotel stays, golf, fishing charters, or any other benefits. All *OOA* participants will be as punctual and cooperative as your days in basic training. http://www. operationopenarms.com/

Purple Heart Ranch (Sterling City, TX) - Military Warriors Hero Support Foundation: Purple Heart Ranch is open exclusively to combat wounded heroes and to Gold Star families. The ranch is also open to children of combat wounded heroes and those who have a parent currently deployed to a combat zone. Both the families of the wounded heroes and the parents of the children are encouraged to come and enjoy the experience with the hunters. There is fishing available at both properties and many other activities for the families. Both ranches are rich in history and are littered with Native American artifacts, especially arrow heads. http://militarywarriors.org/skills4life

RnR Oasis: The mission at RnR Oasis is to assist disabled and wounded U.S. combat veterans in returning to as normal a life as possible, in the least amount of time. It has been their experience that healing and closure takes place around a campfire. Combat brothers and sisters, helping each other on the road to recovery. RnR Oasis provides a safe camping experience with other Veterans to maximize the environment that promotes healing and closure. To that end, RnR Oasis currently rents or leases campgrounds, provides all gear and equipment, food and even fire wood for up to 50 veterans at a time. There is no cost to the veteran for this program. www.rnroasis.org

The Pathway Home: A California residential recovery program created for OIF/OEF Veterans, as well as veterans of the global war on terror who served in other locations. Treatment includes relaxation to help reduce physical responses to tension and stress, and practical instruction in skills for coping with anger, stress and other problems. For more information you can call (707) 948-3031 or go to www.thepathwayhome.org.

Retirees/Veterans

Sadly, after the Vietnam and Korean Wars there was not much support for our troops, much understanding of what they were going through and little outlook or guidance. Their suffering laid the groundwork, in my eyes, for many positive support systems to emerge. I hope some of these organizations will come in useful and hopefully help not only our past service members but the present and future in some way. Those service members should never have been forgotten.

Emergency and Financial Assistance

American Patriot Heroes Fund: Provides emergency assistance to ALL veterans from past, present and future armed forces. http://americanpatriotheroesfund. org/

Armed Forces Foundation: The Foundation is dedicated to providing comfort and solace to members of the military community through financial support, career counseling, housing assistance and recreational therapy programs. They provide assistance to active duty and retired personnel, National Guard, Reserve Components, and their loved ones. http://www.armedforcesfoundation.org/about.php

National Veterans Services Fund, Inc: Provides case-managed social services and limited medical assistance to Vietnam-Persian Gulf War Veterans and their families, with focus on families with disabled children. http://www.angelfire.com/ct2/natvetsvc/

*Operation Once in a Lifetime: This organizations mission is to make the dreams of service members and their families come true by providing free financial and moral support. Operation Once in a Lifetime was created by a service member to help other service members; created on the bases that "a service member knows what a service member needs," And a service member does not need to worry about providing beds for his kids, worrying if his electricity will still be on when he goes home or if his house will be foreclosed on when serving his/her country. A service member needs a program that will provide free financial assistance regardless of his rank, race, branch of service, physical condition or his deployment status. A service member needs a program that can help make a life altering contribution when he/she is in their greatest need. *This is a wonderful organization; I wish I would have heard about them earlier in my past positions. Michigan soldiers could use this organization. I will be passing this information on to the Family Assistance Coordinators.* www.operationonceinalifetime.com

Operation Second Chance: Committed to serving our wounded, injured and ill combat veterans, give support while recovering in hospitals. Please read site for more details. http://www.operationsecondchance.org/

Operation Welcome Homes: Started as a pilot program in Door County, *Operation Welcome Homes* has given free vacations to retired Iraq and Afghanistan vets and their families from all across America. www.operationwelcomehomes.org

*Operation We Are Here: This is a wonderful website that offers information and links to resources for military families and veterans about retreats, books, emotional, marriage, and much more. Please review the site at http://www.operationwearehere.com.

Overview of VA Pension and Health Care Benefits: This site is an article that discusses veteran benefits often overlooked by veterans and their surviving spouses. These benefits include pensions, payments for nursing home or home care, prescription drugs, reimbursement for the cost of adapting a home or car for disability, and more. http://www.va.gov/healtheligibility/library/pubs/healthcareoverview/

Rebuilding Together – Veterans Housing Initiative: Fills the gaps in housing modification and repair services for retired and active duty service members and strives to provide safe and accessible housing for all low-income veterans. Partners with Project H.E.R.O. (Homes Eliminated of Restrictions and Obstacles), an innovative program to make homes accessible to disabled veterans across the United States. www.rebuildingtogether.org/section/initiatives/vet and another branch to this is Rebuilding Together Quad Cities-Rehabilitates the homes of low-income homeowners, particularly the elderly, disabled and families with dependent children. www.rebuildingtogetherquadcities.org/

Supportive Services for Veteran Families: Under this program, the certain agencies in the state of Michigan will be able to provide a range of services to eligible low income veterans and their families. This will include services for rent, utilities, deposits and moving costs. http://www.va.gov/HOMELESS/SSVF.asp

*VFW Military Assistance (MAP): A quality of life initiative focusing on easing the financial emergencies of deploying service members and supporting them and their family through the hardships of deployments. They offer grants for emergency situation and at different locations assistance with job search and scholarships for children. *Wonderful organization, I have worked with them in the past.* http://www.vfw.org/Assistance/Family-Assistance/

Veterans Assistance Foundation: Operates programs designed to assist veterans who are homeless or at risk of becoming homeless to maintain or improve their status in society by providing safe and secure environment through which they can access a wide array of human services. http://vafvets.org

CAREER/JOBS

AMVETS: Strong advocate for American Veterans on important issues such as employment and training, mandatory funding for government-provided health care and other benefits. http://www.amvets.org

Center for Veteran Enterprise (Veteran Business Opportunities): Vetbiz.gov is a Veteran resource information web site designed to assist veteran entrepreneurs who want to start and expand their businesses in the Federal and private marketplace. This site provides up to the minute information from the federal government as it pertains to service disabled and veteran owned small businesses. http://www.vetbiz.gov/

Employer Partnership of the Armed Forces: Connects qualified reservists and veterans with civilian employers to achieve a mutually beneficial relationship. Reservists and National Guard members can take advantage of the programs online portal. Employer Partnership offers career support to soldiers, dependents, and retirees along with resume tips and career development advice. There are over twenty program support managers located throughout the nation to assist service members with job placement and in some cases working one-on-one. For more information, visit the website at www.employerpartnership.org.

E-VETS: Assists veterans preparing to enter the job market. It includes information on a broad range of topics, such as job search tools and tips, employment openings, career assessment, education and training, and benefits and special services available to veterans. The e-Vets resource advisor will provide a list of web links most relevant to your specific needs and interests. http://www.dol.gov/elaws/evets.htm

Hire Vets First: A comprehensive career website for hiring veterans. No matter your occupation, you will find the resources you need for matching employment opportunities with veterans. http://hirevetsfirst.do/gov

Military Franchising (JOBS): If you are looking to earn extra income on the side and operate a business out of your home, a home-based franchise may interest you. This website is a list of home-based franchise opportunities for military spouses and veterans. Find "military-spouse/veteran friendly" home-based franchise opportunities that are looking for you! http://www.militaryfranchising.com/spouse/default.aspx

*Military to Medicine: Offers an easy way for service members and military families to gain a career in health care that can move with you. Whether you have experience and/or education currently or just starting out this program can help you. Military to Medicine's online training is in partnership with The Claude Moore Health Education Program and provides students with real-life job standards and role expectations.

Both students and healthcare employers can feel confident that Military to Medicine course work demonstrates realistic, healthcare workplace skills. Military to Medicine is committed to participants' long-term career success. Before specific career courses begin, Military to Medicine assesses each student's interests and abilities, this information helps students set career goals and select career courses.

At the writing of this book, tuition for the initial assessment was $599, for the career-specific courses (front office medical assistant or medical records and health information assistant), the tuition was $1,850. The tuition includes the eBooks, eLearning materials and completion certificates, Scholarships are available. This program is available for military spouses, wounded warriors and their caregivers, veterans, National Guard, Reserve and their Spouses and service members transitioning to civilian employment. For more information go to www.militarytomedicine.org.

OPM – Veterans Employment Information: Provides a site that deals with vets hiring vets. Please review site for more information and requirements. http://www.fedshirevets.gov

SBA Patriot Express: The SBA "Patriot Express" loan program helps the military community open their own small business. SBA loans up to $500,000 and may be used for business startup, expansion, equipment purchase, working capital, inventory or business occupied real estate purchase. Interest rates generally are 2.25% to 2.75% above the prime rate, based upon the amount and maturity of the loan. Veterans' business development officers man SBA district offices in every state. They can provide lists of area Patriot Express lenders as well as additional small business advice and resources.

In addition, the Veterans Business Outreach Program provides entrepreneurial development services such as business training, counseling and mentoring to eligible veterans owning or considering starting a small business. Check into your local SBA and see what all they have to provide for you and your family. Patriot Express Loans are available to veterans, service-disabled veterans, active-duty military eligible for the military's Transition Assistance Program, Reservists and National Guard members, current spouses of any of these groups, and surviving spouses of members or veterans who died during service or from a service-connected disability. http://www.sba.gov/content/patriot-express

Spouse Fellowship: The FINRA Foundation Military Spouse Fellowship Program gives military spouses the opportunity to earn a career enhancing credential-the accredited financial counselor certificate-while providing financial counseling to the military community. Spouses of active duty, retired and reserve service members are eligible. http://www.saveandinvest.org/Military/SpouseFellowships/index.htm

Veterans Employment and Training Service (VETS): VETS assists veterans and service members with resources and expertise to assist and prepare them to obtain meaningful careers, maximize their employment opportunities, and protect their employment rights. For more information, go to http://www.dol.gov/vets/.

VetJobs: This website assists veterans, spouses and family members find quality jobs with employers worldwide. Vetjobs is partially owned by VFW and has been endorsed by various other veterans' service organizations. Vetjob employment assistance section has all the tools and guidance needed to find jobs. It will start out with an career assessment, assistance on interviewing, writing resumes and other services. It also lists all legitimate job boards by occupation and location in the U.S. For employers, VetJobs is a flat-fee site that has the largest reach possible into the veteran job-candidate market. Additionally, VetJobs has been effective for those employers who need candidates with security clearances. For further information go to www.vetjobs.com.

Veteran Job.com: This site takes you to Orion International, which is one of the nation's largest military recruiting firms that specialize in placing today's top military leaders, engineers, and technicians into America's Fortune 500 and beyond. There offices are located throughout the United States with an all-veteran recruiting and sales team. Orion strives to be the firm of choice for Junior Military Officers, Noncommissioned Officers, and Technicians separating from the military, as well as America's top companies seeking to hire the best. http://www.veteransjobs.com

EDUCATION ASSISTANCE

Anchor Scholarship Foundation: For dependents of active duty or retired personnel who served in commands under the administrative control of Commanders, Naval Surface Forces, US Atlantic or Pacific Fleets for a minimum of 6 years. You can call 843-757-2806 for further information and an application.

Department of Veterans Affairs: This site covers various information regarding education, burial, disabilities, home loans and more. http://www.va.gov/ For veterans who are looking for VA opportunities, the job postings are **ONLY** open to veterans and related job status. http://www.va.gov/vecs

eMilitary.org: The homepage is provided to veterans to access the information they need, and to help veterans network with other veterans. Provided Forums, Chat along with other assistance. Soon they will be providing other resources online. http://www.emilitary.org/usvet.php

Joseph A. McAlinden Divers Scholarship: Offered specifically to Navy and Marine Corps Divers, whether active duty or retired, and their eligible family members. This scholarship provides financial assistance for full-time undergraduate and graduate students, who must be participating in one of the following areas of study: Oceanography, Ocean Agriculture, or Aquaculture. The McAlinden Scholarship also assists with Department of the Navy approved advanced diver training, qualifications and certifications. The scholarship is need-based and ranges from $500 up to $3,000 per academic year, for the eligible students education. There is no deadline for this program; you may apply at any time. http://www.nmcrs.org/education.html

Stateside Spouse Education Assistance Program (SSEAP): This scholarship program assists Army spouses obtain a four year undergraduate degree. Spouses of active duty soldiers, spouses of retired soldiers, and widows or widowers of soldiers who died either on active duty or in a retired status are eligible. http://www.aerhq.org/education_spouseeducation_StateSide.asp

Reserve Officers Association of the US: This program is designed to assist deserving members of ROA, ROAL, their children, or grandchildren who wish to attend or who are now attending accredited U.S. colleges or universities. This scholarship is funded through the Henry J. Reilly Scholarship trust, which states that preference will be given to those pursuing a military career. ROTC cadets, midshipmen and currently serving military graduate students are strongly encouraged to apply. This scholarship is granted to 30 applicants. For more information about ROA or this scholarship go to http://www.roa.org/.

OTHER RESOURCES

American Coalition for Filipino Veterans: Veterans advocacy organization with 4,000 members working to restore official recognition and provide equitable VA benefits to surviving veterans in the Philippines and in America. http://usfilvets.tripod.com

American Military Retirees Association (AMRA): Is a wonderful organization the works on behalf of military retirees and their families, to protect their rights and benefits under the law, and to lobby on their behalf in Washington, DC and elsewhere. Check out the website and learn more about their efforts and other resources they have available. Their latest in 2010 was the Associations Scholarship fund. Through the current generosity of AMRA members, the Associations annually present $35,000 in scholarships to AMRA members, their spouses and dependents, and their grandchildren. They hope to grow the program so they can award more scholarships in the future. Go to http://amra1973.org to learn more about this organization.

Guardian Angels for Soldier's Pets: This organizations mission is supporting our military, veterans, and their beloved pets to ensure the pets are reunited with their owners following a deployment (combat or peace-keeping mission) in harm's way to fight the global war on terrorism or unforeseen emergency hardship impacting their ability to retain their pet's ownership rights. Please go to the website to get further information on eligibility. http://guardianangelsforsoldierspet.org

Honor Flight Network: A non-profit organization created solely to honor America's veterans for all their sacrifices. They will transport our heroes to Washington, D.C. to visit and reflect at their memorials. Top priority is given to the senior veterans—World War II survivors, along with those other veterans who may be terminally ill. For more information, go to http://www.honorflight.org/.

Iraq and Afghanistan Veterans of America: Dedicated to improving the lives of OIF and OEF veterans and families. Has various resources linked to their website on lots of different subjects. http://iava.org/membership

Mesothelioma: Veterans from all branches of the military have served their country in times of war and peace, giving their time, effort and sometimes their lives. Mesothelioma cancer, a disease with no known cure, has fallen upon many U.S. veterans, and the rights of these veterans to receive compensation for this work related disease should be upheld. Learn more about asbestos news at http://www.asbestos.com/veterans.

National Association of American Veterans: Assists all veterans and families from WWII, Korean War, Vietnam, Desert Storm, Enduring Freedom, Iraqi Freedom and the current war in Afghanistan who come home severely wounded by helping access health benefits, improving communication and coordination and collaborating among health agencies, medical professional organizations, educational organizations and the public. http://www.naavets.org/

National Association of County Veterans Service Officers, Inc. (NAVCVSO): NACVSO's mission is to actively promote the rights of veterans and dependents of the United States through a progressive legislative platform. They work collaboratively with the Department of Veterans Affairs and other nationally chartered veteran's organizations to assure that veteran and their dependents receive the entitlements they deserve for the sacrifices they endured. http://www.nacvso.org/

National Association of State Directors of Veterans Affairs (NASDVA): The National Association of State Directors of Veteran Affairs (NASDVA) is an organization with a history dating back to 1946. In the aftermath of World War II many veterans earned State and Federal benefits which required coordinated efforts to assure that veterans received these entitlements. Thus, States developed a Department or Agency designated as the "Office of Prime Responsibility" for veteran services and programs. The members of NASDVA are the Chief Executive Officers or State Directors of Veterans' Affairs in each State as well as the District of Columbia, American Samoa, Northern Mariana Islands, Puerto Rico and the Virgin Islands.

It is important to note that collectively state governments commit more than $4 billion annually of their own resources to support of our nation's veterans and their families. States are second only to the federal VA in providing benefits and services to the men and women who defend our nation. Although each state is unique, with its own traditions, programs, and resources, they are united by the common goal to make a difference in the lives of our veterans. Please go to the website to review a 50 state benefit analysis spreadsheet. http://nasdva.net/

National Veterans Organization of America: http://www.nvo.org

National Association of Veterans Program Administrates: http://www.navpa.org

National Resource Directory: A revitalized Department of Labor online directory promises access to "thousands" of services and resources for wounded troops, veterans and their families. The National Resource Directory provides links to national, state and local sources that support "recovery, rehabilitation and community reintegration." The site offers information for vets seeking education, training and employment. It also provides help for employers who want to hire veterans, understand employment laws and make workplace accommodations for disabled vets. For more information go to http://www.nationalresourcedirectory.gov.

Retired and Annuitant Pay - Cost of Living Allowance (COLA): The cost of living adjustment or COLA is a pay adjustment provided to military retirees and annuitants that help maintain purchasing power. The adjustment is based on a 12 months average increase in the cost of market basket of non-discretionary goods and services, as measured by the consumer price index for urban and clerical workers. http://www.dfas.mil/

Returning Service members (OIF/OEF): Covers information about health care, education, job search, and much more. http://www.oefoif.va.gov/index.asp

Stars and Stripes: Their mission is to fly WWII veterans and terminally ill veterans from other wars to see their memorials in Washington, D.C. They also work closely with schools throughout Wisconsin to ensure that the heroic stories of veterans are built into the curriculum so that future generations will fully appreciate the sacrifices made on their behalf. http://starsandstripeshonorflight.org/

The Center for Women Veterans: This organization assures women veterans receive benefits and services on a par with male veterans, encounter no discrimination in their attempt to access these services, are treated with respect and dignity by VA service providers, and to act as the primary advisor to the Secretary for Veteran Affairs on all matters related to programs, issues, and initiatives for affecting women veterans. http://www.va.gov/womenvet/

The Mission Continues: Mission is to build on America where EVERY returning veteran, wounded or otherwise can serve again as a citizen leader, and where together they honor the fallen by living their values through service. http://www.missioncontinues.org

Veterans Plus: The only non-profit whose mission is the financial education and empowerment of those who have served. Veterans Plus will teach you how to create a household budget, how to pay off your debts in a responsible way and how to teach your children about money. They will help you to understand how your credit rating is established and how it can affect nearly every significant financial transaction you make or consider. They will teach you how to save for a new home or how to keep the home you have. Remember Veterans Plus does not loan money, nor does it sell or offer investment advice or sell insurance or any product of the kind. Instead, they believe that the way to financial **independence is through education and understanding.** For more information go to http://www.veteransplus.org/programs.htm.

Veteran Affairs of Government: http://www.va.gov and http://www.seamlesstransition.va.gov/res_guard.asp

*Veterans Network: This is a casual environment of information for the veterans and their families. *I found the site very enjoyable and I would not mind being on the show one day. Everyone should check this site out!* http://veteransnetwork.net

Veterans Support Center: Is a non-profit 501(c)3 organization that is NOT a government agency or affiliated with any government agency or government department. Veterans Support Center receives no federal, state, or local tax aid. Please visit this website to see the resources that are available for you. Go to http://veteransupportcenter.org/.

Vietnam Veterans of America (VVA) and PTSD and Substance Abuse: PTSD is one of the key issues in why VVA was founded, the history of VVA and its PTSD/SA Committee are linked together. The mission is to support and advocate actively for health care—diagnoses, clinical practices, clinical research, treatments, specialized programs, and related educational efforts—necessary to meet the needs of veterans with PTSD, substance addictions, and other debilitating psychological reactions to trauma resulting from military service. This also supports health care for family members of such veterans. http://vva.org/ptsd_vva.html www.helpguide.org and http://www.veteranstoday.com

A Warrior's Wish Foundation: The Warrior Wish Foundation enhances the lives of United States Military Veterans and their families who are battling a life-limiting illness. Through the fantastic financial support of generous donors, the financial contributions of Veterans' Service Organizations, our volunteer network and our wonderful corporate partnerships, we are able to grant the wishes of those who have served this great nation of ours. A wish may be as simple as a new hearing aid or scooter chair, or as involved as one last family vacation or reunion. http://awarriorwish.org

Women Veterans of America (WVA): Women veterans face their own array of issues after they have finished active duty. WVA was created to be a resource for women veterans and for the families and friends who support them. On this site you can learn about women veteran's health issues, information on military sexual trauma, and the balancing of motherhood with service. The site will provide assistance with understanding military benefits and direct you towards organizations and resources advocating for women veterans. These resources are for current and past members of the military service. http://www.womenveteransofamerica.com/about.

RETREATS/HEALTH

Air Force Enlisted Village: The Air Force Enlisted Village was founded in 1967 to provide a safe, secure and dignified place for indigent surviving spouses of retired Air Force personnel. The Village's primary goal and focus is to "Provide a Home," and financial assistance to these women. The surviving spouse with the greatest need is cared for first and none are refused assistance due to financial status. Low pay and frequent military moves leave some spouses without careers, home equities, retirement plans or any significant assets. Surviving spouses requiring financial assistance live here among peers sharing memories of Air Force life without the stigma normally associated with subsidized housing facilities. Explore the site for more details http://afenlistedwidows.org/.

Fly-Fishing Therapy Resources: These organizations are here to help wounded soldiers get back their life and rebuild skills and goals for the future.

- **Project Healing Waters:** www.projecthealingwaters.org,
- **Trout Unlimited:** www.tu.org (800) 834-2419
- **Federation of Fly Fishers:** www.fedflyfishers.org (406) 222-9369
- **Warriors & Quiet Waters Foundation:** www.warriorsandquietwaters.org

- **River of Recovery:** www.riversofrecovery.org (303) 801-8022
- **Sun Valley Adaptive Sports** www.svasp.org (208) 726-9298

HOMELESS VETERANS

Homeless veterans have existed since wars have been fought. Sadly, many are forgotten and the reasons for their homelessness put to the side. A mental condition that many homeless veterans share is Post Traumatic Stress Disorder (PTSD), which has also been known as "shell shock," "combat fatigue," and during the Civil War, it was known as "Soldier's Heart." It is estimated that around 40% of the homeless are veterans and this number is expected to rise. I am listing several programs that will hopefully help with this situation. Remember, "No service member or their family should be forgotten!"

Compensated Work Therapy: In VA's Compensated Work Therapy/ Transitional Residence (CWT/TR) Program, disadvantaged, at-risk, and homeless Veterans live in CWT/TR community based supervised group homes while working for pay in VA's Compensated Work Therapy Program (also known as Veterans Industries). Veterans in the CWT/TR Program work about 33 hours per week, with approximate earnings of $732 per month, and pay an average of $186 per month toward maintenance and up-keep of the residence. The average length of stay is about 174 days. VA contracts with private industry and the public sector for work done by these Veterans, who learn new job skills, relearn successful work habits, and regain a sense of self-esteem and self-worth. http://www.cwt.va.gov/

Department of Housing and Urban Development/VA Supported Housing: The Department of Housing and Urban Development and VA Supported Housing (HUD-VASH) Program provides permanent housing and ongoing case management treatment services for homeless Veterans who require these supports to live independently. HUD has allocated over 20,000 "housing choice" Section 8 vouchers to Public Housing Authorities (PHAs) throughout the country for eligible homeless Veterans. This program allows veterans and their families to live in Veteran-selected apartment units. The vouchers are portable, allowing Veterans to live in communities where VA case management services can be provided. This program provides for our most vulnerable veterans, and is especially helpful to veterans with families, women veterans, recently returning veterans and veterans with disabilities. http://www.va.gov/ HOMELESS/HUD-VASH.asp

Domiciliary Care for Homeless Veterans: The Domiciliary Care Program is designed to provide state-of-the-art, high quality residential rehabilitation and treatment services for Veterans with multiple and severe medical conditions, mental illness, addiction, or psychosocial deficits. http://www.va.gov/ HOMELESS/DCHV.asp

Drop-in Centers: Drop-in centers provide a daytime sanctuary where homeless veterans can clean up, wash their clothes, and participate in a variety of

278   OPERATION: MILITARY RESOURCES

therapeutic and rehabilitative activities; linkages with longer-term assistance are also available. These are not provided in all states so check with your state office.

Final Salute: Mission is to provide homeless female veterans with safe and suitable housing. Final Salute will work with the female veteran in establishing a plan towards independence through programs that focus on prevention of homelessness, emergency shelter, transitional housing, emergency financial assistance and a goal for independence. http://www.finalsaluteinc.org/

Grant and Per Diem Program (GPD): This program is offered annually (as funding permits) by the VA to fund community-based agencies providing transitional housing or service centers for homeless veterans. Under the Capital Grant Component VA may fund up to 65% of the project for the construction, acquisition, or renovation of facilities or to purchase van(s) to provide outreach and services to homeless Veterans. Per Diem is available to grantees to help off-set operational expenses. Non-Grant programs may apply for Per Diem under a separate announcement, when published in the Federal Register, announcing the funding for "Per Diem Only." http://www.va.gov/HOMELESS/GPD.asp

Healthcare for Homeless Veterans: The mission of this program is to perform outreach, provided by VA social workers and other mental health clinicians, to identify homeless veterans who are eligible for VA services and assist these veterans in accessing appropriate healthcare and benefits. In addition to its initial core mission, HCHV also functions as a mechanism to contract with providers for community-based residential treatment for homeless veterans. http://www.va.gov/HOMELESS/HCHV.asp

Health Care for Re-entry: The Health Care for Re-entry Veterans (HCRV) Program is designed to address the community re-entry needs of incarcerated Veterans. HCRV's goals are to prevent homelessness, reduce the impact of medical, psychiatric, and substance abuse problems upon community re-adjustment, and decrease the likelihood of re-incarceration for those leaving prison. http://www.va.gov/HOMELESS/Reentry.asp

Homeless Veterans Chat: www.va.gov/homeless and the National Call Center is 1-877-424-3838 for live 24 hours a day, 7 days a week.

Homeless Veterans Dental Program: The Homeless Veteran Dental Program increases accessibility to quality dental care to homeless Veteran patients and to help assure success in VA-sponsored and VA partnership homeless rehabilitation programs throughout the United States. http://www.va.gov/HOMELESS/dental.asp

National Call Center for Homeless Veterans: VA has founded a National Call Center for Homeless Veterans to ensure that homeless Veterans or Veterans at-risk for homeless have free, 24/7 access to trained counselors. This hotline is intended to assist homeless Veterans and their families, VA Medical Centers, federal, state and local partners, community agencies, service providers and others in the community. To be connected with a trained VA staff member in your area call 1-877-424-3838 and the website is http://www.va.gov/HOMELESS/NationalCallCenter.asp.

National Center on Homelessness among Veterans: Is a forum to exchange new ideas; provide education and consultation to improve the delivery of service; and disseminate the knowledge gained through the efforts of the Centers Research and Model Development Cores to VA, other federal agencies, and community provider programs that assist homeless populations. http://www.va.gov/HOMELESS/NationalCenter.asp

National Association of American Veterans: Assist all veterans and families from WWII, Korean War, Vietnam, Desert Storm, Enduring Freedom, and Iraqi Freedom severely wounded by helping to access health benefits, improving communication and coordination and collaborating among health agencies, medical professional organizations, educational organizations and the public. http://www.naavets.org/

Non-VA Resources for Assistance: This site provides links to websites to other federal and community resources that could be helpful to those who are homeless or at risk of homelessness. http://www.va.gov/HOMELESS/NonVAResources.asp

Opening Doors-Federal Strategic Plan to Prevent and End Homelessness: This plan outlines an interagency collaboration that aligns mainstream housing, health, education, and human services to prevent Americans from experiencing homelessness. As the most far-reaching and ambitious plan to end homelessness in our history, this Plan will both strengthen existing partnerships-such as the combined effort of HUD and the Veterans Affairs to help homeless Veterans-and forge new partnerships between agencies like HUD, HHS, and the Department of Labor. http://www.va.gov/HOMELESS/docs/OpeningDoors2010FSP.pdf

Operation Second Chance: Committed to serving our wounded, injured and ill combat veterans, give support while recovering in a hospital. See site for more details. http://www.operationsecondchance.org/

Project CHALENG: Project CHALENG (Community Homelessness Assessment, Local Education and Networking Groups) for Veterans, an innovative program designed to enhance the continuum of care for homeless Veterans provided by the local VA and its surrounding community services agencies. The guiding principle behind Project CHALENG is that no single agency can provide the full spectrum of services required to help homeless Veterans become productive members of society. Project CHALENG enhances coordinated services by bringing the VA together with community agencies and other federal, state, and local governments who provide services to the homeless to raise awareness of homeless veterans needs and plan to meet those needs. http://www.va.gov/HOMELESS/Chaleng.asp

Supportive Housing: Like the HUD-VASH Program identified in this chapter, staff in VA's Supported Housing Program provides ongoing case management services to homeless veterans. Emphasis is placed on helping Veterans find permanent housing and providing clinical support needed to keep veterans in permanent housing. Staff in these programs operates without benefit of the specially dedicated Section 8 housing vouchers available in the HUD-VASH Program but are often successful in locating transitional or permanent housing through local means, especially by collaborating with Veterans Service Organizations. http://www.va.gov/HOMELESS/GPD.asp

Supportive Services for Veteran Families Program (SSVF): This program is a new VA program that will provide supportive services to very low-income veterans and their families who are in or transitioning to permanent housing. VA will award grants to private non-profit organizations and consumer cooperatives who will assist very low-income veterans and their families by providing a range of supportive services designed to promote housing stability. For more information go to http://www.va.gov/HOMELESS/docs/Prevention_FACT_Sheet_11-22-10.pdf and for additional details about Notice of Fund Availability (NOFA) go to http://www.va.gov/HOMELESS/SSVF.asp .

Swords to Plowshares: Their mission is to heal the wounds, to restore dignity, hope and self-sufficiency to all veterans in need, and to significantly reduce homelessness and poverty among veterans. Founded in 1974, Swords to Plowshares is a community-based, not-for-profit organization that provides counseling and case management, employment and training, housing and legal assistance to more than 1500 homeless and low-income veterans annually in the San Francisco Bay Area and beyond. They promote and protect the rights of veterans through advocacy, public education, and partnerships with local, state, and national entities. *Swords to Plowshares* is the only veteran's service agency in the U.S. that provides a full continuum of care. They help vets, as well as families of vets, in the following areas:

- Health & Social Services – drop-in center provides emergency shelter, mental health services and referrals to homeless veterans.

- Housing – residential programs provide housing, rehabilitation and counseling to veterans in need.

- Employment & Training – Through direct training and job referrals, *Swords to Plowshares* helps veterans re-enter the workforce.

- Veterans Academy – formerly homeless veterans can live in a supportive community.

- Legal – provides free attorney representation and advocacy to veterans seeking benefits.

For more information please visit the website at http://swords-to-plowshares.org/.

Veteran Justice Outreach (VJO): The purpose of VJO initiative is to avoid the unnecessary criminalization of mental illness and extended incarceration among veterans by ensuring that eligible justice-involved veterans have timely access to VHA mental health and substance abuse services when clinically indicated, and other VA services and benefits as appropriate. http://www. va.gov/HOMELESS/VJO.asp

Veteran Stand Downs: Stand Downs is one part of the Department of Veterans Affairs efforts to provide services to homeless veterans. Stand Downs are typically one to three day events providing services to homeless Veterans such as food, shelter, and clothing. Health screenings, VA and Social Security benefits counseling and referrals to a variety of other necessary services, such as housing, employment and substance abuse treatment. http://www.va.gov/ HOMELESS/standdown.asp

**As of October 1, 2011 Military retirees will pay more for their health care and more cost increases are on the way. Individuals who enroll in the retiree program as of October 1, 2011 will pay $260 annually, up from $230, and it will be $520 annually for a family, up from $460. Retirees already in the program will not see any increase until the next year because they have already paid for the full year. Annual increases are planned for the future.

Retirees/Veterans

MICHIGAN ASSISTANCE
CONTACT INFORMATION

Since I am from Michigan, I have a list of resources available to Michigan military residents. Very soon I will start compiling information for other military states to provide the best list of resources for you. Check back often to www.MilitaryResourceBooks.com for more information and updates.

Claims for Disability: To claim disability, you will need to sit down with a state veteran's service officer or county veteran's counselor to review your service and military medical records. You can find the contact information for service officers at www.michigan.gov/veterans in the federal benefits section; find county counselors contact information at www.macvc.net.

*Cooley Law School: Free legal assistance for military service members and their families. Contact Mrs. Heather Spielmaker at 517-371-5140 extension #4112 or email spielmah@cooley.ed. *I have used this resource to assist military families and they are a great group of attorneys who volunteer their time.*

DD FORM 214: Is your certificate of release or discharge from active duty. Call 517-373-3130, if you returned to Michigan from federal active duty in the past thirty years and they may have a copy of your DD214. If they don't, they will refer you to the National Archives at www.archives.gov. Usually a copy will be in the mail within a couple of days; the archives take up to a couple of weeks.

DEERS Site Locator for Michigan:

- **110th FW Michigan ANG Battle Creek ANGB:** (269) 969-3216

- **127th Wing Michigan ANG Selfridge ANGB:** (586) 239-4516

- **300 MP BDE Inkster:** (313) 561-9400

- **334th Med GP Grand Rapids:** (616) 735-4050

- **645th RSG Southfield:** (248) 359-2000

- **ANG HQ Michigan:** (517) 481-8360

- **Alpena Combat Readiness Training Center:** (989) 354-6220

- **Camp Grayling:** (989) 344-6100

- **Defense Logistics Information Service:** (269) 961-7002

- **HQ 1st BDE, 84th DIV (IT) Livonia:** (734) 367-2400

- **NAVOPSPTCEN Grand Rapids:** (616) 363-6889

- **NMCRC Lansing:** (517) 482-9150

- **NRC Saginaw:** (989) 754-3091

- **US Army TACOM Warren:** (586) 282-5941

- **USCG Air Station Traverse City:** (231) 922-8227

- **USCG SFO Grand Haven:** (616) 850-2517

- **USCG Sector Sault Ste. Marie:** (906) 635-3401

Department of Military and Veterans Affairs/Michigan Military Family Relief Fund: Provided for Army National Guard Soldiers for the state of Michigan ONLY. Need based grant-providing up to $2,000 emergency financial assistance and is for active duty, title 10 deployed soldiers and their families in emergency situations. Applicant must provide a copy of orders, soldiers current last two LES, current military ID card, POA (if requested) letter explaining situation, copy of estimates and/or all bills, and other information as needed. http://www.stclaircounty.org/Offices/veterans/forms/Emerg_Relief_Application_Form.pdf, Fax information to 517-481-7644.

D.J. Jacobetti Home for Veterans: The primary mission of the D.J. Jacobetti Home for Veterans is to restore health and maintain existing functions, enabling residents the opportunity to enjoy their remaining years to the fullest. The D.J. Jacobetti Home for Veterans is a modern nursing home that serves and encourages its veterans to function at their maximum level. The home's staff places great emphasis on tailoring its care plans to a member's individual needs and to encourage their independence, rather than dependence. Every person admitted to the Home is thoroughly evaluated by a physician, social services, nursing, activities and for dietary and physical therapy needs in terms of abilities and disabilities. This comprehensive assessment results in an "interdisciplinary Care Plan" issued within the first seven days of admission. The D.J. Jacobetti Home for Veterans provides 182 nursing care beds, two infirmary beds and 59 residential beds. D.J. Jacobetti is located at 425 Fisher Street, Marquette, MI 49855 and their phone number is 906-226-3576. For more information please go to http://michigan.gov/dmva/0,1607,7-126-2362_2763---,00.html.

Emergency Grants: The Michigan Veterans Trust Fund provides temporary assistance to war-era veterans and family members with 180 days or more of federal active duty. This is provided to all branches of service and assists temporary unforeseen emergency financial hardship. You apply to a committee of volunteers in the county where you live. Eligibility requirements for Emergency Grants can be found at the Department of Military and Veterans Affairs web site. Michigan's Department of Military and Veterans Affairs is located at 3423 N. Martin Luther King Jr. Blvd, Lansing, Mi 48906. Telephone: 517-335-6523/Fax: 517-241-0674. You can call 517-373-3130 for the contact information for your county.

Employment and Career Information: The state's Department of Energy, Labor and Economic Growth provides help and information on the web at www.michigan.gov.veteranjobs or you may call them toll free at 1-800-455-5228. Call 517-373-3062 for information about the state's Civil Service Commission procedures for veteran preference.

Forgotten Eagles of Michigan: This wonderful organization works to heighten awareness and to publicize the POW/MIA issues, to educate the public on the plight of POW/MIA's, to advocate for the fullest possible accounting of all of America's POW/MIAs, to heighten awareness and education of the public on the effects of Agent Orange/Dioxin and of the chemical, biological and radiological weapons testing on the U.S. military personnel. To promote physical and cultural improvement, growth and development, self-respect, self-confidence and usefulness of America's veterans and families, to assist America's disabled in-need veterans, their dependents and the widows and orphans of deceased veterans, and to help not-for-profit organizations that have similar interests at heart. Please view the website for other useful information and resources. http://forgotteneagles.org/

Michigan Department of Military and Veterans Affairs: The department has a complete list of contacts to help you find the assistance in all areas of before, during and after deployment along with assistance you need to seamlessly transition from military to civilian life. The list of contacts is available at the State of Michigan website or by calling 517-335-6523 to speak to the Veteran's Benefits office. http://www.va.gov/

Michigan Education and Financial Assistance Benefit: Michigan's Tuition Grant Procedure Brief is a program administered by the state's Higher Education Assistance Authority that provides tuition assistance to eligible dependents of Michigan veterans. With undergraduate grants of up to $2,800 a year, the Tuition Grant Procedure Brief was designed to make it easier for military orphans and dependents of Michigan veterans to secure the skills necessary to succeed in a range of civilian careers. Awards may be applied to participating online schools, vocational programs and campus-based universities in Michigan. Please go to the website for more information on rules and eligibility information. http://www.worldwidelearn.com/military/state-veterans/michigan/tuition-grant-procedure-brief.html

Michigan Family Support Centers, Army National Guard: Provides support and information to families of deployed service members including military and civilian programs and benefits, telecommunication services such as video conferencing, broadband internet access, support groups, home and car repair assistance, transportation, child care referrals, food and clothing assistance, counseling and more. www.milfamily.org/

*Michigan Military Family Relief Fund: Provides emergency financial assistance to families of title 10, active duty soldiers who live in the state of Michigan. Must have current ID card. Grant is up to $2000. There is currently no website at this time. All application can be mailed or faxed. You can download the application from google by typing in DMVA Form 10-1. The address is: Department of Military and veterans Affairs, Office of Financial Services, Reserve Forces Service Center, 3423 North Martin Luther King Blvd, Lansing, Mi 48906. Attn: Military Family Relief Fund. Military Family Relief Fund Coordinator is Mrs. Kathy A. Enderle at 517-481-7646. *I will recommend this organization, they are a wonderful caring group of people that work there and it is a decent turnaround when needed. I used this organization myself back in 05/06 when my roof leaked through 3 floors of my house and my furnace broke. They were VERY helpful.*

Michigan National Guard Family Program: Provides up to a $500 grant to soldiers and airmen and their family members who encounter financial hardships as a result of deployments, military injuries, or just hard times. Some items that qualify include emergency loss of income through activation for military duty, inability to maintain employment due to injury or sudden illness, or job loss; unexpected medical expenses; pay problems; or the accumulation of legitimate bills (e.g. rent, mortgage, electric, oil, gas, etc.) and/or the inability to pay for basic needs: food, shelter, utilities, clothing, medical bills, and transportation due to unforeseen circumstances. Applications are required to be submitted with the necessary documentation. http://www.michguard.com/family/FinAsst.asp

Michigan National Guard Family Support Funds: Created to assist Air and Army National Guard families, the Michigan National Guard Family Support Funds provides a grant of up to $500 to soldiers, airmen, and their family members. The fund helps families that have experienced financial hardship by providing temporary emergency financial assistance. It also provides funds for programs and training to improve and boost the quality of life of Michigan National Guard families. http://www.michguard.com/family/FinAsst.asp

*Michigan Rehabilitation Services: Disabled veterans should check out the State of Michigan Rehabilitation Services program, which may supplement U.S. Department of Veterans Affairs allowances for vocational rehabilitation in cases of special need or for placement, tools, and equipment. http://www.michigan.gov/lara/0,1607,7-154-25392---,00.html *I have put the site for Michigan; each state has their own site.*

Michigan State Housing Development Authority: Provides information on affordable housing, home loans and rental programs. www.michigan.gov/mshda

Michigan Veterans' Employment Services: Michigan offers veterans a large array of employment services including job fairs, career portals and job boards. All can be easily found at the Michigan Veterans Employment Services website. http://www.vfwmi.org/veteranjobs.htm

Other Military Education Benefit Programs: There are several federal education alternatives for veterans, military spouses and military families to receive education and training, such as the Veterans Affairs Vocational Rehabilitation and Employment program, and the Veterans Affairs Work-Study Program. Traditional avenues to receive tuition assistance include the Federal Pell Grant Program. http://www.online-education.net/military/index.html, http://www.militaryta.com/state_education_benefits/michigan-military-education-benefits.shtml, and http://www.gibill.va.gov/

Montgomery GI Bill/Montgomery GI Bill Kicker: The MGIB program gives veterans as much as 36 months of education benefits that can be used to pursue degree and certificate programs, on-the-job training and online graduate degree programs. The MGIB Kicker can increase your monthly GI Bill payment rate by as much as $950 a month. Payout information can be found at the Department of Veterans Affairs website. http://www.gibill.com/ benefits/mgib-sr-kicker,   http://www.gibill.va.gov/post-911/montgomery-gi-bill/active-duty.html, and http://www.military.com/education/content/gi-bill/ the-gi-bill-kicker.html

Tuition Assistance/Tuition Assistance Top-up: Armed Forces Tuition Assistance can pay up to 100 percent for tuition expenses. If you qualify for Montgomery GI Bill benefits and plan to use Tuition Assistance, and your service does not cover 100 percent of tuition and fees, you can use MGIB Top-up to pay the balance. Top-up is a good option for military personnel pursing online degree programs.   http://www.gibill.va.gov/resources/education_ resources/programs/tuition_assistance_top_up.html,   http://www.gibill.com/ benefits/tuition-top-up/ and   http://www.military.com/education/content/gi-bill/tuition-top-up-program.html

Patriot Fund Endowment: Is sponsored by The American Legion Department of Michigan and is offered to Michigan Veterans of all eras and their families in times of financial hardship especially those who may not qualify for assistance under the existing Legion, County, and VA programs. Funds get distributed after approval of the State Adjutant in concert with the State Reconnect Chairman. For more information go to http://www.michiganlegion.org/pdfs/ endow_fund.pdf and/or your local American Legion office for assistance.

State of Michigan Veterans Booklet: This booklet has been compiled especially for veterans and their families to provide information regarding federal, state and local agencies and provides veterans and their families with links to direct sources, both computer-based and professional, knowledgeable counselors, for answers to specific questions and hopefully to assist veterans in communicating more effectively with their elected representatives. http:// www.michigan.gov/documents/dmva/VBS-Booklet_Instructions_190078_7. pdf

VA Healthcare: The US Department of Veterans Affairs (VA) provides healthcare to more than 126,000 Michigan veterans at five medical centers and 21 community based outpatient clinics. If you have returned from Iraq or Afghanistan you can enroll at https://www.1010ez.med.va.gov/sec/ vha/1010ez/. Find locations at http://www.2.va.gov/directory/guide/home. asp?isflash=1. If you live along Michigan's southern border, South Bend or Toledo may be better choices.

Remember to share about this book with your friends
on Facebook and Twitter!

For updates and more information please visit my website at:
http://MilitaryResourceBooks.com

Notes:

Notes:

Notes:

Notes: